CHAWTON HOUSE LIBRARY SERIES

WOMEN'S TRAVEL WRITINGS IN IBERIA

CONTENTS OF THE EDITION

Chawton House Library Series: Women's Travel Writings

Series Editors: Stephen Bending and Stephen Bygrave

Titles in this Series

Women's Travel Writings in Revolutionary France
Women's Travel Writings in Italy
Women's Travel Writings in Post-Napoleonic France

Forthcoming Titles

Women's Travel Writings in North Africa and the Middle East
Women's Travel Writings in Scotland

WOMEN'S TRAVEL WRITINGS IN IBERIA

Volume 5
Sarah Ellis, *Summer and Winter in the Pyrenees* ([1841])

EDITED BY

Eroulla Demetriou

Routledge
Taylor & Francis Group

LONDON AND NEW YORK

First published 2013 by Pickering & Chatto (Publishers) Limited

Published 2016 by Routledge
2 Park Square, Milton Park, Abingdon, Oxon OX14 4RN
711 Third Avenue, New York, NY 10017, USA

Routledge is an imprint of the Taylor & Francis Group, an informa business

BRITISH LIBRARY CATALOGUING IN PUBLICATION DATA

Women's travel writings in Iberia. – (Chawton House library series. Women's
travel writings)
1. Iberian Peninsula – Description and travel. 2. Travelers' writings, English –
Iberian Peninsula. 3. Women travelers – Iberian Peninsula – History – 19th
century – Sources.
I. Series II. Demetriou, Eroulla editor of compilation. III. Ruiz Mas, Jose
editor of compilation. IV. Lopez-Burgos, Ma. Antonia (Maria Antonia) editor
of compilation. V. Baillie, Marianne, *c.* 1795–1831. Lisbon. VI. Chatterton,
Georgiana, Lady, 1806–1876. Pyrenees. VII. Ellis, Sarah Stickney, 1799–1872.
Summer and winter in the Pyrenees.
914.6'0472'082-dc23

ISBN-13: 978-1-85196-647-9 (set)

Typeset by Pickering & Chatto (Publishers) Limited

CONTENTS

BIBLIOGRAPHY

[Anon.], [Review], *Eclectic Review* (1841), pp. 235–6.

—, [Review], *Home Missionary Magazine* (1841), pp. 260–1.

—, [Review], *Literary Gazette and Journal of the Belles Lettres, Arts, Sciences, for the Year 1841*, 1274 (19 June 1841), p. 388.

—, [Review], *Monthly Review* (1841), pp. 430–40.

—, [Review], *Taits's Edinburgh Magazine* (1841), pp. 534–7.

—, [Review], *Churchman's Monthly Review* (January 1842), pp. 474–8.

Ballantyne, J. W., *Green's Encyclopedia of Medicine and Surgery*, vol. 1 (Edinburgh and London: W. Green, 1906).

Baring-Gould, S., *A Book of the Pyrenees* (London: Methuen & Co., 1907).

Berdou d'Aas, B., *Jeanne III d'Albret. Chronique (1528–1572)* (Biarritz: Atlantica, 2002).

Birkbeck M., *Notes on a Journey through France, from Dieppe through Paris and Lyons, to the Pyrennees, and back through Toulouse, in July, August, and September, 1814: Describing the Habits of the People and the Agriculture of the Country* (London: William Phillips, 1814).

Bourloton, E., G. Cougny and A. Robert (eds), 'Pierre Anastase Torné', *Dictionnaire des parlementaires français, de 1789–1889*, 5 vols (Paris: Bourloton, 1891), vol. 5, p. 430.

Boddington, M., *Sketches in the Pyrenees, with some Remarks on Languedoc, Provence, and the Cornice*, 2 vols (London: Longman, Rees, Orme, Brown, Greene, 1837).

Chandler, D., *Dictionary of the Napoleonic Wars* (New York: Macmillan, 1979).

Cholakian P. F. and R. C. Cholakian, *Marguerite de Navarre: Mother of the Renaissance* (New York: Columbia University Press, 2006).

Colbert, B., 'Bibliography of British Travel Writing, 1780–1840: The European Tour, 1814–1818 (excluding Britain and Ireland)', *Cardiff Corvey: Reading the Romantic Text*, 13 (Winter 2004), pp. 5–44.

Conolly, J., J. Forbes and A. Tweedie (eds), *The Cyclopaedia of Practical Medicine*, 4 vols (London: Sherwood, Gilbert, and Piper, and Balwin and Cradock, 1835), vol. 4, p. 485.

Cortés, A, and J. Pérez de la Riva, *La isla de Cuba en el siglo XIX vista por los extranjeros: en 1820* (La Habana: Biblioteca Nacional 'José Martí', 1966).

Costello, L. S., *Béarn and the Pyrenees. A Legendary Tour to the Country of Henri Quatre* (London: Richard Bentley, 1844).

Cotea, L. (ed.), *Vers l'Orient européen: Voyages et images Pays roumains, Bulgarie, Grèce, Constantinople* (Bucureşti: Editura Universităţii din Bucureşti, 2009).

Courteault, P., *Histoire de Gascogne et de Béarn* (Paris: Boivin, 1939).

Coverdale, J., *The Basque Phase of Spain's First Carlist War* (Princeton, NJ: Princeton University Press, 1984).

Coxe, H., *The Gentleman's Guide in his Tour through France; Being Particularly Descriptive of the Southern and Western Departments [...]* (London: Sherwood, Neely & Jones, [1817]).

Cummings J., *The Hound and the Hawk: The Art of Medieval Hunting* (London: Weidenfeld & Nicolson, 2001).

Cursente, B., 'La question des "cagots" du Béarn. Proposition d'une nouvelle piste de recherche', *Les Cahiers du Centre de Recherches Historiques*, 21 (October 1998) at http://ccrh.revues.org/2521 [accessed 10 May 2012].

Defour, A., *Théodore de Béze, poète et théologien* (Genève: Droz, 2006).

Dartigue, C., *Histoire de la Gascogne* (Paris: Presses Universitaires De France, 1951).

Diccionario de la Real Academia de la Lengua (Madrid: Espasa Calpe, 1992).

Disraeli, B., *Home Letters written by the Late Earl of Beaconsfield in 1830 and 1831* (London: John Murray, 1885).

Dugenne, A., *Panorama historique et descriptif de Pau et de ses environs* (Pau: Imprimerie et lithographie de E. Vignancour, 1839).

Ellis S., *Fireside Tales for the Young* (London: Peter Jackson, Late Fisher, Son, & Co., 1849).

Extramiana J., *Historia de las guerras carlistas* (San Sebastián, 1978–9).

Faget de Baure, M., *Essais historiques sur le Béarn* (Paris, Imprimerie Denugon, 1818).

Favier, F., *Bernadotte. Un maréchal d'Empire sur le trône de Suède* (Paris: Ellipses, 2010).

Ford R., *A Handbook of Travellers in Spain, and Readers and Home*, 1st edn (London: John Murray, 1845).

—, *Gatherings from Spain* (London: John Murray, 1846).

Freer, M. W., *Jeanne d'Albret, Queen of Navarre, 1528–1572* (London: Hurst and Blackett, 1861).

Glover, M., *The Peninsular War 1807–1814* (London: Penguin, 2001).

Grosvenor, E. M., *Narrative of a Yacht Voyage in the Mediterranean during the Years 1840 and 1841*, 2 vols (London: John Murray, 1842).

Hackett, F., *Francis The First* (New York: Doubleday, Doran and Company, Inc., 1937).

Holt, M. P., *The French Wars of Religion 1562–1626* (Cambridge: Cambridge University Press, 2005).

Hooper, R., *A New Medical Dictionary* (Philadelphia, PA: M. Carey & Son, Benjamin Warner, and Edward Parker, 1817).

Hugues Detems, J. F. (Abbot), *Le Clergé de France ou Tableau historique et chronologique des Archevêques, Evêques, Abbés, Abbesses & Chefs des Chapitres principaux du Royaume, depuis la fondation des Eglises jusqu'à nos jours* (Paris: Delalain, 1774).

Hummel, P., 'Paul-Jérémie Bitaubé, un philologue binational au XVIIIe siècle', *International Journal of Classical Tradition*, 2:4 (Spring 1996), pp. 510–35.

Inglis H. D., *Spain in 1830*, 2 vols (London: Whittaker, Treacher and Co., 1831).

— [Derwent Conway], *Switzerland, the South of France and the Pyrenees in 1830* (Edinburgh: Constable and Co., 1931).

Jameson, R. F., *Letters from the Havana, during the Year 1820* (London: John Miller, 1820).

—, *Aperçu statistique de l'Île de Cuba; precede de quelques lettres sur la Havan* (Paris: P. Dufart, 1826).

—, *Notices of the Reformation in the South-West Provinces of France* (London: R. B. Seely and W. Burnside, 1839).

Keightley, T., *Secret Societies of the Middle Ages* (London: William Clowes and Sons, 1837).

Laval S. A. Rev., *A Compendious History of the Reformation in France and of the Reformed Churches in that Kingdom from the First Beginnings of the Reformation to the Repealing of the Edict of Nantz, with an Account of the Late Persecution of the French Protestants under Lewis XIV*, 2 vols (London: H. Woodfall, 1738).

Lyman Roelker, N., *Queen of Navarre: Jeanne d'Albret, 1528–1572* (Cambridge, MA: Belknap Press of Harvard University Press, 1968).

Maritain Center, J. 'Barnabites' at http://www.newadvent.org/cathen/02302a.htm [accessed 24 April 2012].

Michel, F., *Histoire des races maudites* (Paris: A. Franck, 1847).

Milford, J., *Observations, Moral, Literary, and Antiquarian: Made during a Tour through the Pyrennees, South of France, Switzerland, the Whole of Italy and the Netherlands in the Years 1814 and 1815*, 2 vols (London: T. Davison, Whitefriars, for Longman, Hurst, Rees, Orme, and Brown and J. Hatchard, 1818).

Moody S. A. (ed.), *Life and Letters of Elizabeth Last Duchess of Gordon* (London: J. Nisbert and Co., 1865).

Mueller J. and J. Scodel (eds), *Elizabeth I: Translations, 1544–1589* (Chicago, IL: University of Chicago Press, 2009).

Oman, C., *Wellington's Army, 1809–1814* (London: Greenhill, [1912] 1993).

Ostolaza Elizondo, M. I., 'Fernando el Católico y Navarra. Ocupación y administración del reino entre 1512–1515', *Aragón en la Edad Media*, 20 (2008), pp. 559–78.

Palliser, Mrs B., *Historic Devices, Badges, and War-Cries* (London: Sampson Low, Son & Marston, 1870).

Pitts, V. J., *Henri IV of France: His Reign and Age* (Baltimore, MD: The Johns Hopkins Press, 2009).

Porqueres I Gene, E. 'La chaleur des cagots. Lèpre et inscription généalogique de la marginalité', *Les Cahiers du Centre de Recherches Historiques*, 21 (October 1998) at http://ccrh.revues.org/2523 [accessed 10 May 2012].

Puech A., *Histoire de Gascogne* (Auch: Dessaint, 1914).

Putnam, S., *Marguerite of Navarre* (New York: Grosset & Dunlap, 1936).

Robb. G., *The Discovery of France: A Historical Geography from the Revolution to the First World War* (New York and London: W. W. Norton, 2008).

Romer, I. F., *The Rhone, the Darro and the Guadalquivir: A Summer Ramble in 1842*, 2 vols (London: R. Bentley, 1843).

Russell, H. (Count), *Pau and the Pyrenees* (London: Longmans, Green and Co., 1871).

Sarasa Sánchez, E. (ed.), *Sancho Ramírez, rey de Aragón, y su tiempo (1064–1094)* (Huesca: Instituto de Estudios Altoaragonenses, 1994).

Saulnier. C. de, and A. Strubel, *La poetique de la chasse au Moyen Âge: les livres de chasse du XIVe siècle* (Paris: Presses Universitaires de France, 1994)

Scott W. (Sir), *Guy Mannering or The Astrologer*, 2nd edn (Edinburgh: James Ballantyne and Co, 1815).

Smith, D., *The Napoleonic Wars Data Book* (London: Greenhill, 1998).

Swain, M., *The Needlework of Mary, Queen of Scots* (Carlton, Bedfordshire: Ruth Bean Publishers, 1986).

Swinburne, H., *Travels through Spain, in the Years 1775 and 1776*, 2 vols (London: J. Davis, 1787).

Tondini di Quarenghi, C., 'Barnabites.' *The Catholic Encyclopedia*, vol. 2 (New York: Robert Appleton Company, 1907) at http://www.newadvent.org/cathen/02302a.htm [accessed 24 April 2012].

Vernier, R., *Lord of the Pyrenees: Gaston Febus, Count of Foix (1331–1391)* (Suffolk: Boydell and Brewer, 2008).

Vignancourt, E. (ed.), *Poésies Béarnaises* (Pau: Vignancourt 1827).

Witson, M., *Spain and Barbary. Letters to a Younger Sister during a Visit to Gibraltar, Cádiz, Sevilla, Tangier* (London: J. Hatchland, 1837).

CHRONOLOGY

1794   William Ellis is born in London into a humble working-class family. He develops a love for gardening and botany in his youth.

1799   Sarah Stickney is born into a tenant farmer's family. She is brought up as a Member of the Society of Friends but becomes a Congregationalist in 1837.

1816   Mr Ellis is ordained. He marries Mary Mercy Moor (9 November).

1816–24   Mrs Mary Mercy Ellis accompanies her husband throughout all his missionary travels in Polynesia and the Hawaiian Islands.

1823   Rev. Ellis publishes *A Journal of a Tour around Hawaii, the Largest of the Sandwich Islands*.

1824   (December) Sarah Stickney publishes her poem 'The Lament of the Peasant's Daughter' in *Kaleidoscope*.

1825   The Ellises return to England due to Rev. Ellis's health problems.

1829   Rev. Ellis publishes *Polynesian Researches, during a Residence of Nearly Six Years in the South Sea Islands*, 2 vols. His work is favourably reviewed by Robert Southey in the *Quarterly Review*.

1830   Rev. Ellis becomes Assistant Foreign Secretary of the London Missionary Society and then Chief Foreign Secretary. He is also the editor of an annual called the *Christian Keepsake*.

1832   Rev. Ellis publishes *Polynesian Researches, during a Residence of Nearly Eight Years in the South Sea Islands*, 3 vols (2nd edn). He establishes himself as a successful and well-known geographical and travel writer. Sarah Stickney publishes *The Negro Slave* and *Contrasts, a Series of Twenty Drawings Designed by S. Stickney*.

1833   Sarah Stickney publishes *Pictures of Private Life*.

1835   (January) Mary Ellis dies. She leaves four children to the care of Rev. Ellis.

1835   Stickney publishes *The Poetry of Life*, 2 vols. It is reviewed relatively unfavourably by Edgar A. Poe in *Southern Literary Messenger* (January 1836). It receives another unfavourable review in the *Knickerbocker* (August 1843). It is also reviewed in *Athenaeum* (29 February 1840).

1836   Rev. Ellis publishes a biography of his wife Mary, *Memoir of Mrs. Mary Mercy Ellis*. Stickney publishes *Home, or the Iron Rule, a Domestic Story*, 3 vols.

1837   Sarah Stickney marries Rev. William Ellis.

1838   Rev. Ellis publishes *History of Madagascar: Comprising also the Progress of the Christian Mission Established in 1818, and an Authentic Account of the Recent Martyrdom of Rafaravavy, and of the Persecution of the Native Christians, Compiled Chiefly from Original Documents*, 2 vols.

1839   Mrs Ellis publishes *The Women of England: Their Social Duties and Domestic Habits*.

1839   (December) Rev. and Mrs Ellis travel to the south-west area of the French Pyrenees. They spend eleven months in Béarn due to an undisclosed ailment of Rev. Ellis.

1839   (27 December) The Ellises travel from Paris to Bordeaux. They stop at Tours.

1839   (28 December) They leave for Pau, passing through Mont-de-Marsar and Aire.

1840   (1 January) They reach Pau and decide to settle there.

1840   (February to March) They go on excursions to visit Orthez, Jurançon, Gan, Rebenac, Louvie, Nay and Eaux Chaudes. They always return to Pau.

1840   (April) They visit Gelos, Urzein, Lescar and Bilhere.

1840   (May) They visit (and spend some time) in Eaux Bonnes, Eaux Chaudes and Gabas. They go back to Pau.

1840   (mid-June) They leave Pau for visits to Bizanos, Betharram, Argelez, Pierrefitte, Cauterets, Luz, St Sauver, Garvanie, Gédre, Barégan, Trasmesages, Grip and Bagnéres de Bigorre.

1840   (End of June until August) They reside at Bagnères and make excursions to St Paul and Campan.

1840   (Beginning of September) Bagnères, Cauterets, Lourdes, Pont d'Espagne, Pierrefitte, Luz and St Saveur.

1840   (Mid-September) Campan, Barèges, Bagnères.

1840   (End of October) They go back to Pau. They visit Tarbes.

1840   (November) Pau. They go on excursions to Oleron, Bidos, Bedous, Osse, Accous, Eggum and Urdos.

1840   Mrs Ellis publishes *The Sons of the Soil, a Poem*.

1841   (2 April) Mrs Ellis finishes writing her preface to *Summer and Winter in the Pyrenees*.

1841   First edition of Mrs Ellis's *Summer and Winter in the Pyrenees*.

1841   Mrs Ellis publishes *Family Secrets: or, Hints to Those who would Make Home Happy*, 3 vols.

1842   Mrs Ellis publishes *The Daughters of England: Their Position in Society, Character and Responsibilities* and *Dangers of Dining Out, or Hints to Those who would Make Home Happy.*

1843   Mrs Ellis publishes *A Voice for the Vintage, or the Force of Example. Addressed to Those who Think and Feel; The Wives of England: Their Relative Duties, Domestic Influences and Social Obligations.* Reviewed in *Athenaeum* (24 April 1858). She also publishes *The Mothers of England: Their Influence & Responsibilities* and *Mrs Ellis's Housekeeping Made Easy.*

1843–4 Publication of *The Select Works of Mrs Ellis.*

1844   Publication of *The Prose Works of Mrs Ellis; The Brother and Sister and Other Tales; The Juveline Scrap-book; The Minister's Family, or Hints to Those Who would Make Home Happy; The Irish Girl and Other Poems,* and *The Family Monitor and Domestic Guide.*

1843–6 A series of jokes at Mrs Ellis's expense appear in *Punch*: 1843 (vol. 5); 1844 (vol. 6); 1844 (vol. 7); 1845 (vol. 8) and 1846 (vol. 10).

1844   Rev. Ellis publishes vol. 1 of *History of the London Missionary Society.*

1844   Rev. and Mrs Ellis retire to their country house ('Rose Hill') in the village of Hoddesdon (Hertfordshire) due to the former's ill health.

1845   Mrs Ellis publishes *The Family Monitor and Domestic Guide: Women of England; Daughters of England; Wives of England; Mothers of England* and *Look to the End, or the Bennets Abroad,* 2 vols, reviewed in *Athenaeum* (15 February 1845) and *The Select Works of Mrs Ellis* and *The Young Ladies' Reader, or Extracts from Modern Authors,* reviewed in *Athenaeum* (10 May 1845).

c. 1845 Mrs Ellis publishes a school prospectus titled 'Progressive Education for Young Ladies'.

1846   Mrs Ellis publishes *The Island Queen, a Poem* and *Temper and Temperament: or, Varieties of Character,* 2 vols.

1847   Mrs Ellis publishes *Prevention Better than Cure: or, the Moral Wants of the World We Live In* and *Guide to Social Happiness.* Second edition of *Summer and Winter in the Pyrenees* is published.

1848   Mrs Ellis publishes *Rawdon House, Hints on Formation of Character,* based on her experiences as a teacher in the educational institution Rawdon House, a school for girls.

1849   Mrs Ellis publishes *Fireside Tales for the Young,* 4 vols and *Social Distinction, or Hearts and Homes,* 3 vols.

1850   Mrs Ellis publishes *Conversations of Human Nature: For the Young; The Morning Call: A Table Book of Literature and Art,* 4 vols and *Fireside Stories.*

1850–2   Mrs Ellis publishes *Self-Deception, or the History of a Human Heart* (serialized in the *Morning Call*).

1853   Mrs Ellis publishes *My Brother, or, the Man of Many Friends* [by an Old Author]. Rev. Ellis is sent to Madagascar as the official representative of the London Missionary Society, but is refused entry. The couple settles in Mauritius. After some attempts, they manage to be allowed entry.

1853–65   Missionary stay in Madagascar.

1854   Mrs Ellis publishes *The Value of Health*.

1856   Mrs Ellis publishes *The Education of Character: With Hints of Moral Training*, reviewed in *Athenaeum* (31 January 1857) and *The Mother's Mistake, a Tale*.

1858   Rev. Ellis publishes *Three Visits to Madagascar during the Years 1853–1854–1856: Including a Journey to the Capital with Notices of the Natural History of the Country and of the Present Civilization of the People*. Mrs Ellis publishes *Friends at their Own Fireside, or Pictures of the Private Life of the People Called Quakers*, 2 vols, reviewed in *Athenaeum* (19 June 1858).

1859   Mrs Ellis publishes *The Widow Green and her Three Nieces*, reviewed in *Athenaeum* (21 January 1859) and *The Mothers of Great Men* reviewed in *Athenaeum* (14 June 1859).

1860   Mrs Ellis publishes *Chapters on Wives*, reviewed in *Athenaeum* (14 July 1860).

1862   Mrs Ellis publishes *Janet, One of Many: A Story in Verse* reviewed in *Athenaeum* (4 October 1862).

1863   Mrs Ellis publishes *Pique, a Novel*, 3 vols; *The Brewer's Family* and *Madagascar: Its Social and Religious Progress*.

1865   The Ellises return to England. Rev. Ellis lectures extensively about his experiences and his travels in Madagascar. Mrs Ellis publishes *William and Mary, or the Fatal Blow* and *Share and Share Alike, or the Grand Principle*.

1866   Mrs Ellis publishes *The Beautiful in Nature & Art*. Reviewed in *Athenaeum* (7 July 1866) and in *British Quarterly Review* 44 (July and October 1866).

1867   Rev. Ellis publishes *Madagascar Revisited, Describing the Events of a New Reign and the Revolution which Followed: Setting Forth also the Persecutions Endured by the Christians, and their Heroic Sufferings, with Notices of the Present State and Prospects of the People*.

1868   Mrs Ellis publishes *Northern Roses A Yorkshire Story*, 3 vols.

1869   Mrs Ellis publishes *Education of the Heart: Women's Best Work*, reviewed in *Athenaeum* (11 June 1870).

1870	Rev. Ellis publishes *The Martyr Church of Madagascar: A Narrative of the Introduction, Progress, and Triumph of Christianity in Madagascar, with Notices of Personal Intercourse and Travel in the Island.*
1872	(9 June) Rev. Ellis dies from a cold. He is buried in the Congregationalists' non-denominational Abney Park Cemetery (London).
1872	(16 June) Mrs Ellis dies a week after her husband. She is buried at Hoddesdon (Hertfordshire).
1873	John E. Ellis (Rev. Ellis's son) and Henry Allen publish a biography of William Ellis: *Life of William Ellis, Missionary to the South Seas and to Madagascar.*
1889	Mrs Bayley publishes *The Life and Letters of Mrs Sewell*. Mrs Sewell was Mrs Ellis's sister-in-law. This biography of Mrs Sewell includes a few minor anecdotes related to Mrs Ellis. An entry on William Ellis is included in the *Dictionary of National Biography, 1885–1900*, vol. 17, written by William Garden Blaikie. This entry also alludes to Mrs Ellis and her literary works.
1893	Publication of *The Home Life and Letters of Mrs Ellis Compiled by her Nieces.*
1905	The Anglo-Australian Agnes Grant Hay (1838–1910) publishes *Afterglow Memories,* where she occasionally speaks about her acquaintance with Mrs Ellis.
2004	An entry titled 'Ellis, Sarah (1799–1872)' appears in the *ODNB*.

SARAH ELLIS

Sarah Ellis, née Stickney, (1799–1872) was famous not for being a travel writer, but for being a writer of female conduct books, her most well-known being *The Wives of England* (1843), *The Women of England: Their Social Duties and Domestic Habits* (1839), *The Mothers of England* (1843) and *The Daughters of England* (1842), as mentioned in the general introduction to this series. Born into a family belonging to the Society of Friends, in 1837 she joined the Congregational church before marrying Rev. William Ellis, whose ill health was the cause of their journey to the Pyrenees from December 1839 until November 1840, during which time they settled in Pau.

All the reviews of this travel book are anonymous and, save the first review mentioned below, are lacking a title, headed merely with the publication details of the work. The edition of *Summer and Winter in the Pyrenees* presented here is the first edition of 1841, published by Fisher, Son and Co. Although it does not contain the year of publication, the fact that it was reviewed in the *Literary Gazette and Journal of the Belles Lettres, Arts, Sciences, for the Year 1841*[1] leaves no doubt that it had been published just before this date. This review states that Mrs Ellis's work is 'a pleasant guide to the baths', showing that perhaps its anonymous author had not read the work in its entirety. Indeed, this review's main asset is to give a clue as to the work's date of publication, as apart from the above-mentioned comment, all it does is reproduce a few passages from the book.

The book's moralistic and religious tone was discussed in several texts. In the *Churchman's Monthly Review*,[2] which was published in January 1842, the reader is assured that Mrs Ellis 'has produced a very lively, agreeable and interesting work'[3] whose 'chief recommendation' is 'the high tone of moral and religious feeling, by which it is pervaded'.[4] The reviewer commends the author for the fact that her evangelical observations 'rise naturally from the scenery or objects which she is contemplating, and come, therefore, with double effect'.[5] In line with this comment, a short mention of Mrs Ellis's book in *Home Missionary Magazine* also credits the work for being 'the production of a christian writer, and therefore perfectly safe in the hands of juvenile readers, whose standards of morality, might not be raised by every exhibition of foreign habits and manners'.[6] Also, in the 'Literary Register' of *Taits's Edinburgh Magazine*, where large passages of the book are reproduced, the reviewer makes the following comment about Mrs Ellis:

> If any shall condemn her for English prudery and narrow views, in the threatened danger to morals and religion, which she predicts, from intercourse with our continental neighbours, and from breaking up of our domestic habits, they may be consoled by learning that her work furnishes the antidote, in showing that travel may be a healthful and improving exercise for both body and mind. [7]

The reviewer in *Eclectic Review* states that Mrs Ellis is 'Free from the absurd prejudices of many English tourists, yet deeply sensible of the paramount importance of religious truth'[8] and concludes by recommending the work as 'a safe guide'.

Another interesting review, published in the *Monthly Review*, is perhaps slightly more critical than the ones mentioned above, although the reader is assured that the work 'requires, and admits of, very little criticism'.[9] Despite placing Mrs Ellis on a par with Countess Blessington, whose work *The Idler in France*[10] is also reviewed in the same volume of the *Monthly Review* by the same anonymous reviewer,[11] and calling them 'two accomplished women speaking at the same time',[12] the reader is told that Mrs Ellis had 'less knowledge of our Gallic neighbours, and therefore deals more with appearances than essentials, – with external signs than principles'.[13] The reviewer admits that the book's content about Protestants in Pau and other places 'will interest some readers'.[14] Her book is likened to a 'guide-book' and descriptions which the reviewer decides are 'lively or distinct'[15] are reproduced.

It is necessary to make an observation that is pertinent to the content of Mrs Ellis's travel book. Like other writers of the age, she borrows freely from other sources without quoting them. Such examples are to be found in the editorial notes whenever they have been located. One such example of this 'borrowing' corresponds to Dugenne's *Panorama historique et descriptif de Pau et de ses environs*, which Mrs Ellis merely justifies as 'related by a French writer' (p. 72). Another instance is the information she gives 'on good authority', which the anonymous reviewer in the *Monthly Review* refers to sarcastically, attributing her comments on the expenditure of the English in France to mere guesswork.[16] My own opinion is that she was copying this information from some unidentified source.

The second edition of *Summer and Winter in the Pyrenees* was published in 1847 as part of the Fisher, Son and Co. Englishwomen's Family Library series. It is identical to the first in its pages and page numbers, and like the first edition the date of publication is not shown. It only differs from the first edition in the expression 'Second Edition' on its title page after the quote by Inglis.

Notes

1. *Literary Gazette and Journal of the Belles Lettres, Arts, Sciences, for the Year 1841*, 1274 (19 June 1841), p. 388.
2. *Churchman's Monthly Review* (January 1842), pp. 474–8.
3. Ibid., p. 474.
4. Ibid., p. 477.
5. Ibid., p. 476.
6. *Home Missionary Magazine* (1841), pp. 260–1.
7. *Taits's Edinburgh Magazine* (1841), pp. 534–7, on p. 537.
8. *Eclectic Review* (1841), pp. 235–6, on p. 36.
9. *Monthly Review* (1841), pp. 430–40, on p. 430.
10. M. Gardiner, Countess of Blessington, *The Idler in France* (London: Henry Colburn, 1841).
11. Ellis's review states that 'In reviewing the "Idler in France", we saw that ...' (*Monthly Review*, p. 430).
12. *Monthly Review*, p. 430.
13. Ibid.
14. Ibid., p. 434.
15. Ibid., p. 436.
16. Ibid., p. 438.

Drawn by Mrs Ellis.

The Chateau of Pau and Bridge of Gavarzcan.

FISHER, SON & Co LONDON & PARIS.

Engraved by J.C. Bentley.

SUMMER AND WINTER

IN

THE PYRENEES.

BY THE AUTHOR OF

"THE WOMEN OF ENGLAND," "THE SONS OF THE
SOIL," AND "FAMILY SECRETS."

" I know of no pleasure that will compare with going abroad,
excepting one—returning home."—*Inglis.*

FISHER, SON, & CO.
NEWGATE STREET, LONDON; RUE St. HONORÉ, PARIS.

PREFACE.

———◆———

IT is one of the duties we owe to society, that the pleasures we enjoy, and the difficulties we encounter in our own experience, should be made conducive to the benefit of others, who may in future be similarly circumstanced with ourselves. Deeming it probable that many individuals under the necessity of hastening from England to the south of France, may wish to know something of the climate, the scenery, and the inhabitants of that salubrious region, it is my desire in offering the present work to the public, not only to supply information to such travellers; but to afford amusement, interest, and I would

fain hope, some degree of instruction, to those
whose circumstances or inclination detain
them at home.

In this attempt, I have been chiefly stimu-
lated by the inconvenience I myself experienced in leaving England, without being
able to meet with any work containing the
information of which I was in want; for
amongst the few writers who have made the
Pyrenees the subject of their observations,
there is, I believe, not one who has written
more recently than eight or ten years ago;
while the annual influx of strangers into this
part of France, the increased facilities for
travelling, and the improvements in general
accommodation are now so great, that the
neighbourhood of the Pyrenees can only be
said to be the same as it was ten years ago,
in the simplicity of its peculiar people, the
luxury of its delicious climate, and the almost
unrivalled beauty of its majestic and varied
scenery.

In alluding to the writers in whose steps it would have been presumption for me to tread, but for the circumstance already stated, I must not omit to mention the lively and spirit-stirring narrative of Mr. Inglis, whose talent for description would have left little for others to say on this subject, except that his notice of the Pyrenees appended to that of Switzerland is so short, as to occupy not more than a hundred pages, in which there is no mention of some favourite situations amongst the mountains now much frequented, and only a slight and passing notice of Pau. Besides which, his book is rendered at once more interesting, and less useful, to the common order of travellers, by the enterprising spirit and indefatigable energy of the writer having led him rather over the summit of mountain ranges, than along the beaten tracks, which steps less practised and less vigorous are condemned to travel.

In the following pages, I have made no

pretension to observations either of a scientific or a political nature. Mine is a simple detail of impressions made upon my own mind, from the scenes and circumstances around me; and although the egotism of this style of writing may need some apology, I believe it is the only prudent and useful method, by which persons of no considerable attainment in science or philosophy, can transmit to higher and more gifted minds, such facts as they may not have the same opportunity of witnessing, but from which they may thus be enabled to draw important conclusions.

Trusting that the seeming trifles here recorded, and which have been collected from a journal kept on the spot, and transmitted at different times to my friends in England, may now afford gratification to a wider circle, I can only wish, that all who read these pages may participate in the pleasure I have enjoyed, while they escape the fatigue and

inconvenience by which such pleasure is
necessarily accompanied; and that they may
feel, on behalf of themselves and their friends,
the same gratitude for those attractions of
scenery, and advantages of climate, which
will always be associated with my recollections of a residence of fifteen months amongst
the Pyrenees.

Pau, April 2nd, 1841.

CONTENTS.

CONTENTS.

CHAP. IV.

CHAP. V.

CHAP. VL

CHAP. VII.

CONTENTS.

CHAP. VIIL

CHAP. IX.

CHAP. X.

CHAP. XI.

CONTENTS.

CHAP. XII.

CHAPTER I.

DEPARTURE FROM PARIS—TRAVELLING IN FRANCE—
ARRIVAL AT BORDEAUX—CLIMATE OF THE SOUTH
—FRENCH BREAKFASTS—JOURNEY FROM BORDEAUX
—DEPARTMENT OF THE LANDES—FIRST SIGHT OF
THE PYRENEES—ARRIVAL AT PAU.

THE friendly relations which for the last five and
twenty years have so happily subsisted between
England and France, together with the increased
facility for travelling on the Continent, which
the general tranquillity of Europe has afforded,
have left little to be added to our information respecting France and the French nation in general.

There are, however, sections of that country,
scarcely rivalled by any other in their grandeur
and beauty, inhabited by communities whose simplicity of manners, and characteristic peculiarities,
cannot fail to interest; yet whose situation, widely
remote from the routes most frequently pursued by
English travellers through France, Switzerland, and

B

2   SUMMER AND WINTER

Italy, renders them in many respects, an unknown
people; while the beautiful scenery by which they
are surrounded, remains comparatively unexplored.

One of these delightful regions, the neighbourhood of the French Pyrenees, Mr. Ellis and myself
were induced, for the recovery of his health, to visit
at the close of the year 1839; and, deeming it most
prudent, as the season was so far advanced, not to
linger by the way, we decided upon travelling by
the Malle Poste from Paris to Bordeaux, after remaining only a few days in the former city.

It was on the 27th of December, at seven in the
evening, that we commenced this journey, having
been told that if the roads were good, we should
perform it in thirty-six hours.   With so many miles
of constant travelling before us, it was no small
satisfaction to find that we had the carriage entirely
to ourselves, and that besides this, it was so roomy
and commodious, as to admit of almost any change
of position.   There was, however, one inconvenience in travelling by the Malle Poste, for which,
happily, our kind friends in Paris had prepared us.
We were only permitted to stop for refreshment
once, by the way; so that without the provision of
cold fowl, bread, and water, which we only happened
to think of the moment before setting out, our situation would have been somewhat deplorable.

After the acquaintance we had made with French diligences and all their equipments, on the road from Boulogne to Paris, we considered ourselves as setting out in great style in the Malle Poste, with four respectable white horses; and the night being dark and rainy, we were not conscious until the morning, how far our whole set-out had fallen short of the expectations at first excited. We then found that although our carriage was drawn by five horses instead of four, they were of the most grotesque description,—raw-boned and shaggy, with their tails tied up in bunches; and their heads, necks, and bodies, hung about with harness consisting of thongs of leather neither tanned nor cleaned, and arranged in such a manner as would baffle the ingenuity of any but a Frenchman. In addition to all which, they had immense collars hung about with little tinkling bells, which to an English ear, would seem to announce a merry andrew, rather than a mail coach.

The postilions too, were as remarkable as the animals they drove; and like them, were changed about every five miles. Sometimes these men sat in the dicky; sometimes on one of the horses; sometimes they wore smart blue jackets ornamented with silver lace; sometimes the short blue frocks of the peasants; and sometimes they had the skins of

B 2

4   SUMMER AND WINTER

dogs or calves tied round them. But whatever
their garments were composed of, they always
floated about in the wind, as wild and loose as
possible. Most of these men wore the wooden shoes
of the country, turned up at the toe, with a sharp
point, and sometimes, also, finished off behind with
a high sharp heel, with which they trod on the
backs of the horses as they clambered up and down.

If any one should be disposed to doubt the real
difference of national character between the French
and the English, they need only look at such public
conveyances, to be convinced in a moment, that
there is something radically dissimilar in their
modes of thinking and feeling; or perhaps, I ought
rather to say, in the impressions they receive from
the same object. Polite as we all allow them to
be, and celebrated as they justly are for their good
taste, the French look every day without a smile,
or a wish for improvement, upon some of the most
outlandish machines that ever were constructed for
the conveyance of passengers; and which, if they
were driven along the streets of London, would
unquestionably attract a mob.

How many passengers a diligence is intended to
carry, is not easy to ascertain; for what with its
three apartments within, its piles of luggage on the
top, the number of persons who scramble up to a

receptacle in front of the roof, and the additional number who insist upon having taken their places, and have to be pulled out by main force to make room for others, a French diligence might be supposed by a stranger, to be transporting the inhabitants of a whole village. And then the shouting, whooping, cracking, and coaxing, with which the whole affair is kept going!

The variety of trappings which compose the harness of French horses, would scarcely be expected, from its appearance, to hold together for a single mile; and the fact is, that something always does give way about every ten minutes. Such accidents, however, unless more than commonly serious, occasion no delay; for the driver hangs his reins upon a hook on the dicky, descends like a monkey, and then runs sideways as fast as the horses can go, adjusting the broken harness all the time. The great beauty of the whole affair is, that the horses go just as well when he is not driving, as when he is; nor does the breaking of a trace or two seem to make the least difference in the movement of the vehicle.

After all, we must not be too ready to smile at a French diligence, when it possesses two points of excellence, which some of our public conveyances of far higher pretensions, would be much improved

6   SUMMER AND WINTER

by adopting.   In the first place it is extremely easy;
and in the next, it is so constructed that the driver
or conducteur can lock the hind wheel without
descending from his seat, which, in a hilly country,
or in a case of danger, is an amazing advantage.

The first night we spent in the Malle Poste, was
certainly the most comfortable I ever experienced
in travelling.   On looking out the following morning at early dawn, we found that a wide river was
rolling its cold blue waters beside us.   It was the
Loire, on whose banks we travelled for many miles,
our road being a straight, and apparently interminable line of mud, with rows of tall poplars on
each side, and the low country all around us under
water; so that it was sometimes difficult to say
which was the exact course of the river.

Very little variety of scene presents itself in this
route in the winter; for even the washerwomen,
who at first look so strange and so picturesque, are
so numerous and frequent, that you soon learn to
look at them, as you do at the straight roads and
poplars, only as necessary parts of the scene.   I
had been accustomed to think that English artists,
in drawing continental scenery, put in the washerwomen and the linen by way of effect.   But of
such frequency and importance is this process,
carried on in the open air, that amongst the first

objects which attracted my attention on the banks
of the Loire, were ranges of rafts and rudely constructed vessels, appropriated exclusively to the
washerwomen; while long lines by the sides of the
water displayed the clean white linen, sometimes
hanging in terraces one above another up the sides
of the hills.

Throughout the whole of our journey, we had
looked in vain for what we should call in England
the houses of the gentry. Chateaux, ancient and
modern, were here and there to be seen, but not
those neat and comfortable dwellings of a somewhat
lower grade, which grace the whole of our native
isle. Indeed the French have no idea of the *countenance* of a house, or that a good front door, and
respectable entrance, give as much character to the
appearance of a house, as a nose and mouth to
that of a human face. Thus you see in a French
house an excellent roof and plenty of windows, the
middle row particularly good, while the doors are
like barn doors, and the filth and forlornness of the
way up to them beyond all description. Cow
houses, and stables in England, are approached
more agreeably; and all this is found where the
furniture of the first floor consists of marble and
wood of the finest polish, and curtains arranged
with the nicest regard to elegance and taste.

8   SUMMER AND WINTER

Among the ancient and often dilapidated chateaux, whose gloomy looking towers appeared to us
to frown on the neighbouring country, the Castle
of Blois, so rich in historical associations, is altogether one of the most grand and imposing I
remember to have ever beheld. The city of Blois
occupies a commanding situation on the slope of a
hill, extending down to the banks of the Loire,
which is crossed by a handsome bridge; but it is
the princely castle which claims more particularly
the attention of the traveller, and which we especially regretted not having time to visit.

Before reaching Tours, which is the next place of
importance in this route, a curious scene presents
itself. On the opposite side of the Loire, is an
extensive line of rugged limestone rock, not only
clothed with vines trained about in every possible
variety, but actually hollowed out into human
dwellings, for apparently a very considerable population; so that you see doors, and windows, balconies, and those innumerable staircases that wind
up the outside of almost all the old houses in
France, mingled with the light drapery of the vines,
which even as we saw them, without their garniture
of leaves, looked picturesque, and almost beautiful.

Attracted, as all travellers must be, by the fine

old Cathedral of Tours, and by the noble bridge
which spans the river, we would gladly have stayed
here to make further observations upon both—to say
nothing of the desirableness of a breakfast, after
twelve hours' travelling, an idea by no means unlikely to occur to an English traveller. No such
indulgence, however, was allowed us. The letters
were handed out, and away we drove again, truly
rejoiced to think that we were not wholly unprovided. Nor was it until seven in the evening that
we were permitted to descend from our vehicle, for
half an hour, to dine at a miserable looking inn,
where, in a little room scarcely large enough for a
table, we had the usual profusion of dishes, followed
by an excellent dessert.

We had been told that we should reach Bordeaux
about six the following morning; but such was the
state of the roads, that when the light of day again
dawned, we were far from the end of our journey;
and what made us less reconciled to our situation,
it was Sunday. Rain was still falling heavily, and
the atmosphere having become milder as we advanced southward, we seemed to be travelling
through a region of steam; while the country
people, regardless of the heavy rains, were as
busy and as brisk as ever. Notwithstanding the

10   SUMMER AND WINTER

Sabbath too, they were buying and selling, and in some places even working in the fields, the same as on other days.

It was here, I think, we felt most forcibly that we were far from England, and widely separated from those sacred privileges which a Sabbath in our native land affords. Instead of " the sound of the church-going bell," and the country people walking quietly in family groups to the place of worship, the father with his youngest child, and the mother with her Bible in her hand, all serious, orderly, and respectable, here in every village through which we passed, there was held a sort of market; while the falling rain, the dirt of the roads, and above all the indescribable filth of the doorways, gave an aspect of disorder and dis-comfort to the whole country. Well might we exclaim, " Is this the laughing France which tra-vellers have painted in such glowing colours? "

It was early on the second day of our journey that we crossed the Dordogne, a broad river, over which a beautiful suspension bridge has just been erected; which, for want of more solid foundation, is said to be already giving way. The road over the bridge not then being opened, we were driven at great speed through a little dirty village on the banks of the river; and the masons employed about the new works, having nearly blocked up the way with masses of stone and timber, we had to tack about amongst the deep mire, avoiding with some difficulty the cottage walls, notwithstanding the heaps of rubbish which generally form a sort of embankment at every door. Yet on we went, without ever stopping, slashing and clattering, with the usual whoop and jingle, down a steep narrow way, directly on board the ferry boat which was to convey us across the river; and here the opportunity was deemed eligible for changing horses, after which process we were left, with the new set, standing close to the edge of the boat; so that a single unruly movement would have plunged them and us into the water.

The road from this place to Bordeaux appeared to us most dreary; but the rain having now softened into a warm steamy haze, we could not for some hours see many yards before us. The weather began to clear, however, before noon, when the road turning suddenly round the side of a hill, we saw before us the noble city of Bordeaux, with the no less noble Garonne, bearing on its bosom the merchandise of many lands. It was a splendid sight, and repaid us for much of the discomfort of our journey.

Seldom have travellers arrived at a resting place

more weary and forlorn than we were at Bordeaux;
but, soon located at a comfortable hotel, we were
in a condition to enjoy the full benefit of cold
water and excellent coffee, as well as to appreciate
the kind services of one of those pretty French
women, who wait upon you with a sort of intuitive
notion of all your wants.

But for the tact of the French, and their general
disposition to oblige, it would be impossible for
the numbers of English who know nothing, or
next to nothing of the language, to penetrate as
they do into every part of this country. The
language of Babel could not exceed, nor can
imagination conceive anything to equal the jargon
of utterance to which the French will not only
listen without a smile, but with the kindest wish to
attach some possible meaning to the sounds conveyed; but no sooner does the idea strike them,
than they finish the sentence for the stammering
stranger, and act upon it before he has had time
to blush. It is, perhaps, unnecessary to say, that
not only the totally ignorant, but many who consider themselves pretty well fortified by an English
education against the difficulties of travelling
abroad, are often placed in this situation; for it
is not merely an acquaintance with French literature, that will be found necessary in arranging the

business of hotels and public conveyances. Far more valuable to the traveller would be the familiar use of the names of domestic utensils, and the usual mode of reckoning money, with the general phraseology of inns and waiters. I must not, however, undervalue a previous knowledge of the general construction of the language.

One of our first objects on arriving at Bordeaux, was to send off some of our letters of introduction, which were soon followed by a visit from an excellent Swiss gentleman, whose residence is at a little distance, but who spends the Sunday with his family in the city, for the advantage of attending Protestant worship. After cheerfully undertaking for us every act of kindness which such entire strangers could require, he left us under an engagement to join his family and a few French and English protestants, at his house in the evening, where a religious service is regularly held.

On our way to the house of this gentleman, we had to cross a large public square, or place, containing about five acres of ground, surrounded by avenues of acacias already budding, as they do with us in the months of April or May. On this place were assembled groups of people apparently from all countries, and clothed in as many varieties of costume. But the climate—the atmosphere !—

14   SUMMER AND WINTER

what words can describe the almost magical change
to us from that of England! It seemed as if
storm and tempest never had been there. The
most bland and silent summer's evening in our
country about the hour of nine, is not so soft and
balmy; besides all which, the sunset glow of the
warm south gave to the whole scene a brilliancy
of effect beyond what can be imagined in our
northern clime.

Before us the broad river was sleeping, blue and
clear, without a ripple or a wave, crowded on both
sides with shipping from all the countries of
Europe, the dark sides and white masts of the
vessels reflected in the clear deep water; while
every sail and oar remained as motionless as death.
Far away, to the left, stretched the noble quay,
curving with the line of the river, and forming an
unbroken crescent more than three miles in extent,
composed of irregular but handsome buildings,
diversified by many beautiful towers and spires
which rose behind; and all constructed of that
yellow kind of stone which gives to architecture
the richest tints of colouring, when mixed with the
venerable grey of hoary time.

No wonder that this spacious promenade should
be thronged with loitering visitors, when it offers
such a view. It is true the·people who sauntered

there were idle, but they were not disorderly; and the attractive costume of the women, particularly their head-dresses, and their clear, soft, and glowing complexions, made them all look lovely to strangers suddenly transported, as we were, from the cold and drizzle of an English winter, to this region of beauty and balm, where it was a perfect luxury to stand still, and breathe the soft evening air, without a shudder or a chill.

The common people of France, throughout the whole of our journey, had appeared to us remarkably good looking. Their long and well-formed noses, dark eyes and hair, neat mouths, white teeth, and more than all their complexions, not fair, but rich, like the fresh bloom of a peach,—neither red nor yellow, but just such a mixture of both as can only be described by a perfect glow; yet all the while so delicate, as the sunset tints of the western sky, though rich in colouring, are delicate in the extreme. I have seen hundreds of country-men in France, whose portraits would have graced a picture gallery; and perhaps an equal number of women, any of whom a painter would have been glad to place on a balcony open to the setting sun, and wreathe about with roses. But a really interesting face, such a face as carries the imagination home with it—a face to remember,

16   SUMMER AND WINTER

and to wish to meet again after many days;—such a face I have seldom found in France. They are pictures all; and whether young or old, the people wear such dresses, and place themselves in such positions, that one longs perpetually to transmit them to canvass.

It was a beautiful sight, for example, to see the women by the side of the road we travelled, tending their little flocks of sheep, with their knitting in their hands, or more frequently spinning with the old-fashioned distaff; often seated on a bank, with two or three brown goats beside them, and a large shepherd's dog sleeping at their feet.

I have said that the head-dresses of the French women are becoming, yet doubt whether an exception must not be made of the caps worn by the old and middle-aged women in Bordeaux and the neighbourhood, which are of such enormous dimensions as almost to baffle description, and defy belief. One would think it impossible to maintain such a fabric of stiff muslin in wet weather, but that in France neither men nor women are ever separated from their umbrellas, especially in the south, where they are used to keep off the sun as well as the rain, and are often of a bright red colour. The narrow streets of Paris, seen as I first beheld them, in heavy rain, gave me the idea of rivers of umbrellas; and I was afterwards amused to see the peasants of the south using these inseparable accompaniments on horseback. Even the men who break stones by the roadside have their umbrellas, which I have no doubt they would hold in one hand, while they used the hammer with the other, but that they all have screens, made of straw worked into a wooden frame, which they set up to shelter them from the wind and rain.

Besides the complexions of the people above described, every person, every object in Bordeaux seemed to wear a colouring entirely new to me; for the effect produced by a southern climate upon the aspect of nature, is such as no art can imitate, no pen describe. In short, it must be seen and felt, to be really understood. I am aware, that much of the vividness of an impression is sometimes owing to its being the first of the kind received; yet I believe all travellers agree that Bordeaux is one of the most splendid cities in the world; its public buildings many of them unrivalled; while the busy, cheerful aspect of its numerous population, is one that never tires.

The Garonne at Bordeaux is between six and seven hundred yards in breadth; and the bridge of seventeen arches, by which it is crossed, is one hundred and nine feet longer than Waterloo

18   SUMMER AND WINTER

Bridge. The construction of this bridge is singular : it has not only an aqueduct by which water
is conveyed into the city, but a sort of interior
passage, or covered way, by which one may pass
along over the arches, the whole length of the
bridge.

Novel and interesting as the whole scene presented by the river, the quay, the bridge, and the
spacious promenade was to us, we were not reluctant to repair to the house of the kind Swiss
gentleman, at the appointed hour. Here we found
a congregation of about forty or fifty persons assembled, who had already commenced the evening
service by singing some of the sweetest hymns I
ever heard. The lady who took the lead in the
music was a daughter of Dr. Malan, of Geneva, with
the same intelligent countenance, and marked by a
strong resemblance to her father. Her husband, who
was son to the gentleman of the house, delivered a
short but impressive address ; and the meeting then
closed with prayer and another hymn : after which
the party separated, and we returned to our hotel,
well pleased to have found a little community of
kindred minds, so distant from our native land.

We had, on the following day, great pleasure in
visiting a depository of the Holy Scriptures in this
place. The situation is in one of the most public

and frequented parts of the city, and the depository well supplied with Bibles and Testaments in nearly all the European languages; but especially in those most likely to be useful here. The excellent agent of the Paris Bible Society, who has the care of this depository, informed us that the circulation of the Scriptures was not publicly prohibited by the priests; and that at one time frequent applications for copies had been made.

It is unquestionably the part of wisdom, in cases where conscience is not concerned, to follow the popular maxims, and conform to the habits of the people amongst whom you live. I had heard that in France it was customary to have but two meals in the day, but doubted the possibility of regulating my notions of comfort by this rule. On farther observation, however, I found it not so difficult as I had at first supposed; and the public breakfast table at our hotel at Bordeaux afforded me a view of this case, by no means discouraging.

While we thought ourselves faring substantially on mutton chops and coffee, a comfortable old gentleman, who sat near us, regaled himself first with a plate full of oysters, and what the French always breakfast with,—plentiful libations of wine. He then had another plate full of sausages, another of mutton chops, and a large bowl of coffee, with

bread in proportion, which in France is three
times the quantity we eat in England. After such
a breakfast, and a dinner to correspond, I had no
difficulty in understanding how it would be possible
to be satisfied with two meals a day.

On descending to the table d'hote at five o'clock
in the same room, I felt all the unpleasantness of
being the only lady amongst fifteen or twenty of
the nobler sex. Nor was my native shyness at all
abated, by finding myself seated beside the finest
man I ever saw, all rings and ruffles, brooches and
beard. The dinner as usual consisted of a vast
variety of dishes, many of them altogether new to
me, amongst which our friend of the breakfast table
played as active a part as any of the company. If
the scene altogether had felt strange to me at first,
it was no less so in its conclusion; for the dinner
being ended, many of the gentlemen filled their
mouths with water, and after rinsing them
thoroughly, made use of their plates instead of
finger-glasses; after which a glass full of tooth-
picks being handed round, we all rose at our
pleasure, and left the table.

If on this, as well as many other occasions, my
English prejudices were startled by the perfect
ease, perhaps I might say, the want of nicety, in
the manners of the French, I must, on the other

hand, observe that their habits in some respects
are such as might put ours to shame. Nothing,
for instance, can exceed the whiteness and cleanliness of the whole of their table service, the assiduity with which their plates are changed almost
every instant, and the quantity of clean linen and
napkins with which not only their tables, but their
bedrooms are supplied.

As the diligence for Pau did not leave Bordeaux
until Tuesday evening, we had an opportunity of
seeing more of this magnificent city, about whose
splendid streets and squares we walked until
thoroughly wearied; for the general interest of
the scene, increased by its being the resort of so
many foreigners, was such as to lead us on, from
hour to hour, and from place to place, without our
being aware of the lapse of time, or the distance
we had walked.

At six in the evening of the last day of the year,
we left Bordeaux, and again were so fortunate as
to have that part of the conveyance which we occupied entirely to ourselves. The last few days
had been so bland and warm, that we were little
prepared for a sharp frost, which then set in; and
having put away a quantity of spare clothing, I
was too cold to sleep; a circumstance not much to
be regretted, as my wakefulness enabled me to

witness, what I might otherwise have missed, the
first dawn of morning in the wide, uncultivated
Landes, a district of country thinly inhabited, and
stretching to a vast extent, southward of Bordeaux.

In wintry weather, the aspect of this part of the
country must be one of dreariness beyond description, and many are the stories told of travellers who
have been lost or bewildered amongst the forests of
this apparently interminable waste. To us, however, the impression was one of a different nature,
and the roads being at that time excellent, we
were at liberty both to admire and enjoy our novel
situation. By the first light of morning we discovered that we were in the midst of an immense
pine forest, interspersed with venerable oaks. No
human dwelling was to be seen, nor trace of man,
except that here and there a solitary woodcutter
was lighting his fire in the wilderness, while a
cloud of white smoke could just be seen curling up
amongst the trees. As the light increased, we
could distinguish, from the higher ground, leagues
beyond leagues of these dark pine thickets, with
valleys of white mist between them ; and in many
places, breaking the monotony of the scene, wide
tracts of heath and fern, which looked like purple
and silver in the sunshine and hoar frost.

But the wonders of this scene were not fully

revealed until we had looked for some time to the south, where the horizon was terminated by a long line of blue, which, from its broken and irregular outline, I at first imagined to be a ridge of clouds. At length, however, we found, as the morning advanced, that it was the noble range of the Pyrenees, the first really mountain-range I had ever beheld. Not like our English hills, resembling in the distance a drove of giant cattle, each endeavouring to raise its back higher than the rest; but so varied in the colouring, and at the same time so rugged and massive, as to convey the idea of their having been the waves of a chaotic world, suddenly arrested in their foam and fury, and fixed for ever, a spectacle to wondering ages.

Had our journey been through a mountainous, or even a hilly country, this magnificent spectacle might possibly have been less striking; but we were well prepared, by the many leagues of level ground we had passed, the long straight roads, the interminable avenues of poplars, and the low marshes covered with winter floods, to gaze with feelings of admiration and delight upon the splendid scene before us. The Pyrenees too differ from most other mountains, in rising almost immediately from a plain not much above the level of the sea: thus their real height suffers no apparent diminution by their being based upon elevated ground, or by rising in the midst of inferior mountains. As an object of grandeur and sublimity they stand alone; and from their situation, as well as from their height, appear to belong to the purer atmosphere of another world,—a barrier between earth and heaven,—a pathway through the skies, which at that far distance it might well be deemed presumption for any human foot to tread.

Absorbed as we were for some time in the contemplation of this scene, our attention, as the day advanced, was attracted by objects of a different, though scarcely less interesting character. The peasants of the country, whom we met, already wore the look of Spain; the brown flat cap, perhaps more resembling the Scottish bonnet, and cloaks of the same colour thrown gracefully over one shoulder. The little oxen, too, so peculiar to this part of France, of one uniform, fawn colour, approaching to buff, and perfect in their symmetry, we saw here for the first time, drawing small carts of wicker-work, many of which have a light arched covering of thatch, which is easily taken off in fine weather. The oxen are always yoked in pairs, exactly of the same size, their heads being fastened by the horns to a kind of frame or yoke, by which they are held together, and by which also they draw their burdens, having no other harness or fastening. If one, therefore, puts his head to the ground, the other must do the same, or be content, as I have sometimes seen them, to have his nose jerked up in the air.

Whatever the treatment of the horses may be in this part of France, that of the oxen is most careful and kind; as a proof of which, they are always in good condition, and almost universally, when employed in labour, are covered with neat white sheets. In addition to this covering of white linen sheet, they usually have a sort of rug, of sheep or dog's skin, laid across their heads, though whether for use or ornament I have not been able to discover. The manner of conducting a team of oxen is rather curious, for the driver, as we should call him, always walks before, carrying in his hand, and often extending over his shoulder, a long straight stick, with a small goad at the end; this stick he holds out, between the heads of the cattle, in a somewhat graceful manner, and by a slight application of the goad, indicates the direction he wishes them to take. The animals themselves are extremely docile and gentle, which may be owing to their being yoked together in the same manner while only calves, in which state they are brought to market. Still there must be some-

C

thing in their nature, as well as in their education, different from ours, as they are never heard to bellow or low. Whether in the fields, the markets, or yoked to their little carts, they are peaceful, tractable, and perfectly silent. These oxen, which are much more frequently used in field labour than horses, constitute a great portion of the wealth of the peasants, being valued at from 300 to 400 francs each.

The day which had dawned so brightly upon us in the Landes, was the first of the year, and every peasant we met, whether man or woman, was carrying poultry, eggs, or some other produce of their little farms, to the nearest market town; nor were we sorry to find that we ourselves were approaching the ancient looking town of Mont-de-Marsan; for strange and interesting as the aspect of the Landes may be at first, its monotony soon wearies, while its very loneliness creates a longing for more social and familiar scenes. At Mont-de-Marsan, where we stopped to breakfast, a vast concourse of busy-looking country people had assembled to dispose of their goods, which consisted chiefly of pigs, poultry, and coarse earthenware.

Having found the women so beautiful at Bordeaux, I had formed the idea that in advancing southward, especially towards the borders of Spain, they would be more and more attractive; what then was my surprise, to find the market of Mont-de-Marsan crowded with women, the exact opposite of what my imagination had pictured,—old and young, without exception, sallow, coarse, and vulgar. Much of this, however, might be attributable to their peculiar costume, for in the south of France, a few leagues, or a single mountain, will often make a wide difference in the dress and habits of the people. At this place, all the women wore their thick black hair tied down upon their foreheads, almost as low as the eyebrows, and then turned back over the string, and combed down short and straight into the neck behind. Surmounting this heavy mass, was a low thick cap, of coarse white linen, sufficient of itself to extinguish the beauty of a Hebe.

From Mont-de-Marsan to Aire, the road runs through a perfectly flat, but cultivated country. Here the effects of a totally different climate from our own, were visible in the dust, which the men who have the care of the public roads were scraping into heaps by the sides. Even had this not been the case, we had sufficient evidence in the clearness of the atmosphere, and the brightness of the sunshine, which blazed into our carriage so as to compel us to let down the blinds. All this was the

more striking to us, the more magical in its effect
upon our feelings, in consequence of the dreary
autumn we had spent in London, as well as from
the fact of the whole of our journey from that place
to Bordeaux having been performed without one
gleam of sunshine.

The town of Aire is situated on the river Adour,
which winds its way to Bayonne, after receiving
the waters of many tributary streams from the
Pyrenees.   We little thought at that time, how intimate would become our acquaintance with this
river, in some of its earlier and more irregular
wanderings.

On leaving Aire, we ascended a long steep hill,
and after passing to our left an old college, which
appears to be a place of some importance, we
gained the high ground, where, a little to our right,
on the 2nd of March, 1814, four days after the
battle of Orthez, a part of Marshal Soult's army,
under General Clauzel, were attacked by the
British, under General Hill, and after an obstinate
combat, which lasted until nightfall, were driven
back, through the town of Aire, and compelled to
leave their magazines in the hands of the victors.

From this height we had again before us the
glorious spectacle of the whole range of the Pyrenees, now so much nearer, that we could see they

were sheeted in the purest snow. The sky was without a cloud, and the air so fresh and balmy, that it was a luxury to recline even in a French diligence, and feel that we were advancing nearer to a region of such beauty and grandeur. There are feelings which no words can express, and ours were certainly of this order; when, as the day declined, we gazed upon the sky, and watched the different tints of purple and gold literally burning and red; until, as the deepening shades of evening fell around us, we could see nothing but this blaze of light beyond the outline of the mountains, stretching far away to the west.

Having left home too hastily to obtain any particular information respecting the place at which our journey for the winter was to terminate, we had strangely made up our minds to expect that Pau was a little, irregular, dirty town, like many of those we had seen in our journey through France; it was therefore with little interest that we found our carriage clattering, with the usual shout, and slash, and jingle, down a steep descent, into the middle of the town, where we soon found ourselves, for the first time after leaving England, situated in a dirty hotel. For the first time on our journey too, we had no carpet in our bed-room, though in other respects it was ornamented in the

30   SUMMER AND WINTER

usual style, with marble tables, handsome furniture, and excellent beds; and the people of the house being extremely kind and attentive, we had little to complain of.

CHAPTER II.

GENERAL APPEARANCE OF PAU — VISITORS — PUBLIC
PROMENADES—CLIMATE—GENERAL APPEARANCE OF
THE SCENERY — ASPECT OF THE TOWN — ANCIENT
CHATEAU OF HENRY IV.

ON the morning after our arrival at Pau, we
were surprised, on first looking out, to behold a
wide, handsome square, with regular buildings on
each side, noble avenues in the distance, and, as the
day advanced, a tide of respectable and fashionable-
looking English people, setting in towards a certain
point, which looked extremely inviting. The same
bright sunshine still blazed upon the scene, and
there were ladies in light dresses, with their para-
sols, without which it is scarcely possible to look
steadily at any object when the sun is shining
here; while others rode forth in happy looking
parties, with their hats and habits, just as in Hyde
Park, only somewhat differently mounted. Nor
was there wanting the usual proportion of dandies,
still evidently English, notwithstanding all the
pains they had taken to look French. And here,
if I might presume to venture a remark upon this

class of my countrymen, it would be to observe
upon the futility, as well as the bad taste, of all
such endeavours.   The English countenance, if
not good in itself, can never be made so by the
garniture which the military habits of Frenchmen
may have rendered more appropriate to them; and
amongst the many anomalies which arrest the attention of the traveller abroad, it is by no means
the least, to meet the light complexion, fair hair,
rosy cheeks, and long upper lip, of a native Briton,
under a disguise which only serves to render his
identity more striking.

Impatient to become acquainted with a place
where we expected to spend some months, I took
the earliest opportunity of quitting the hotel, and
following the tide I had observed, soon found
myself at the entrance of a spacious and noble
avenue of trees, leading to a promenade, which is
justly celebrated as being one of the most beautiful
in the world.   It is called the Parc, and consists
of a range of high ground, running from east to
west, parallel with the river Gave ; thickly covered
with magnificent trees, chiefly beech, and laid out
in walks of every variety, some straight, and others
serpentine ; some leading along the highest ridges,
and commanding the most extensive view, while
others wind along the foot of the eminence, be-

neath the shadow of the loftier trees; and others, still narrower and more intricate, are nearly lost amongst thicker foliage and closer underwood; as if to suit the different tastes and dispositions of the many strangers from distant lands, who meet here to enjoy the luxury of this delicious climate.

And a motley concourse they are: invalids of every stage, from mere delicacy down to hopeless disease, are seen basking in the sunshine, or leaning on the arms that would be stretched forth, if it were possible, to snatch them from the grave. It is a melancholy, yet in some respects a cheering sight, to meet this class of our fellow-creatures in such a scene; melancholy, to contrast the symptoms of waning life, exhibited in the human frame, with the glow, the richness, and the exuberance of the landscape smiling around; melancholy, to see the solitary invalid pacing to and fro, as if he was endeavouring to outstrip his mortal enemy, or chasing the phantom of health, which still eludes his grasp; and melancholy too, to see the fondly cherished females, the wives, the daughters, and the sisters, who come here, perhaps, to die. Yet, on the other hand, it is a spectacle which scarcely can be contemplated without feelings of gratitude and joy, to think that there is such an atmosphere, and such a scene, accessible to so many of the inhabitants of less genial climates; and that the health and vigour, of which so many are in search, so often is restored to them, beneath these sunny skies. Nor are such feelings rendered less intense, but rather deepened in their interest, by a longer acquaintance with these favourite walks; for if, on the one hand, we then behold the glow of health, the firm step, and the renovated frame, where we had been accustomed to the aspect of disease; on the other, we see the sable weeds, or the solitary mourner, left to tell that all has been in vain.

Amongst the many objects of novelty and interest which attract the attention of the visitor in Pau, we must not omit to mention the variety of characters and costumes by which the Parc is enlivened. Here are to be seen travellers from almost every country, but chiefly Spaniards, with their long dark cloaks, lined with red, and gracefully thrown over one shoulder, Italians, English, Scotch, and Irish, officers of different ranks, soldiers, Bearnais peasants, monks, and nurse-maids, with here and there a non-descript, to whom it is impossible to assign " a local habitation and a name." Amongst this class we were at first inclined to place a very singular looking old gentleman, who we afterwards learned was a Spanish bishop, compelled, from the nature of his political sentiments, to escape to the north of the Pyrenees. This individual, who certainly has something majestic in his deportment, wore a pea-green hat, with low crown, and brim of enormous magnitude curled up on both sides, so that its real circumference can only be known by a profile view, while his figure is enveloped in a rich purple cloak, lined also with pea-green.

At the foot of the woody range of high ground, forming the promenade above described, runs the broad shallow river Gave, with a perpetual low murmur that lulls the senses to repose. It is, in fact, the only sound we hear, for there is so little wind in this climate, that not a leaf is seen to move, and we therefore distinguish at a greater distance the toll of the matin and the vesper bell in the neighbouring villages, and the tinkling sounds which tell when the flocks are led to and from the fields. There appears, at first, a sort of mystery in this universal stillness. It seems like a pause in the breath of nature, a suspension of the general throb of life, and we almost feel as if it must be followed by that shout of joy, which the language of poetry has so often described, as the grateful response of nature for the blessings of light and life. And never, surely, could this response

be offered more appropriately than from such a
scene as this rich and fertile land presents.

The river I have described is not broken into
falls and eddies, as in its higher and more mountainous course; but here it winds along a woody
and well-cultivated valley, adorned in the spring
with every variety of green, as the different
kinds of grain begin to shoot above the ground.
Villages and farm-houses are scattered along its
banks, as far as the eye can reach, to the east and
west; while to the south, the valley is bounded, at
a short distance, by a line of vine-covered hills,
running parallel with the Pyrenees, and extending
to the foot of the mountains.   Amongst these villages, Jurançon, situated immediately opposite the
Parc, is at once the most picturesque and the most
important, being justly celebrated for the richness
of its wines.   It stands at the entrance of one of
the many beautiful valleys which open up amongst
the mountains, and has a fine back-ground of
oaks, and other lofty trees, which separate it from
the hills immediately beyond.   These hills are
covered with vineyards, and clothed with the richest vegetation; while many of their most commanding heights, as well as many of the loveliest little
dells by which they are intersected, are studded

with gentlemen's seats, and adorned with orchards and gardens.

Beyond these hills, at a distance of twenty or thirty miles, rise the majestic Pyrenees, the most eastern groups of which are only visible in certain states of the atmosphere, but, from their being almost always covered with snow, it is evident that they are of no inconsiderable height. The entire chain of the Pyrenees extends from the Mediterranean to the Atlantic; and the length of the barrier, which it forms between France and Spain, is stated by Inglis to be nearly 270 miles; its greatest breadth, which is near the centre, 69, and its general range of elevation from 7000 to 11,000 feet.

Far surpassing, in the beauty and sublimity of its outline, all the other mountains of this range, as they appear from Pau, is the Pic du Midi de Bigorre, which, far to the eastward, stands out from the rest, in the most commanding situation, with a fine back-ground of rugged peaks and snowy pinnacles, running to the south-west, and connecting it with the general chain. This mountain is 9721 feet in height, but from the circumstance of its rising almost immediately from a plain, it strikes the beholder as being more majestic and higher

than it really is.   Its summit is in the form of one
corner of a triangle, and the descent on the northern side is so extensive and precipitous, that snow
never rests upon it.   It therefore seems to frown
upon the world with a dark and inaccessible brow,
though immediately beneath this descent, wide
tracts of silvery snow are sleeping, which catch the
sun-light, and seem to melt into every possible
tint of aërial beauty.   This mountain is chiefly
visited, by travellers from Bagnères and Baréges,
and is more frequently ascended than any other
of the high Pyrenees, on account of the position
it holds, as jutting out from the general range,
and thus commanding a more extensive and unin-
terrupted view to the north, north-east, and north-
west.

Next in importance to this mountain, from the
peculiarity of its form and situation, is the Pic du
Midi de Pau; and perhaps no one of the range
appears more striking, when beheld for the first time.
It seems indeed, from its very singularity, to be
separated from the general mass, the mountains on
either side falling back to the right and the left, as
if to leave it alone.   From a mass of irregular and
broken pinnacles, of no great elevation, it rises like
a mighty cone, with a cloven summit, on one entire
side too steep for the snows to rest.   It is a re-

markable feature in this mountain, that it catches almost every passing cloud, so that, when higher ranges are perfectly clear, it is often wrapped in mist, and never looks more singular, or more sublime, than when the vapour forms a sort of belt around it, while its cloven crest is seen towering into the sky. But the most beautiful characteristic of this mountain, is the noble vista, through which it is seen from the Parc at Pau. First, a wide opening in the vine-clad hills, with Jurançon immediately to the right; then other green and fertile hills, tufted with wood, and their outlines intersecting one another; then a more majestic range of hills of dark rock, and pine, too high for cultivation, and yet below the region of snow. Beyond these is seen for many miles, extending to the foot of the Pic, a misty valley, with purple rocks rising in bold dark promontories of precipitous descent on either side, and extending far up into distant heights of untrodden snow. This is the valley which leads to two of the favourite watering places, Eaux Chaudes and Eaux Bonnes; it is called the valley d'Ossau, and the name has been explained to us by a native, as meaning " the valley where the bears come down."

Perhaps one of the most imposing aspects under which the Pyrenees are seen from Pau, is when the

40   SUMMER AND WINTER

state of the atmosphere, and the light is such, that
we see in, as it were, amongst them, and are able
to trace the different valleys by which they are divided, beginning with some of the lower hills which
rise from the woody plain on the banks of the Gave,
and following them up to their snowy summits,
until lost in the distance, or intercepted by some
other range.   It is then that we are able to form
some idea of the real extent and magnitude of these
stupendous mountains; the eye then wanders on,
from one lofty pinnacle to another, tracing out the
blue and silvery outline of the sublimest heights;
or, returning by some lower chain, it takes a down-
ward course, and penetrates into those deep, mysterious hollows, where the purple shadows fall
obliquely, so that here and there a bold and broken
rock stands forth and catches a sort of golden
light.

It is scarcely possible, however, where the sunshine is so brilliant, and the atmosphere so clear as
in the climate of the Pyrenees, to say under what
aspect they are the most beautiful; nor have we
ever been able to decide whether they appear to
the greatest advantage in the morning or the evening, for at mid-day there is, in the brightest weather,
a sort of silvery haze which always renders them
more or less obscure.   Perhaps the appearance

they present in the morning is the most brilliant; but the evening is the time when associations are the strongest, and consequently there is more to think of, and to feel, if not actually more to admire, in connexion with their grandeur and beauty, at the close, than at the commencement of the day.

This is the time we have usually chosen for walking in the Parc, and after the wonted concourse of visitors have retired, we have enjoyed more fully the gratification of feeling that we were alone with nature. The old chateau of Pau, which forms a conspicuous object from the eastern extremity of the Parc, with its irregular pile of ancient towers, is then tinted with the golden hues of the glowing west. The river, which as it wanders at the foot of this venerable edifice, is spanned by a massive and ancient bridge, is then seen winding its way in the distance, like a silver thread; while the mountains look more clear in the sunset—more immediately present to the scene; and the line of vine-clad hills is painted against the evening sky, with that distinctness of outline, which renders visible every tree upon their summits, and one might almost fancy, every leaf.

It is said, there is a certain latitude at which beautiful sunsets begin. We are I fancy south of this latitude at Pau; at all events, I feel convinced

that nothing can exceed the beauty of the sunsets
from this point of view; which, besides the mountain
range, commands a vast extent of country towards
Bayonne, along which the hills more immediately
beneath the rays of the setting sun are tinged with
all the glories of the sky, until, melting away in
the distance into a faint blue line, they leave the
fertile plain, with all its woods, and fields, and
cottages, and with the many serpent-bendings
of the Gave, between its tufted banks, to blend
together into one vast lake of gold.

It is true the colours of evening in this climate
are more evanescent than with us; but while they
last, they are also much more varied and intense.
Even the snow on the distant mountains, though
it still retains its purity, partakes of the colouring of the scene, so that sometimes on looking up,
you suddenly behold them wrapped in a mantle of
pink, or lilac, changing to crimson—gold—and
then the palest yellow, until one peak after another
loses the parting radiance of the sun, and all are
again clothed in that cold blue, and colder white,
which has been well described by a distinguished
traveller, as resembling the aspect of death,
when the spirit has but just departed. Nor is it
until night advances, that we lose the outline of
these mountains; even then, if the moon is shining,

and the sky is clear, you may at the same distance distinguish every peak, and trace out every valley, with the same exactness as before, though a more mysterious and aërial aspect is spread over the whole.

Arriving, as we did, at the leafless season of the year, we remained of course for some time ignorant of the summer beauty of the scenery in the neighbourhood of Pau. To us, however, there seemed nothing wanting, for the purity of the atmosphere, and the brilliance of the sunshine, tinged with beauty every object upon which the eye could rest. And it is this very distinctness, and vividness of colouring, which sometimes leads me to question the boasted superiority of Swiss scenery over that of the Pyrenees. I know that the mountains are higher, and that the whole aspect of the country, so far as regards vastness and sublimity, bears no comparison with this; but I am yet to be convinced, that in detail, and in beauty of colouring, the scenery of the Pyrenees is surpassed by that of any other country.

It must not however be supposed, that on the mountains alone, the stranger looks with interest, while tracing out the various promenades by which Pau is surrounded. The town itself, or more properly the city, contains about 14,000 inhabitants, and is not only respectable, but imposing, in its general appearance and situation, being built upon the same range of high ground as the Parc, with the river and its many tributary streams watering the plain immediately below. That side of the city which presents a southern aspect, and which is consequently parallel with the river, consists almost entirely of handsome houses, with their gardens, pleasure grounds, and green fields spotted with sheep and lambs, and fringed with weeping willows, sloping down to the sides of the water ; and between some of these fields, and one of the streams which hurry on to join the Gave, is an avenue of oaks, which form a shady and pleasant promenade.

At the eastern extremity of the town is an old college, once a monastery, a massive and venerable pile of building, with the same high roofs of black slate which are seen upon every edifice of antiquity and importance in this part of France. About half way between this building and the west end of the town is another promenade, called the Place Royale, commanding a view to the southward, as fine, or finer, than that from the Parc ; and it is here we may at once discover the favourite resort of the French, because it is perfectly flat, without a blade of grass, shaded by trees in regular rows, surrounded on all sides but one by houses and shops; but above all, because it is the place where you may meet with all the world! for this last recommendation constitutes in reality the crowning point of excellence with every one in France. Whatever you are in search of, in the way of situation, either for comfort or for health, for sorrow or for sickness, their highest commendation will be, that it places you in a position where all the world may either be seen, or heard, or come in contact with, in some way or another.

At the southern extremity of this promenade, and situated on the slope which commands an extensive view of the mountains, are the baths, two regular and handsome buildings, flat at the top, and from their whole character and situation looking more Italian than French. Beyond these, to the west, are terraces and trees extending down to the river, on the banks of which, and connecting with the bridge, is another group of houses, apparently some of the oldest in the town, while above them, on the same ridge of high ground as the Place Royale and the Parc, and raised still higher by an artificial mound, stands the venerable chateau, the birth-place of Henry IV., with the church of St. Martin to the eastward, on the same line.

The general aspect of this chateau, where the sovereigns of Navarre formerly held their court, is

46   SUMMER AND WINTER

more venerable than picturesque, although the advantages of its situation could not well be surpassed.
It appears at first sight to be composed of a pile of
irregular roofs and towers, facing different directions, not at right angles, but rather standing out
so as to command the most extensive view of the
heights and valleys by which it is surrounded;
all these towers are surmounted by those high
black roofs, slightly curved inwards, which give a
Moorish character to the whole. Like most ancient
castles, it is constructed with a wide court-yard in
the centre, from whence you look up to ranges of
irregular windows, and carved masonry, all worn
and grey, and sometimes even black with time.
Yet even here, such is the redundant luxuriance of
this fertile clime, that wild weeds are waving from
the hoary heights, with the blossoms of thyme, and
other flowers, leaves of the brightest green, and
twigs and sprays of a thousand different plants
shooting up from the old mortar, even before it
crumbles from the walls.

Immediately at the foot of the artificial mound
upon which the chateau stands, there is a broad
terrace, where French taste has planted a sort of
garden, with regular rows of plane trees, as regularly
despoiled of their branches each time they have
arrived at a certain height; and again below this

terrace is the most ruinous, but at the same time the most interesting part of the chateau. It is now detached, but was once connected with it by an arched way over a little stream, which still works a water mill called the Mill of Jeanne d'Albret, the mother of Henry IV. This ancient and humble-looking building also boasts the honour of having formerly supplied the court with flour. The square tower above alluded to, which rises by the side of the stream, is now a mere shell, the roof and interior being almost entirely ruinous; while from the massiveness of the outer walls, it appears capable of resisting all further attacks of time. Of the roof, which reached to a level with the terrace above, but little remains, and the deep cornice of heavy masonry by which it was surrounded, is now clothed with the richest drapery of fern and ivy, intermingled with plants of a more delicate and fragile nature, weaving altogether a garland of beauty and of life, which seems to mock the "hoar austerity" of the grey ruin beneath.

Whether this tower was originally built for any other purpose than to protect the entrance to the chateau from the bridge, near which it stands, and still nearer to the ruins of a bridge of earlier date, or whether its lower apartments were appropriated

48   SUMMER AND WINTER

to the purpose of a dungeon, it is not easy at the
present day to ascertain; but history of a later date
is clear, that it was at one time used as a mint; and
what adds still greater interest to its present character is, that when the seeds of the Reformation
were beginning to take root in this part of France,
it was in one of the chambers of this building, that
Calvin preached to a little faithful band of his
friends and followers, amongst whom the most
distinguished was Marguerite of Valois, sister of
Francis I., and then Queen of Navarre.

In addition to the sacred cause thus fostered
under the protection of her court, there is much
in the character of Marguerite to hallow the remembrance of scenes with which she was so intimately associated, much in the tenderness of her
devoted affection, much in her high intellectual
attainments, but more in the depth and sincerity of
her religious faith, which supported her to the last,
when all else had failed.   It is not the least touching feature amongst the many beauties with which
her character is adorned, that she possessed so
strong a hold upon the heart of her brother, the king
of France, who, in the playfulness of his affection,
used to call her his " Marguerite of Marguerites,"
or daisy of daisies.   And well did she repay this
tenderness, by her heroic flight to the court of

Madrid, when he was a prisoner there after the battle of Pavia, by her patient watch at the side of his sick bed, where she read the scriptures to him until his heart was almost convinced, and by her earnest intercessions for him with the cold-hearted monarch, whose captive he then was, and with whom she pleaded so fearlessly, as to be obliged to fly from his kingdom for her life, accomplishing the journey from Madrid to the frontier with a speed almost incredible for a delicate female. Nor were the accomplishments of her mind and manners much inferior to the high qualities of her heart. Adorned with the title of the " fourth grace, and the tenth muse," she presided over her little court at Angouleme, where our unfortunate Anne Bolleyn bloomed amongst her maids of honour; and while residing in the chateau of Pau, her love of literature, and patronage of the fine arts, drew around her the society of men of letters, and distinguished artists, from her own and other lands. A deeper bond of sympathy, however, appears to have existed between Marguerite of Valois and some of the most eminent of the early reformers, amongst whom may be added to the name of Calvin already mentioned, those of Erasmus, Roussel, Lefevre d'Etaples, Marot, Caroli, Dolet, and many others.

D

CHAPTER III.

SETTLEMENT AT PAU—LODGINGS—DOMESTIC COM-
FORT—SERVANTS—GENERAL EXPENSE OF LIVING—
APPEARANCE OF THE PEOPLE—HORSES—WOMEN—
COSTUMES—MARKETS—PRICE OF PROVISIONS.

OUR first business on arriving in Pau being to
secure lodgings until the season should be so far
advanced as to allow us to proceed nearer to the
mountains, we gladly took advantage of the kindness of a friend, to conduct us to some of the most
eligible that were still at liberty.   The situation we
chose was by no means unexceptionable ; yet such
was the number of strangers, especially English,
who had fixed their residence at Pau for the winter,
that our friends thought us fortunate in the home
we had secured.

Impressed as we had been, and as English people
generally are, with an idea of the cheapness of
living abroad, we were not a little surprised to find
that we must pay in most instances as much for the
necessaries of life, as in our own country ; and that
for every article we purchased in the shops, or the

market, we must give at least twice as much as it was worth, and much more than the owner expected finally to take, unless indeed we chose the other alternative of bargaining and disputing for half an hour on every article we bought.

Our lodging—thanks to an English clergyman who had preceded us—was supplied with a carpet; but our sleeping room had only the usual bed-side fragment, which is all that must be expected here. The floors, both of the bed-rooms and the salons, are however preserved from the cold, comfortless aspect which bare boards would otherwise present, by a custom which prevails of first staining them red, and then, after a coating of wax, brushing them until they become brown and bright. With regard to their cleanliness, it is not necessary to say more than that they are never washed.

It was in our search for lodgings, that we were most struck with the difference between French and English houses, in the extreme disorder and discomfort of the doors and passages by which the former are approached. It is such in fact, that no one who can help it, thinks of living on the ground floor; such apartments are therefore almost entirely appropriated to shops and other offices. In many instances I should certainly have supposed that the entrance to a respectable house

would lead to a place for horses or cattle; and
the stairs too being also never washed, and common to all the families who live on the different
stages or flats, are often dirty and disgusting in the
extreme.   Yet no sooner is the door of a salon or
bed-room thrown open, than you see the walls
adorned with beautiful paper, handsome slabs and
fire-places of marble, elegant time-pieces and
other fancy ornaments, with looking-glasses in
gilt frames, in great variety and number.   In addition to which, the window curtains are almost
invariably arranged with taste; and over the beds,
which are covered with silk, or curiously knitted
counterpanes, hang rich canopies, chiefly of crimson, composed of festoons and fringes, as handsome
as they are often inappropriate.

It is then, without carpets, and without comforts
of a thousand kinds, that English people are content to live abroad; and I am inclined to think
that this is the grand secret of being able to live at
less expence in France than in our native country,
—because we are satisfied to do without a vast
number of things which we imagine to be essential
to respectability at home.   And perhaps we are
sufficiently repaid for our self-denial, where the
climate is like that of the south of France.

For the want of cleanliness, and the general discomfort in the appearance of the houses, I had been in a great measure prepared; but I confess there was one privation which it baffled my philosophy to sustain, and that was the want of tea; I therefore made it a great point in settling in our new abode, to lay in a large stock of this precious article, and with the satisfaction of a true Englishwoman, I ordered it to be brought up, on the first evening of our arrival at our lodgings. What then was my surprise, to find that there was no such thing as a kettle in the house, that there never had been, and that neither the wants nor the wishes of a French family included this important and familiar accompaniment to an English fire-side !

Nor was this all. Water may certainly be boiled without a kettle, but it is said there is not a servant in all France who understands the virtue of boiling water. Warm water they will bring you, because it is sufficient for all their purposes; but you must stand over it yourself, and that every time it is required, to see that it actually does boil, or it will be brought to you of the temperature of new milk. Ours was of this temperature on the evening I had ordered tea with such pleasant anticipations, and the servant having put in a few leaves of tea, and told me it was ready, I poured it out, as clear and colourless as if it had been pure water. Nor was

our next attempt much more successful, for the tea-
pot was then filled with this lukewarm water, in
expectation that I should add to it the necessary
quantity of tea. A few evenings after this, however, a veritable kettle was brought for our accommodation, and as a proof how little the people of
the house were acquainted with the use of it, it
was always brought up to us, and placed flat upon
the table with the tea-cups.

But the greatest disappointment in connexion
with this social meal, remains to be told. There is
no tea to be found in Pau, or indeed nearer than
Toulouse, that is worthy of the name; and the stock
we had purchased with so much satisfaction, proved
to be nothing better than some kind of astringent
herb, with a strong flavour of turpentine. I ought
to add that good green tea may certainly be had,
this being the only kind which the French ever
drink, but out of regard to their nerves they take
it so weak as to differ little from pure water.

A far more serious grievance than the want of
tea, I had already found in the sourness of the
French bread, which, although extremely light, is
made with leaven instead of yeast, and is always
more or less sour; but as most of the bakers in
Pau sell what they call English bread, this inconvenience is easily avoided.

The month in which strangers settle for the winter in Pau, is September. About this time the price asked for lodgings is very high. A few months later they are much more reasonable, and towards the spring, may be had for still less. It is not easy to give a very exact idea of this portion of the expence of a winter in Pau, because the price of lodging depends here, as in every other place, upon the situation, point of view, as well as upon many other points of taste and fancy. Good accommodations for a family of four or five persons, may be found at the rate of 100 or 120 francs per month. For handsome furniture, elegant salons, carpets, and first-rate situation, it will be necessary to pay four times that sum.

It does not appear to be the custom with French families residing here, ever to take individuals to share at the same table, or in other words to board with them; nor indeed would such a plan be very congenial to English habits. It is consequently necessary to hire your own servants, and these may be had at the following rate. A good cook at from twenty to twenty-five francs per month; a femme de chambre at from ten to fifteen. Of the former it is said that they are all cheats. I am unable to add my testimony to this sweeping statement, having found much kindness, and a fair average of

honesty, amongst the French servants.   Still it is
customary, and therefore desirable, to keep such
things as sugar and coffee out of their reach, and to
endeavour to ascertain the actual price of what the
cook may purchase, lest she should appropriate a
certain commission on each article herself.   As
regards the direct taking of money, or indeed of
anything of importance, there is certainly as little
need for suspicion here, as in England.

   In case of the family circumstances of the visitor
rendering the trouble of a cook undesirable, it is
easy to adopt the alternative of having dinners
sent from any of the hotels, or the restaurateurs,
from whence they can be had according to order,
at any time, of any quality, and consisting of any
number of dishes you may desire.   The following
is the rate at which tables are usually supplied.
For six persons in the salon, and two or three in
the kitchen, at six francs per day, without wine or
dessert.   We were supplied at one time for three
francs per day, and much better afterwards for
two and a half, with one dish of meat, one of
excellent vegetables, and one of pudding, or some
other kind of sweet dish.   Our best provision was
from Tourné.   I am unable to say whether he is a
descendant of the famous Tourné, restaurateur of
this place, of whom it is related by a French writer,

that such was the excellence of his establishment *artistique*, that a French gastronome exclaimed in an ecstacy of enthusiasm, " The city of Pau has produced but two great men, Henry IV., and Tourné !"

The provision of a table for French servants need make no part of the stranger's calculation. Let them have their bread, which is one of the cheapest articles of consumption, or a certain allowance for buying it, the wine of the country, which may be had at four sous per bottle, their vegetables, and lard, and they will be much happier than if fed from your own table. They are so obliging too, that if any physical or moral power could operate so as to make them clean, they would deserve to rank high amongst this class of their fellow-creatures.

Perhaps it will convey the most correct idea of the state of things in the sort of menage I have described, to say that in the items included in fitting up a kitchen, no kind of pail finds a place, no dust cloth, and no apparatus by which the floors can possibly be washed; and when we add to this, that the servants are in the habit of pouring out all spare slops, wherever they may be, either in the kitchen, on the stairs, or even in the salon, the state of the floors, especially that of the kitchen,

may more easily be imagined than described.   In
the case of any particular overthrow, they take a
long brush with which they are provided, and just
sweep together dust, ashes, and water, leaving the
floor to dry how, and when it can.   Instead of being
annoyed by any of these disasters, a smile, and a
shrug, and a remark that it is of no consequence,
is the only indication you perceive of their regarding it.

As a proof of their comfortable indifference to
what we regard as points of propriety, a friend of
ours told us that his servant, finding one night
she had left a candle burning at the bottom of the
stairs, very coolly took the kettle, and from a height
of some hundred steps, poured the water down to
extinguish it, altogether regardless of the ascent
of other lodgers at the same time.

In addition to all this, the stranger in the south
of France must be prepared for a degree of familiarity in the manners of the servants, at first rather
startling to our English reserve.   I ought scarcely
to call it familiarity either, for on no occasion, by
look, word, or act, do they betray the least desire
to place themselves on a level with those they
serve.   There is a line of demarcation between
these two grades in society, which they may be
safely trusted never to pass; and if they come often

into your room when they think you are lonely, and take every opportunity to chat with you, and tell you the news, it is purely with a good-natured desire to keep you from dullness, as well as from the natural impulse of their own vivacity, which irresistibly impels them to talk. In other respects they seldom annoy. Their wants are so few, their accustomed indulgences so limited, that they never come to you with complaints that they cannot do one thing, or put up with another; and while the language and gesture of vehement passion is not unfrequent amongst themselves, I have never heard of a word, or even tone of rudeness being used towards their employers.

After all, there is something in the cheerfulness and contentment of a people who have so few of our artificial wants, and consequently so few of our repinings, from which we might, if we would, learn many a useful lesson; and never is this difference in the habits of the two countries more striking, than in mixing amongst the happy looking peasantry who meet in busy crowds on a market day at Pau.

The first time we beheld this amusing spectacle, we supposed it was a fair; but found it repeated every Monday with the same appearance of activity, liveliness, sociability, and general good-will.

60   SUMMER AND WINTER

One of my favourite amusements, the good taste
of which might possibly be questioned as a matter
of gentility, has been to walk along some of the principal roads on a market day, and meet the peasants,
either coming from, or returning to their homes,
on which occasions I have often observed that no
one goes alone.   All are gathered into groups; for
in France there seem to be but two evils greater
than nature is able to sustain—loneliness, and
bitterness.   Many are the offers I have had, not
impertinently, but kindly meant, of companions by
the way, accompanied by a few words of condolence
that I was *all alone.*

In connexion with the peasantry, it is necessary
to mention the horses, of which I have yet said
nothing; and which, unlike the oxen, appear to be
hardly treated, and worse fed.   The horses in this
part of France differ almost as much as animals of
the same species can do, from those in the neighbourhood of Paris, and Boulogne.   They are longer,
and more slender, with narrow chests, small legs
that seem to bend under them, and long lankey
tails, sometimes tied up in knots at half their length,
in which state the animals seem to have a curious
propensity to carry them pointing straight out.
Although some of them are tolerably well shaped,
those used by the peasantry are for the most part

miserable and grotesque looking creatures, having been made to work and carry burdens while mere foals, never tasting corn, and being doomed to hard usage to the end of their lives.

I have never seen more pitiful objects than some of these animals, when flogged up the streets of Pau, with heavy loads behind them; and there is a particular kind of cart here, which renders the evil greater than it would otherwise be. It is a narrow frame of prodigious length, with wheels proportionately high, drawn by six, and sometimes seven horses, one before another. But the great evil is, that, carrying an immense load, and filled from one extremity to the other, they can with difficulty be drawn up a hill without injury to the horse in the shafts; and I have actually seen a large animal in this situation, entirely lifted off the ground, while the others were struggling as if for their lives.

Mounted upon one of the miserable gaunt look-ing horses I have described, with its tail tied up in knots, and pointing straight out behind, the reader must imagine one of the peasants of Bearn, riding to market, with a high saddle such as they always use, an immensity of trapping about his horse's head, a rusty curb to his bridle, sometimes huge wooden stirrups, made in the form of half a shoe,

62   SUMMER AND WINTER

and such a load of bags and property of various descriptions, strapped on before and behind him, that the rider forms but a small part of the whole set-out. He himself has a flat brown woollen cap, and a cloak of the same material, wide enough at the bottom to cover his own legs, and then extend backwards over the tail of the horse, so as to make them look like one animal. The most curious part of the cloak however, is the hood, which in bad weather he draws over his head, when the breadth which the cap gives it, the flat top, and the long point extending out behind, in the form of a funnel, render the outline of his person very extraordinary.

In addition to this figure, the attention of the stranger is attracted by an object still more remarkable,—the female peasant who pursues her way to market seated in the same style. The first I saw of this description was a large, stout, respectable looking woman, with a neat frilled cap, and lace collar; while the lower extremity of her person displayed a pair of plaid trowsers, and spurs. It is however much more common to see the country-women with the long white or red capulet or hood upon their heads, and all have wide blue aprons, which make a kind of riding skirt. Nor is the pace at which they ride less strange to us than their appearance. It is invariably a long trot, probably more easy than it looks, as neither men nor women ever rise in their stirrups, but keep their seats with great dignity, particularly the latter.

And well may they assume an aspect of dignity, if general usefulness can entitle them to do so; for in this part of France, it is the women who do all the work. Even on their way to market, we see them carrying on their heads the heaviest burdens, and it is said they can carry as much as 150 lbs.; while the men go swaggering along with nothing but a stick. It would be an easier task to enumerate the kinds of labour in which women are not employed, than those in which they are. In the country they are to be seen every day at this season of the year, ploughing and harrowing, and spreading or carting manure; at other seasons, mowing, reaping, and carrying the hay home on their heads; while in the market we find them selling their corn, and every other produce of their farms. In the towns, besides being employed in sweeping the streets, and cleaning the lamps, they act as labourers to the paviors, bricklayers, and stone-masons; and carry on the work of glaziers, and almost every other duty, both in doors and out, except that of serving as soldiers.

It may readily be supposed that the women suffer much in their appearance from such habits of

64   SUMMER AND WINTER

hard labour, and constant exposure to the weather. The consequence is, they look old before middle life, and in real old age, the loss of their teeth, their naturally hard features, and complexions, dry, leathern, and all over wrinkles, combine to render them hideous in the extreme. Still they seem to enjoy life, especially as they go home from market, munching their dry bread or roasted chestnuts along the road, and chatting in noisy groups, about the business of the day. Yet I must confess, when I have seen one of these old women riding like a man, at a hard launching trot, I have longed to place her in a comfortable arm chair by the fire-side of an English cottage, to put a neat cap upon her head, and a bible in her hand, and so leave her to pass the remainder of her days in peace.

If it should be asked, where are the children all the while the women are thus employed, I must answer, that I cannot tell. Compared with England, and especially with Ireland, the number of children in the south of France is so small, that one wonders the more to behold the multitude of peasants who flock to the fairs and markets. Those we do see, are sometimes very beautiful, for the French countenance wants nothing but the softness and sweetness of extreme youth, to render it lovely and attractive. The features of the Bearnais, both amongst the men and women, are generally well formed, and remarkable for the just proportion of the three divisions which the laws of beauty have assigned to the length of the human countenance ; whereas in England, there is scarcely one face in a hundred, of which the lowest third, extending from the end of the nose to the lowest line of the chin, is not by far the longest. The Bearnais too have invariably thin and delicately formed lips, but there is, especially amongst the men, a breadth of jaw from ear to ear, which, in addition to the hard sharp lines of the nose and nostrils, gives them an expression of countenance always coarse, and sometimes almost savage.

These defects, however, offend but little in the countenance of youth, and the children of Pau, but particularly the young girls just growing into women, are certainly amongst the prettiest I have ever seen. Much of the charm of their appearance is no doubt attributable to the neatness, and appropriateness of the dress worn by the poorer classes, above all to that which adorns the head, and which always consists of a coloured handkerchief, more or less tastefully arranged. The eye is never shocked here, as in England, by the slovenly cap, the shabby bonnet, or the mock finery which too frequently disfigures this class of women in our native land. Whether the Bearnaise women are engaged in house, or field labour, their dresses are

66   SUMMER AND WINTER

always appropriate, and their colours, which are much more striking and brilliant than ours, almost invariably well chosen.

Of these colours, the most tasteful are generally displayed in the handkerchief, which forms the head-dress. It is of a manufacture peculiar to the country, which neither fades nor crumples. The middle is usually of a drab, fawn, or brown colour, with a broad border suited to it. It is adjusted so as to give a Grecian contour to the head and face, and I suspect, notwithstanding its appearance of artless simplicity, that there are degrees of coquetry by which it is arranged, so as best to suit the countenance of the wearer. Beneath this handkerchief we see soft bands of dark hair carefully parted on the forehead, and placed against the cheek, so as to contrast in the best manner, with a complexion at once glowing and delicate, healthy and pure. Add to this, the neatest little collar round the neck, the universal shawl pinned down in front, over which the hands in curiously coloured mittens are closely folded, and you see ninety-nine out of a hundred of the young women in this part of France.

The peasant women, besides the handkerchief above described, wear generally, when out of doors, a kind of hood, called a capulet. It is made of white or scarlet cloth, of the finest texture, often bordered with black velvet, and has an extremely

picturesque and striking appearance, whether hanging loosely from the head to the shoulders, over
which it extends, or folded thick and flat on the
head, as we often see it in Italian pictures.

Instead of the capulet, the women frequently
wear, in bad weather, and almost always when they
go to church, a large cloak of black or blue stuff,
lined with red, which entirely conceals the figure,
and, sombre as it is, looks not inappropriate, when
they are kneeling in the churches.

Neither of these dresses are, however, so much
used in the country, on common occasions, as in the
town: the capulet being generally folded up, until
the peasant woman enters the market, where, of
course, she wishes to appear to the greatest advantage. When on horseback, too, they much more
frequently wear, in addition to the handkerchief
already described, another tied loosely over their
heads, simply to preserve them from the glare
of the sun, to which neither men nor women
allow their heads to be exposed. The capulet
would also be less convenient for the many burdens they have to carry, especially one we have
sometimes seen, which is a pig round the back of
the neck, with the legs held together in front; and
whatever this may be to the bearer, it looks comfortable enough to the pig. For the manner in

68   SUMMER AND WINTER

which lambs are carried I cannot say so much, for
I have often seen them with their four feet tied
together in a bunch, and the woman's arm slipped
through them, so that the animal hung down like
a basket.

But it would be as vain to attempt to enumerate
the strange things that women will carry, as the
trifles which furnish an excuse for taking them to
market.   One fowl, and I have heard it said, one
egg, will take them many miles to sell it; while
two men almost invariably, make it their business
to take a calf, one of them to pull it on, and the
other to push behind.

The rest of their dress is of the simplest and
coarsest description, usually consisting of a thick
woollen petticoat, of brown or blue, with a stripe
of a different colour; a blue cloth jacket, tight to
the waist, and a cotton shawl or handkerchief
pinned over it. This dress being dark and durable,
and exactly suited to their occupation, never looks
either dirty or shabby; nor is there such a thing
as a ragged garment to be seen, even upon the
poorest, or the most infirm.

With regard to shoes and stockings, they are not
particular. Indeed, both seem to be luxuries, of
which they make parade on public occasions, for
we often see the women stopping to put them on

before they enter the town, and taking them off again on their return, in order to pursue their way with less incumbrance. The peasants and the mountaineers wear universally rudely shaped shoes of wood, immensely thick, but turned up with a pointed toe. They are said to keep the feet warm, by being half filled with straw.

In addition to the costume above described, the French servant at Pau appears to be inseparable from her basket. Whether she goes to buy or sell, and often when she has no such object, she must have her basket, either hanging on her arm, or placed upon her head; and it is in the latter situation that we see the baskets flat and shallow, but of such prodigious circumference, that the wonder is, how they are able to pass along the busy streets. The women also carry on their heads, as they go to and from the different fountains, a peculiar kind of cruche, or water-pot, of brown earthenware, so formed as to give the bearer a very classical and picturesque appearance.

Nor must we omit, amongst the medley groups which throng the streets and promenades of Pau, the stately priest, with his long black robes, and silken sash of the same colour. Whether worn by the young or the old, there is something in their dress which gives them the same venerable and

patriarchal look; increased, no doubt, by their
wearing their hair cut very short in front, and
hanging long behind, as well as by the large cocked
hat, fastened up on three sides with strings or
stays. At funerals, and on other public occasions, this hat gives place to another, in the shape
of a cone, with a large bushy tuft at the top; while
the black robe is covered with one of thin muslin,
apparently well starched; long bands of which
material fall down from the shoulders, and of these
some are curiously crimped, I suppose to indicate
the office or the dignity of the wearer.

With an aspect scarcely less solemn than the
priest's, and clothed in a costume more curious, we
see occasionally the Sisters of Charity, moving
along the streets on their errands of kindness. Of
this order there are eleven residing at Pau, and
they have under their care an hospital for the sick
and the aged, as well as for unfortunate children,
not acknowledged by their parents. These women,
who are all extremely stout and comely, notwithstanding their arduous duties, wear the dark cloth
dress of nuns, with a string of large beads, and
crucifix suspended by their side; and having, from
the nature of their occupations, to be so frequently
exposed to the public gaze, their faces are shaded
by a large bonnet of white linen, so stiff as to re-

semble pasteboard, while from its enormous peak, which projects out in front, are sloping sides, forming a sort of curved brim, so as entirely to shade the neck and shoulders.

We have now to imagine all these figures, and a thousand others, which it would be impossible to describe, passing and repassing along the most crowded parts of the city of Pau, sometimes under the deep shadow of the ancient buildings, whose irregular roofs, black slates, innumerable windows, old balconies, and often overhanging gables, give a peculiarly foreign aspect to the long perspective of the narrow streets; while in other parts we see them gathered into groups, in the full blaze of the sunshine, which brightens into tenfold vividness the rich colouring of their various costumes. Around them too are scattered on the ground, or heaped in baskets, the fresh green vegetables, the fruits, and other produce of this fertile land, in such profusion, that you wonder not at the cheerful sparkling of their bright black eyes, as they look around for purchasers; while with all their natural facility of speech, and their never-tiring gesticulation in full play, they exhibit all the accompaniments of that system of trickery, which seems to form the pastime of a Bearnais market.

For the purpose of selling corn, a handsome and

commodious hall has been erected, in a central
part of the town, and here the women are always
to be seen, as usual, occupying the place appropriated with us exclusively to men. Of all the
different kinds of produce or manufacture to be
sold, each has its distinct and separate place. Potatoes, for instance, which form a much more important article of consumption than we were aware
of, are sold only in one part of the town; flax,
which is extensively grown, in another; earthenware, poultry, cart-loads of wooden shoes, dried
grass for making mattrasses, fuel, rosin, which is
sold to be made into candles, and used by the
country people, all have their proper place of
allotment for display, with many other articles for
sale, too numerous to be named.

We must not, however, forget to mention the
pigs of this country, which furnish the far-famed
hams of Bayonne, and which also have their appointed place. They are of a large species, fat-
tened on chesnuts, and are held in just estimation
for their excellent bacon, which is sold at one
franc per pound. It is curious to see them under-
going their ablutions in the morning of a market-
day, when they are driven down to the river and
thoroughly washed, by having water thrown on
them with a wooden shovel.

Perhaps no articles are seen here in greater abundance, than the different woollen goods manufactured in the country, of every kind, and quality, from the finest merinos, down to the coarse brown worsted of the native colour of the mountain sheep, from which the dress of the peasantry is chiefly made. The art of knitting too, is carried to a degree of perfection, almost incredible to those who have never travelled amongst the Pyrenees; and knitted woollen articles of almost every description, and of all the colours of the rainbow, may be found here upon the various stalls on a market day; though they are to be met with in much greater perfection at Bagneres de Bigorre. Besides these there are all kinds of cotton goods, with a most enticing display of the coloured handkerchieves for the head, as well as the red sashes which the Bearnais peasants wear round the body.

In addition to these attractions, there is always in some part of the town on a market day, a concourse of country people gathered round a man, whose object most probably is, to sell off such articles as need more than common recommendation, and for this purpose he usually mounts upon a cart or stage, and by his grotesque and ridiculous costume, as well as by his extravagant

E

74   SUMMER AND WINTER

and vehement gesticulations, endeavours to attract
the attention of passers by. He is not unfrequently
disguised under a cocked hat, and white wig, while
his face, distorted and swollen by the excess of his
vociferations, gives him all the appearance of in-
sanity; and in England he would certainly be
taken for a mountebank, or a madman.

In the neighbourhood of the Pyrenees, the fruit
is neither so plentiful, nor so fine, as at a greater
distance from the mountains. The grapes however
are excellent, and these may be bought in the
autumn, at the rate of twelve pounds for ten sous,
about five pence, figs, twenty for one sous, medlars,
eighteen for one sous, roasted chestnuts, twenty-four
for one sous, walnuts, twenty for one sous, apples
one sous per dozen.

Butter is generally sold in Pau at one franc per
pound, milk three sous for half a pint, beef and
mutton eighteen sous per pound, which is thirty-six
ounces. A turkey is sold at three francs, a couple
of chickens at thirty or thirty-three sous, a couple
of ducks at three francs, a quail four or five sous.
All vegetables abundant, cheap and good.

One of the first articles of importance with which
the stranger in Pau has to provide himself at
lodgings, is wood for fuel; and this must be purchased early on the market day. It is brought to

the place of sale in small cart loads. For one load which will probably last a small family three weeks he must give ten or twelve francs, not forgetting to add another load of faggots, which may be had at the rate of six sous for each bundle, when bought by the load. Besides which it will be necessary to lay in a stock of charcoal, the grand secret of French cookery consisting in the many vessels they can keep hot, beside their little charcoal fires.

In these, and all his bargainings, the stranger, especially if he be an Englishman, must lay it to account that he will be over charged; for there is an idea prevailing here, that the English people have so much money, they are at a loss how to dispose of it, and consequently the French endeavour to assist them by practising every kind of imposition which promises the least hope of success. Even when dealing with the people of their own country, they are in the habit of asking much more for every article than they expect finally to receive. On their first offer being declined, they kindly invite the purchaser to make his own, after which ensues that scene of bargaining and disputing, which is so well suited to the Frenchman's turn of mind, but for which the English have neither taste nor talent.

It is perhaps from the absence of this talent, and

E 2

in some cases partly owing to ignorance of the niceties of the language, that English strangers form their estimate of the great expensiveness of residing in Pau.   With a perfect knowledge of the language, more especially of the tricks and turns by which a good bargain is effected; with health for personal effort, and with a spirit to trace out and baffle all deception, it would, I imagine, be possible to live much more cheaply here than in England.

An intelligent friend who has resided three years in Pau, has kindly supplied me with the following, amongst many other items of information respecting the state of the country, and the habits of the people.   From his statements, confirmed by general observation, we find that the French have the happy art of managing their affairs, so as to live at much less expense than the English do, either here or in their own country.

" In the city of Pau the wages of a man servant are from twenty to thirty francs per month. A sempstress is paid only eight sous per day, besides her maintenance. A day labourer receives from twenty to twenty-two sous per day; journeymen tailors two francs per day; masons, thirty sous per day, and head masons or builders, two francs; carpenters thirty sous, gardeners the same; cabinet makers and painters, fifty sous per day, which is the highest rate of wages.   Clerks in warehouses, or counting houses, receive from forty to fifty francs per month.   The priests charge five francs for a mass performed for an individual, or at a funeral, and ordinary funerals cost about thirty or forty francs.   Private soldiers receive only one sous per day.

" In the smaller towns of the department of the lower Pyrenees, there are many proprietors who live in a style of gentility upon 2000 or 3000 francs (£80 to £120) per annum; fowls, eggs, bread, and vegetables, forming almost the only provision of country residents.   In the town of Argelés, consisting of 2000 inhabitants, one calf and one sheep were weekly sacrificed to the appetites of the whole town, two English families consuming at least a fourth part of this provision.   During four months (the duration of our friend's experience) no beef was to be met with."

CHAPTER IV.

BURIAL GROUND AT PAU—GENERAL ORDER AND QUIET
OF THE TOWN—DOMESTIC HABITS AND CHARACTER
OF THE COMMON PEOPLE—AMUSEMENTS—FETES—
RELIGIOUS CEREMONIES — NUN TAKING THE VEIL—
PROTESTANT WORSHIP IN FRANCE.

FROM the contemplation of the lively spectacle
which the busy scenes already described present,
we naturally turn to a different view of the picture,
and ask what is the end of all this appearance of
activity and life. The answer is an humbling one,
for how few could we find amongst this energetic
race, so rich in the enjoyment of health, and of all
those faculties which render life a blessing—how
very few who are animated by a wish or a hope
beyond the mere bodily requirements of daily life
—how few who dream of any other kind of usefulness than that which has self for its centre, and its
bound; and perhaps fewer still, whose aims and
whose endeavours have ever been extended beyond
this present life ! It is then but as a moving picture, that the scene can really please, for the mind

is perhaps more than usually impressed with the insufficiency of mere earthly hopes and objects, in a situation where so many strangers come to die; where all, and more than all the accustomed means of restoration so often prove unequal to the purchase of relief from pain; and where the combined advantages of youth, and wealth, and affectionate solicitude, are so often found to be in vain.

Perhaps it is that so many come too late, but I have seldom been more struck with the impotence of mere human means for arresting the progress of disease, than in visiting, on one of the sunniest and sweetest days of our early residence at Pau, the burial ground where so many strangers are interred. It is situated at the outskirts of a high part of the town, on a hill which slopes to the west; the side which would otherwise be most exposed to public view, being protected by a high wall, and screened by an avenue of trees.

The greatest portion of this enclosure is appropriated to the Roman Catholics, whose graves, adorned with flowers, and shrubs, are some of them preserved with the greatest care, while the simple and touching inscriptions on the tombstones, and the little stool at the foot of the grave, where the mourner comes to kneel, would indicate that their memory was still precious to the survivors.

There are others, however, where the taste is
shocked by a display of the meanest tinsel; and
others still, which bear evident marks of forgetfulness, or at least of neglect.

In one corner of the burial ground is the Protestant place of rest. This also is ornamented by
weeping willows, and other plants, and surrounded
by a little hedge of roses. This space contains the
remains of strangers from almost every land, but
chiefly from England, Scotland, and Ireland; and
many of the inscriptions are dedicated to the
memory of married women, between the ages of
twenty-five and thirty-five.

Peaceful and retired as this burial ground appears to be when you have entered it, one can
scarcely say that it is appropriately situated,
from its proximity to the barracks, and perhaps
more particularly from its being immediately adjoining a piece of ground appropriated to the purpose of shooting at a mark, where the first lessons
in the art of duelling are taught, and where the
pupils have a board to aim at, on which is painted
the full-length figure of a man, with a circle of red
and white to indicate the position of his heart.

I confess the purpose, and the situation of this
place, so near to the burial ground, has given me a
feeling of inexpressible repulsion, whenever I have

passed by; more especially, when I have seen a coarse, bold woman, who seems to have the keeping of the ground, and who gives out the powder and the bullets to those who are here learning to become murderers.

At a short distance from the place, and parallel with a noble avenue of trees by which the burial ground is shaded, stand the barracks, a long, regular, and handsome line of building, in a high and healthy situation, with a wide extent of open ground in front, where the soldiers perform their exercise. The whole of this space, with the avenues by which on two sides it is still adorned, was formerly included in the gardens and pleasure grounds of the chateau; and there is still something of its former character, in a beautiful grove of trees at the north-western extremity, under the shade of which the country people enjoy the advantage of placing their cattle, on market and fair days.

It might be imagined that the order and quiet of the town of Pau would be in some degree disturbed by the number of troops usually stationed here. So far from this, however, nothing can exceed the regularity and good discipline of the soldiers, a hardy, healthy-looking set of men, whose simple diet, and scanty allowance of one sous per day, exercise no doubt a wholesome and beneficial influence upon

their general habits.   Nor are there any towns of
the same size in England, where a greater degree
of public tranquillity and order prevails.   And notwithstanding the many little acts of deception and
falsehood for which strangers must be prepared, in
no place is property more generally secure.   Street
broils are also exceedingly rare, and burglaries
neither heard of nor dreaded.

As an exception to the general rule of order,
however, I must not omit one particular kind of
annoyance, which is probably too much in accor-
dance with French taste to have been made a subject of prohibition by the authorities of the place.
It is a habit of screaming, howling, or yelling, I
know not which to call it.   Perhaps a combination
of all three would be most appropriate; and frightful
and discordant as it is, there is seldom an evening
when it is not heard between the hours of six and
eleven.   It seems to be an amusement peculiar to
young men, who begin their performance with a
howling scream, which goes off into a kind of
mock laughter; and it generally prevails when a
regiment of soldiers is about to leave the town.   At
these times also, you are often disturbed early in
the morning, by the drum which beats them up
from their different quarters, as well as by troops
of their friends or comrades, who assemble in the

streets through which they pass, and sing in chorus some wild and boisterous song; which, rousing us suddenly from sleep, as it often has done, in the darkness of a winter's morning, always reminded us of the state of France during the time of the revolution.

An idea of the comparative infrequency of crime amongst the Bearnaise people, may be formed from the following observations, kindly furnished me by an intelligent friend, formerly a judge in one of our colonies, who has resided in Pau during the last three years, and who is the author of a very interesting work on " The Reformation in the South-west Provinces of France."

" There is usually a regiment of the line stationed at Pau, and nothing can exceed the order and quiet discipline of these men. It is the more remarkable that such order and quiet should prevail, since no religious instruction or observance whatever is given to, or required of them. No chaplains have been appointed to regiments in France, since the year 1830. The men are never taken to church, and the Sundays and fête days being selected as periods of military display, or review, they cannot of course individually attend Divine service.

Although the population of Pau amounts to 14,000, the prison is rarely tenanted by more than six *detenus.* The cases are usually what we should term in England petty larceny. No case of capital punishment has occurred during the last twenty-two years.

Yet the criminal laws of France are very severe. There are five classes of prisons.

1. *Les Bagnes,* viz. Toulon, Brest, and Rochefort. In these the condemned criminals are employed in hard labour. Brest receives those condemned for life, or ten years. Their number at present is 25,000. Toulon and Rochefort receive those sentenced to from five to ten years' imprisonment. The first of these has 3,000 forçats, as they are called, the latter 1,600.

2. *Les Maisons Centrales.* Of these there are nineteen in France, for prisoners sentenced to from one to five years' imprisonment.

3. *Maisons de Correction.* There are eighty-seven of these, for terms not exceeding a year.

4. *Maisons d'Arrêt.* These are for prisoners whose offences are not of a grave nature.

5. *Les Depôts.* For those charged with offences and detained for trial.

Notwithstanding this apparently excellent classification, great confusion exists in the administration of the system, on account of the insufficiency of places of detention, and also from the necessity of lodging persons *en route*, at the different prisons. Even the two sexes are not always separated. The average number of criminal prisoners, exclusive of military, is about 50,000.

There is no system of poor laws in France; and though it is part of the business of the municipality of towns to provide for the poor, this is not done with regularity, nor are there any fixed funds for supplying resources. Each winter, or period of distress, a vote of the town council affords more or less towards a charitable fund, and subscriptions are solicited in aid. Assistance is afforded not by money, but by fuel, bread, and clothing, and is seldom continued beyond a few weeks. The very aged and decrepid have a tin badge given them, which is a licence to beg. No other mendicants are permitted. In addition to this public resource, the priests have " quetes" or collections made at the churches, of which there are only two in Pau, besides the hospital chapel; and as these contributions are disbursed solely by themselves, they are enabled to gain, and to retain, a strong influence over the lower orders. There are no parochial divisions in France, in a religious sense; but the curés agree amongst themselves as to the extent of their respective districts.

It is not many months since (1840), that the

cure of St. Jaques being desirous of enlarging his
church, appealed to the people for aid, and in the
course of a few days 10,000 francs were contributed.
On occasion of these public " quetes," the most
distinguished ladies stand at the doors of the
churches, with little tin boxes, which they gaily
shake at the ears of those entering or leaving the
church, and in order to enforce the levy, are not
sparing of intercessions to the gentry.

A considerable sum is daily raised by the priests
from the letting of chairs or seats in the churches.
There are no pews or benches, but single chairs
are let by the sacristan, for one sous each mass.
Masses are performed on festival days every hour,
from six in the morning till mid-day. Sermons
are rarely preached except during Lent, Whitsun-
tide, &c. &c. On these occasions the churches are
filled to overflowing. The priests, besides the
resources of profit they possess, are paid by government, on a scale little superior to the Protestant
ministers."

The general aspect of the population of Pau, as
well as that of all the towns and villages I have
seen in the south of France, would convey the idea
that intemperance was much more rare than in
England; and there is no doubt but cases of gross
or fatal intemperance are much less frequent, a fact

which is the more to be wondered at, when the wines of the country are so cheap, and when excellent brandy may be had at the price of sixteen pence per quart. Still, on making farther observations with strict reference to this subject, we have seen but too many old men led home from market in a state of comparative helplessness, and but too many young ones something more than excited; but, for the honour of the hard-working portion of the community, I must add, that a woman whose conduct excited even a suspicion of the kind, I have never seen.

Indeed they appear to be too fully employed—too heavily laden with the actual burdens of life, to have time for any kind of self-indulgence. We seldom see them, as in England, even surrounded by their children, nor does it appear to be consistent with the taste of French women to derive pleasure from those sources of maternal interest which the helpless state of infancy affords.

It is the custom throughout the whole of France, for mothers to send away their infants to be nursed, almost as soon as they have seen the light; and this custom prevails, not only amongst the higher, but the middle classes, whose children are frequently put out to be nursed at the rate of ten francs per month; and they are often placed with mothers, who, to make way for them, send out their own children at little more than half that expense.

We had been two months settled in our lodgings before we knew that there was a child belonging to the house. At the expiration of that time, the nurse being taken ill, a fine infant was brought home, whose good nature, happy countenance, and playful habits, might have done good to the heart of its mother, or at least might have kept her from some of the balls she was in the habit of attending, at least three times a week, and every Sunday during carnival.

It is remarkable that in the French language there is no word synonymous with our word *home*— no word that even approaches to it, in the magic influence this word possesses over the hearts of those who understand and feel it. The beautiful climate of the Pyrenees, which tempts every one into the open air, may be some apology for the general desertion and discomfort of the houses of the peasantry, and of the poorer classes in general; but certainly there must be some national or constitutional defect in the habits of a people, who seek their amusement and their interest any where rather than at home.

I have said that the women appear to be too busy to find time for any personal indulgence, but the frequent dancing, both in town and country, especially on Sunday, must form an exception to this rule. Through the whole of the Sunday, both men and women seem to give themselves up to the pursuit of pleasure, as earnestly as they do to labour during the rest of the week. It is on this day especially, that the English stranger feels his real distance from his native land, and sighs in vain for the repose, and the quiet, as well as for the many holier associations, with which the memory of the sabbath is sanctified to him.

It is true that in the south of France, the peasants do not go out to field labour exactly as on other days, that the shops in the towns are less frequented, that the common people are generally more neatly dressed, and many of them, especially the women, may be seen in the earlier part of the day repairing to the different churches; but the fact that it is a day set apart for amusement of every kind, amongst which may be enumerated horse racing, horse fairs, plays, dancing, and public shows, sufficiently proves how little idea prevails amongst the people, of the real purpose for which the institution of the sabbath was ordained.

With regard to this day, we were particularly

90   SUMMER AND WINTER

unfortunate in the lodgings we had chosen, being
opposite to the theatre, where a more than common
display is expected every Sunday evening; in addition to which, we were immediately over a room
for drinking wine, for which purpose people continually flocked in between the acts.

Besides the " *spectacle,*" many of the barns, and
public rooms in the town and the suburbs of Pau,
are filled with dancers on the Sunday afternoon and
evening, especially during the carnival; and in
passing along the streets on that day, you frequently see stages erected for the display of some
monster, or the performance of some mountebank;
and with these it is the custom for a party to station themselves at the doors of the churches, during
service, where they beat their drums, and announce
to the people as they come out, what is to be the
amusement of the afternoon or evening.

In addition to all this desecration of the sabbath,
there are other amusements connected with what
are called religious observances, in which the people make it a great point to take part. To us,
however, their religious processions, their fêtes,
and their masques, appeared altogether as devoid
of interest, as on the one hand they were conducted
without reverence, and on the other without wit or
point. I had expected that the masques, and the

tricks of the carnival, would have been such as to excite merriment at least, instead of which the whole is a childish and grotesque piece of buffoonery, as entirely without aim, as apparently without effect, for they do not even laugh themselves.

Indeed I should be at a loss to say what does make the French people laugh. That they smile, and look lively, and good humoured, may be said of almost all, as well as that they are capable of being thrown, on the instant, and from the slightest possible cause, into a perfect explosion of speech and gesticulation enough to strike an English person dumb for an hour; but the hearty, spirit-stirring laugh, which indicates the having got possession of an excellent joke, and which even before its awakening cause is fully told, infects the bystanders, until it echoes from one to another of the merry group —this laugh, or any thing approaching to it, is never heard in France.

Nor, had the French people really any very acute sense of the ridiculous, could they pass with gravity the heterogeneous scenes which daily meet their view. Of this fact a French diligence in all its glory is perhaps the strongest illustration; but there are also carriages of many other descriptions, postilions, equestrians, costumes and customs, not only different from our own, but so grotesque in

themselves, that the wonder is they never excite so
much as a smile.   Amongst these it may not be
inappropriate to mention, that a friend of ours,
saw at Toulouse, a woman, finely dressed, riding on
horseback, in the Bearnais fashion, and preceded
by a herald with a trumpet, announcing that she
had *English needles* to sell.

It is but justice to the Bearnaise to add, that
their anger is as transient and superficial as their
mirth.   When they quarrel it is but for the moment,
and their accustomed appearance of lively good
nature is immediately resumed.   As a specimen of
the only kind of street broils we ever witnessed, I saw
two men one day in the very climax of a passion.
One of them, the most exasperated, started up with
the countenance of a fury, stooped down in the
attitude of gathering up a fist full of strength, and
with his hand clenched rushed at the other, as if to
strike him a deadly blow.   Before his hand reached
the face of the offender, however, his fingers
expanded like a star fish, and the whole thing went
off in air.

Desirous of ascertaining whether the French
were ever really entertained with their own mummeries, I went on the last day of the carnival to
see an exhibition which takes place annually on the
road to Bizanos, a little village situated at the

distance of a mile from Pau. The origin of this custom seems to have had some relation to a fanciful idea of performing the obsequies of the carnival, by burning or burying some kind of effigy, but the whole affair has now dwindled down to a mere promenade on foot, on horseback, or in any kind of carriage, up and down a straight road, for about the distance of three quarters of a mile; in which space you meet nearly the whole population of Pau —rich and poor, high and low, with here and there a few masks; while groups of dancers fill the neighbouring barns, and bands of discordant music help to make ' confusion worse confounded.'

Had we been previously disposed to call in question the power of custom over the habits of the multitude, we might have come here to be convinced of its extent; for what else can induce some of the most respectable families to drive backwards and forwards through such a scene, where, to say nothing of its aimless stupidity, the crowd is such as often to endanger human life? We ourselves were witness to one of the maskers being thrown down by the horses of a gentleman's carriage, and remaining some time in such a position, that a single movement of the horses, either forward or backward, must have been fatal. In all this motley crowd, we looked in vain for merriment.

94　　　　SUMMER AND WINTER

It is true a sharp north-east wind was blowing all the time, and cold is a powerful sedative to animal spirits; but I had certainly expected to see some point, or some purpose in the frolic, and for this I looked in vain amongst the different actors in the scene.　A friend told us afterwards, that he had seen a man swinging about a pot of burning pitch, in imitation of the manner in which incense is burned, and scattered in the churches.

Nor is this idle and aimless parade more destitute of interest, than their exhibitions of a religious character are devoid of reverence or solemn feeling.　A French funeral is a melancholy spectacle, especially if it be that of a person of the poorer class.　I have seen the priest who was about to perform the last act of duty to the dead, walking towards the house of mourning with all the boys of a village about him, one of them carrying the cross, and all chattering and laughing as they went, as if on their way to a merry-making.　A little while after, I have seen the funeral procession advancing at a brisk pace, half a dozen careless-looking country fellows, three on each side, swinging the coffin between them, and talking merrily all the way, while a few old women followed with candles in their hands.

Nor were such funerals of the lowest grade.

There are those of the patients who die in the
hospital, for whom a common coffin is employed,
which is brought back from the grave, after the
body has been deposited there.

The manner of conducting the funeral of a
young person, or a child, appeared to us very
singular the first time we witnessed it. The
procession was conducted, as usual, by a priest
advancing in great state, with his conical hat and
white muslin robe, while a man who walked by his
side, chanted all the way in a loud and sonorous
voice. We were near the burial ground, and
stood still to see the procession pass; but where
the bearers could be, we were at a loss to
imagine. At last we beheld the coffin, balanced
upon the head of a boy, and though apparently
as long as himself, he never put up his hand to
keep it steady, but walked along at a quick pace
behind the priest. All the funerals in this part of
France are conducted on foot, and usually take
place at the expiration of twenty-four hours after
the person's death.

There is now no monastery in Pau, but a small
number of Ursuline sisters occupy a convent in
a central part of the town. To this order there
were three or four additions, during the time of
our residence in the neighbourhood; and, having

96   SUMMER AND WINTER

heard much of the solemn and imposing character
of the ceremony which takes place on occasion of
such accessions, I took an opportunity of witnessing
a spectacle, which there seems to be a tendency
in all minds to invest with peculiar interest.

On entering the chapel of the convent, I found
it already crowded with curious and eager specta-
tors, a considerable number of whom were English.
By securing a place among the crowd more immediately opposite to that part of the chapel which
is appropriated to the nuns, it was not difficult to
see all that took place within the oratory, which is
separated from the body of the church by a
grating, or screen of lattice work; and here we
saw the young ladies of the school belonging to
the convent, seated in regular order, all neatly
dressed, most of them smiling and whispering, and
looking like anything but renouncing the world.
At the sound of a bell, however, they all assumed
a different aspect, and rising from their seats as
the door of the oratory opened, made way for a
procession of solemn sisters, clothed in their long
black robes, and bearing lighted tapers in their
hands.   Between two of these, and bearing also
a lighted taper in her hand, advanced the object
upon whom all eyes were fixed, the nun who was
about to take the veil.   She was a stately-looking

woman, apparently about thirty, dressed in a robe of rich yellow satin, with a splendidly embroidered scarf. Her jet black hair was arranged in ringlets, and on one side was placed a large white rose. She advanced towards a crucifix, and having placed her candle on the altar, performed the usual act of reverence, and then sat down in a crimson chair which had been placed for her, immediately opposite an opening in the lattice which commanded a full view of the altar in the sanctuary, where about a dozen priests, in full costume, according to their different orders in the church, were assembled.

In the mean time the nuns on one side of the oratory had retreated to their seats with their tapers burning, while those on the other side had put theirs out. On the first appearance of the procession, a strain of sweet and touching music had commenced, which ceased soon after the new sister had taken her seat; when one of the priests, ascending the pulpit, delivered a sermon, which, with the prayers which followed, occupied more than an hour. In this sermon, the preacher dwelt chiefly upon the advantages of renouncing the world, and embracing a religious vocation, repeating many times the expression, that Jesus

F

98   SUMMER AND WINTER

Christ had that day taken to himself another spouse.

After the sermon, the new sister was led from the oratory by the lady abbess, preceded by two little girls bearing lighted tapers; and until her return, the time was occupied by a kind of chanting, in which the priests and holy sisters sung by turns, some of the female voices sounding remarkably sweet and soft.

In the course of half an hour the nun returned, dressed in a black robe, again preceded by the two children, and led by the lady abbess, who now took her seat beside the crucifix, where the nun knelt down, and received from her hand a string of black beads. While she remained in the same attitude, the priest whose office it appeared to be to conduct the ceremony, placed upon her head the white veil, and gave her a paper in which was written her new name, saying at the same time, " In the world thou hast been called ——; as a child of God, thy name is now ——." She then rose, and after kissing the lady abbess on both cheeks, went round the oratory, and saluted all the sisters in the same manner. This performance concluded, she seated herself again in the crimson chair, when a wreath of roses was placed upon her

head.   Mass was then said, and the host lifted up
before the kneeling congregation; after which
incense was scattered, and the whole ceremony
concluded.

We were told, a few days after, that a beautiful
young creature had on this occasion devoted herself to the church; but certainly, if one might
venture to judge by physiognomy, the devotee
was one of those who have little to sacrifice in
giving up the world.   There was a firmness, a
hardness, and a determination in the expression
of her countenance, well suited to the austerities
of a convent.   With regard to the general attractions of the scene, I certainly left the chapel
more than ever convinced, that ceremonies of this
kind can offer nothing seductive to a mind in the
slightest degree impressed with the true spirituality
of religion.   Nor is this conviction weakened in
its force on reflecting more seriously upon the mock
sacrifice by which the heart is thus deluded into
a belief of its devotion to God; while its highest
faculties, and its best affections, are withdrawn
from the sphere of duty which He has so wisely
appointed.

I have already spoken of the Sabbath day at
Pau.   Unpleasant as it unquestionably is in some
respects, in others it affords advantages not to be

100   SUMMER AND WINTER

met with elsewhere in this part of France. For
some years the English residents and visitors have
been favoured with the ministerial labours of pious
and excellent clergymen, by whom Divine worship
has been regularly performed twice every Sunday.
Three or four years ago, ground was purchased by
the Duchess of Gordon in an airy and eligible part
of the town, for the erection of a Protestant church,
which is now nearly completed. It is a neat and
strongly-built edifice, the upper part forming a
commodious place for public worship for the
English and French Protestants, while the lower
part is already appropriated to the purpose of
school-rooms for French Protestant children, and
apartments for the master and mistress. The
expense of this building has been defrayed by the
munificence of the Duchess of Gordon, and by the
contributions of the English resorting to this place.

In the mean time the Protestant worship in
Pau has been held in a large room adjoining a
grocer's shop in one of the principal streets; and
the room, though capable of containing nearly two
hundred persons, has generally been found much
too small for the numbers who would gladly attend.

The English morning service on the Sunday
commences at eleven o'clock, and the afternoon at
four. There is also a missionary meeting held

once every month, in furtherance of the objects of the Church Missionary Society. Besides these services, the excellent clergyman, the Rev. J. Ridgeway, who has officiated in English for the last three years, holds a weekly Bible class at his own house, for the instruction of the juvenile members of his congregation.

The building for public worship, now nearly completed, is designed for the use both of the French and the English. At present, the religious services amongst the small number of French Protestants here, are held in the same room as that in which the English meet, and at the house of the truly pious and benevolent French pastor, the Rev. L. J. Buscarlet. There is preaching in French in the public room every Sunday, at two o'clock, when the congregation frequently exceeds one hundred persons. Besides this, religious meetings in French are held at the minister's house in the morning and evening of the Sabbath; on one evening in the week; and there is a meeting for prayer in French and English every Thursday at noon.

There are about two hundred Protestants in Pau, of whom forty are communicants. The stipend of the minister, as well as the maintenance of the instructors in the schools, is provided

by the Société Evangélique de France, an institution worthy of every encouragement, and possessing strong claims on the sympathy and support of
more favoured portions of the Christian church.

There are at present about sixty children in the
schools, of whom twenty are girls. The minister
receives from the Society 1500 francs, or about
£60 per annum; the schoolmaster about £40,
and the schoolmistress £32; and the subscriptions of the English visitors at Pau supply nearly
half this amount. In the year 1839, these donations, aided by a bazaar, amounted to a sum equal
to the entire expenditure. At present, the local
contributions to a considerable amount have been
appropriated to the purpose of fitting up the
newly-erected school-rooms.

At the house of the estimable minister, there is
a good depository of Bibles and Testaments, with
tracts and larger books on religious subjects in
French and Spanish, from which those who are
desirous of diffusing the knowledge of Divine
truth, may supply themselves with the means.

With the commendable desire of interesting his
congregation in the progress of Christianity in
different parts of the world, Mr. Buscarlet has a
missionary prayer meeting at his house on the
first Monday of every month. Mr. Ellis has had

great pleasure in attending these meetings, and in giving to the people there assembled, some account of the missions of the London Society, particularly those to the South Seas. At Orthez, where there are said to be eighteen hundred Protestants, there exists a deep interest in the missionary operations of Christians from this country, increased, no doubt, by the fact of one of the most valuable French missionaries in South Africa, Mr. Casalis, having gone from that town, where his family still reside.

The Protestants of Orthez had sent once or twice to invite Mr. Ellis to pay them a visit; and in the month of February he accompanied Mr. Buscarlet to that ancient town, once the seat of a college for the education of Protestant ministers. Mr. Ellis was received kindly by Mr. Gabriac, the pastor of the church, and with the most friendly hospitality by Mr. Raclus, a pious minister who labours in the neighbourhood. During the forenoon he walked out to the lower part of the town, to see the ancient and picturesque bridge, which spans the deep and rapid waters of the Gave, and afterwards visited the ruined tower of the venerable chateau built by one of the counts of Foix. This spot commands an extensive view of the ground where the battle between the

104   SUMMER AND WINTER

Duke of Wellington and Marshal Soult was fought on the 27th of February, 1814. It was in the same month when Mr. Ellis beheld it. The morning was then fine, the country verdant, and the fields already rich in promise of the coming harvest; while the serenity and cheerfulness of nature formed a strong contrast with what the same scene must have presented on that memorable day.

In the afternoon, Mr. Ellis addressed an assembly of about three hundred in the church, which is a substantial edifice; and in the evening attended a meeting held at the house of Madame Casalis, the widowed mother of the missionary already mentioned; and as Mr. Ellis had had the pleasure of seeing her son when, some time after taking leave of his native place, he visited London, in his way to Africa, and had also accompanied him to the ship in which he was to sail, the mother and her amiable family were deeply interested in hearing all that could be told of one so distant and so dear.

In the department of the Lower Pyrénées, there are about twelve Protestant congregations; but, with the exception of those at Orthez and Salies, they are most of them small; though it is hoped they are increasing here, as well as in other parts of France. The pastors of the consistorial churches and the professors of the colleges, are all paid by the government, the stipends of the pastor being regulated by the population of the places in which they labour. The highest stipend is 3000 francs, or £120; that of the second class is 2000, or £80: of the third or lowest, 1500, or £60. The total amount paid by the French government to Protestant ministers in 1839-40, was £13,000; while to the Catholic priests, the scale of whose stipend is about the same as many of the Protestants, the government paid during the same period £1,100,000. Besides providing the buildings for worship, and paying the stipends of the ministers, the local authorities furnish a residence for the minister, or allow a sum for that purpose. In Pau 500 francs per annum are allowed to each of the Catholic priests for lodgings.

In addition to the ministers of the consistorial churches, the Société Evangélique has a number of faithful and devoted men labouring in almost every part of the country.

There are seven professors and about seventy students at the establishment for educating Protestant ministers at Montauban. The reformed church of France now numbers ninety consistoires, comprising about four hundred pastors, and about

F 3

106   SUMMER AND WINTER

nine hundred lay elders. It is an encouraging fact, that during the last year, their church has opened not less than fifteen new places of worship.

Those visitors at Pau who feel pleasure in visiting the schools, and affording encouragement to the efforts now made, amidst many difficulties, for promoting religious education and piety amongst the people, can scarcely fail to become more interested in the prosperity of the institution by which these efforts are sustained.

The Société Evangélique de France is conducted by gentlemen of benevolence and piety. It has existed about eight years, and has, during that period, exercised a limited, but truly beneficial influence, in several of the most important departments of France. It has opened places of worship, or stationed ministers, in not fewer than thirty towns and cities. Schools have been established, or supported, in twenty places, in which 1600 scholars are receiving instruction. Sixty-eight colporteurs have been employed by the same institution, who have left amongst the people they have visited 14,000 copies of the Holy Scriptures. These, and other operations of this useful society, are sustained entirely by the voluntary contributions of its friends.

CHAPTER V.

EXCURSIONS—LOUVIE—NAY—EAUX CHAUDES.

THE weather in the early part of our stay at Pau being so particularly mild and pleasant, we found it difficult to confine our walks and rides to the immediate neighbourhood of the town. The mountains which looked so beautiful in the distance, perpetually invited us to a nearer acquaintance; and, although frequently told that no one thought of visiting them before the months of May or June, we determined to make the experiment at a much earlier period; but not without first attempting a sort of exploratory excursion to Louvie, a small town situated at the foot of the snowy mountains, and rather more than half way to Eaux Bonnes and Eaux Chaudes.

It was early in the month of February, that we set out one morning to make this excursion, a party of four on horseback, prepared for a ride of thirty miles. The morning was most propitious—bright, but sufficiently cold to render exercise agreeable, and as we passed the old bridge of six arches, which stretches over the river Gave, the vine-covered hills rose before us in all the dewy fresh-ness of early spring. At the termination of this bridge, one enters the Commune of Jurançon, to which belong the numerous groups of houses ex-tending from the river to the foot of the hills. By the side of the road there is still standing a cross, called the "cross of the Prince," which derives its name from the circumstance of Louis XIII. in company with the nobles of his court, having knelt before one erected on this spot, at the time when he visited Bearn for the purpose of re-establishing the Roman Catholic religion.

Jurançon, which forms so beautiful a picture from the Parc, is scarcely less attractive when you pass near the shade of its umbrageous trees, some of the finest which this country affords. They are chiefly oaks, and they cover a wide space of ground appropriated to rural sports, to the village .dance, and, on particular occasions, to the performance of plays, sometimes those of Corneille and Racine, the female parts being sustained by the young men of the village. Whenever I have visited this place, however, I have found it occupied in a very differ-ent manner—by immense herds of swine, the property of the neighbouring farmers, who place them under the care of one herdsman, by whom they are driven to feed upon the acorns beneath these trees.

Leaving Jurançon to our right, we pursued our way along the valley which looks so tempting from the Parc, terminating in the Pic du Midi, and forming one of the principal routes by which Spain is entered from this part of France.

After Jurançon the next village is Gan, formerly celebrated for its mineral spring, now little frequented. Beyond its general aspect of antiquity, it offers little to attract the stranger's eye, and we were glad to hasten on and to leave behind us the long straight road by which it is approached; especially as we found, soon after passing this village, that our route was becoming more varied, and that the little limpid river Neez, which we had seen meandering through the fields, was likely to become more intimately our companion by the way.

We now perceived that we were entering a wilder and more picturesque region; for the range of vine-clad hills which skirt the valley of the Gave, extend to the southward until they blend with the Pyrenees, gradually exchanging their chateaux for the humbler dwellings of the peasants, and their vineyards for the barren rocks, or wastes

110   SUMMER AND WINTER

of untrodden snow. Our view was now becoming more closely bounded by the sides of abrupt and rugged hills, leaving little more than the excellent road over which we travelled, and the now turbulent stream beside it, to occupy the valley between.

The river in this part of our ride, reminded us of the Wharf at Bolton Abbey, in Yorkshire, and there are many places where it chafes and struggles through the rocks, like the Strid, of fatal celebrity. But we wanted the green smooth turf which stretches along the banks of the Wharf; for here all was more rugged, and more wild; though, as a proof of the wide difference between this climate and our own, the hill sides were still covered with vines.

As the day advanced, it proved to be one of the clearest of the many we had enjoyed, with a sun that lighted every thing into life and beauty. There was, as usual, not a breath of wind, though the rush of the rapid stream, and the pace at which we travelled, gave to the air sufficient freshness. All was still, above and around us, except the pure wild torrent beside our path, and the vine dressers, who were busy at their work, and whose voices echoed from hill to hill. Here and there a peak of purest snow was beginning to be visible beyond the frowning crags above us, with which were contrasted the vivid green of the patches of young flax in the valley, and the bright box, and fern, and ivy, that hung in rich profusion amongst the rocks.

At one part of the road, we turned aside to see the source of the river Neez, which wells out of the solid rock, at once a considerable stream. We did not, however, lose this pleasant kind of companionship, for we soon found ourselves tracing the course of another river, from whose banks we were only occasionally separated by rising ground.

We had lost sight of the mountains soon after leaving Gan, but the increasing freshness and coldness of the air, as well as the boldness and height of the crags above our heads, indicated our approach to their vicinity; and at the little village of Rebenac, we again beheld a wider extent of mountainous scenery, though still the Pic remained hidden from our view. On an eminence a little above this village, and commanding an extensive view, a noble mansion is pointed out as the residence of a family, one of the members of which has been distinguished for his elegant translation of Homer.

The road to this place, from its great variety, had appeared to me rather long; and I confess I began to fear, either that we should never find the

112   SUMMER AND WINTER

mountains, or that the view of the Valley of
Ossau, of which some of my companions had
spoken with so much enthusiasm, would end in
disappointment. It was not long, however, before
we ascended a steep hill, from which much was to
be hoped, and passing through the village of Sé-
vignac, we came at once upon a scene that would
have richly repaid us, had our journey been ten
times the length it was.

Immediately before us, to the southward, was the
vista of crags and mountains I had so often contemplated at a greater distance, now magnified in
their grandeur and sublimity, with the giant Pic
rising in sovereign majesty above them all; while
farther to the right and left, were mountains loftier
still, whose rugged masses were now clothed in
virgin snow. But what to me gave the whole
scene a character of the highest sublimity, was the
aspect and colouring of the nearer mountains, on
one side sloping down into the valley with a long
bold outline, on the other almost perpendicular,
except that here and there they were broken into
stupendous masses of dark rock;—on one side
clothed in a rich haze of purple and gold, which
just left visible the pine forests on their summits,
and the villages, and crags, and chestnut woods
along their sides, and at their feet; while on

the other fell the clear light of that magnificent sunshine, which brought out to view all their jutting promontories, and even the glittering box with which they were so richly crowned; while immediately below the eminence on which we stood for a long time to gaze, lay a wide and fertile valley, watered by a broad clear river, and enlivened by innumerable villages and hamlets, stretching as far as the eye could reach, at the foot of the mountains, and along the different openings amongst the lower hills.

Nor was the scene, in some of its wildest features, a distant one. One of the perpendicular mountains to the left, rose immediately from the path on which we rode, so that we quenched our thirst with the icicles which hung from the rocks; while the sun still shone so brightly upon us, that we were sometimes glad to find a shelter from its beams. This, then, was the entrance to the valley of Ossau — the "valley where the bears come down"—the valley where Henry IV. used to come to chase these monsters of the wild—the valley whose inhabitants have scarcely been rivalled by those of any other country, for their industrious hardihood, and for the bold independence with which from time immemorial they have defended their property and their rights.

114   SUMMER AND WINTER

We had seen at different times in the neighbourhood of Pau, a few stray specimens of the figure
and costume of the peasants of this valley; but
here we beheld for the first time, these hardy
mountaineers amidst their native wilds. And a
noble looking race they are, somewhat taller than
the peasantry around Pau, with more vigorous
complexions, and dressed in a costume at once
more primitive and more picturesque. They
wear the same round cap or bonnet of brown
cloth, but their black and flowing hair is always
cut close in front, and left to hang loose upon their
shoulders. They most commonly wear a jacket of
brown cloth, sometimes one of red, and a scarlet or
crimson sash tied about the body. On no occasion
are they seen with trousers, but always breeches of
brown cloth, and worsted stockings of the same
colour, and of their own knitting, not made with feet,
but finished off by a kind of wide border of the
same material, which hangs down over the great
wooden shoe, made in the shape of a canoe, only
more curved underneath, and more turned up at
the toe. In addition to this, they generally have,
somewhere about them, their wide woollen cloak,
with its pointed hood. The shepherds are always
accompanied by a dog, of a kind peculiar to the
Pyrenees, as large as the Newfoundland dog, but

more like a wolf in shape, and always white, with a mixture of buff, or wolfish grey.

These dogs, though large and powerful, have the appearance of being gentle and docile, from their being thin, and badly fed; but that they have a disposition to be otherwise, I can testify, having been twice seized by them, and having also heard of many instances in which they were the terror of the neighbourhood. Mr. Ellis met one day on the same road we were travelling, with a very communicative priest, who told him that he always rode with pistols, to defend himself from these dogs; and not long after our arrival at Pau, an animal of this description was the cause of a sudden and much lamented death. It was that of a young French officer, whose horse took fright at one of these large dogs rushing out, as they always do, without a moment's warning. The rider was dashed to the ground, and his head pitching on a stone, he was killed on the spot. He was aid-de-camp to a general residing in the place, and engaged to be married to his daughter. His funeral was the most solemn we have witnessed, being conducted with military discipline, and attended by all the officers, amongst whom he was much respected.

Perhaps the most singular feature in the character of the shepherd's dog of the Pyrenees, is,

116   SUMMER AND WINTER

that like his master, he always leads, instead of
driving the sheep. He is brought up entirely
amongst them, and sleeps in the same fold. It
is a curious sight to see the shepherd and his dog
coming first out of a field, and the flock following.
The sheep are more slender and taller than ours,
with thick curled horns, and long fine wool; while
the singularity of a long face, with a kind of
Roman nose, makes them look particularly solemn.

On arriving at the inn at Louvie, situated by the
side of the river which waters the valley, we were
somewhat disconcerted to find a scarcity of provision, the season being much too early for visitors
to be expected, and the trout in the river, which
are said to be excellent, not choosing that day to
be caught. With appetites sharpened by the keen
mountain air, we were obliged to be satisfied with
a promise of eggs and bacon, which are as frequently met with here, as in any of the dales of
Yorkshire; and while this repast was preparing, we
walked to a little village on the left side of the
river, situated amongst a group of hills, or rather
scattered rocks, on the summit of one of which,
stand the ruins of an ancient castle, now called
Castel Geloos. As the valley derives its name
from the two latin words *ursi saltus*, this edifice was
formerly called Castellum Ursalticum. It was the

residence of the Viscounts of Ossau, at the time when the valley formed a little state independent of Bearn. And it was here that the Bearnais sovereigns, in later times, used to receive the oaths of the Ossalois, on occasions when they came to render justice in their state.

Near this place is an ancient church, much celebrated for its beautiful columns of marble. It is related of these columns, that Henry IV. finding nothing to equal them in Paris, wrote to request the inhabitants of the village to give up the possession of them to him. Their answer was a remarkable one, and truly characteristic of the people :—" Sire, our hearts and our property are yours, dispose of them as you will; but, as regards the columns, they belong to God. *Entendez-vous-en avec lui.*"

While resting on one of the little craggy hills near the ruins of Castel Geloos, with the majestic Pic du Midi before us,—the mountains veiled in purple haze to our right,—the perpendicular heights to our left,—the old castle in the foreground,—and the river winding at our feet, we were all struck with the peculiar adaptation of the scene to all that an artist requires; and I only regret that no one seems to have made choice of this particular spot.

118   SUMMER AND WINTER

On returning again to the inn at Louvie, which cannot certainly be recommended either for its cleanliness or comfort, we found that the chicken which was to be added to our dinner, had but just received its death stroke. Chicken, however, it was not; for when, in the short space of a quarter of an hour it was placed upon the table, its sinewy structure might have defied the eagerness of appetites even less fastidious than ours; and we were obliged to content ourselves with a dinner of eggs and bacon, at an enormous charge, not having taken the precaution to bargain for our fare beforehand, which is always necessary in travelling in this country.   On remonstrating with the mistress of the house on the disproportion of her dinner and her charge, and referring to the uneatable nature of her chicken, she coolly replied, with the usual French shrug, that it was no fault of hers, that she did not make the chicken.

It was a beautiful evening when we returned to Pau, the sky without a cloud, and the air sharpened by a slight tendency to frost.   Such indeed had been the weather almost every day since the time of our arrival.   Though perfectly calm, it was never sultry, for on turning immediately out of the sunshine into the shade, the contrast was so great, as always to produce a sensation like that of washing the hands and face in cold water on a hot summer's day. The only time when the air was oppressive, was during the prevalence of a south, or Spanish wind; but as these winds seldom continue more than a day, and are then succeeded by rain, they are not much to be complained of. There is usually in the early part of the spring, a month or more of almost constant wet. This year was an exception. There had been, on our arrival at Pau, twenty-eight days without a drop of rain; and as the weather had become much colder by the end of February, and there had only once or twice been rain enough to lay the dust, vegetation was unusually backward, and the public roads by no means in an agreeable state.

We had sufficient experience of this, in an excursion we made during the first week of March, to the little town of Nay, situated about ten miles from Pau, at the foot of the mountains higher up the course of the river. By some mischance we had chosen the day previous to one of the great fairs held at Pau, for the sale of horses, mules, and other cattle; and as the country towards Nay is amongst the richest in agricultural produce, we had the full benefit of finding the dust already set

120   SUMMER AND WINTER

in motion by hundreds of busy peasants, who
hastened on their way to the place of general
rendezvous.

Besides the people of Bearn, these fairs
are the resort of numbers of Spaniards, whose
trade with this country consists chiefly in mules,
with droves of which animals, the roads at such
times are thronged.   They are generally beautiful
creatures, their price averaging from 300 to 700
francs; and the Spaniards by whom they are
accompanied, are the most striking and picturesque
objects I have ever seen.   The usual dress of
these men is a printed cotton handkerchief tied
close round the head, over which they sometimes
wear an enormous hat, with a wide brim curled up
all round; while the better order have a hat of
black velvet with the same broad brim, and a
conical crown, ornamented with bands of velvet,
and tufts of silk fringe.   Their jackets are usually
of blue or purple velvet, or plush, their small-
clothes of the same material, with a silk sash,
and often a thick roll of cloth or linen wrapped
round their loins.   Their stockings are curiously
knitted, blue or white, and they wear veritable
sandals, laced round the leg up to the calf.
Some of the mule drivers have the animal on
which they ride caparisoned in a kind of crimson

cloth, from which is suspended a long rich fringe with tassels of silk.   They are for the most part, however, an abject-looking, lean, and haggard set of people, with thin sharp features, small dark eyes, and invariably frizzled brown hair.   Still there is something commanding in their gait and atti- tude, so that you may know them to be Spaniards at a distance, partly from the custom they adopt of always wearing something slung over one shoul- der, in the fashion of a mantle; and even when this is nothing better than a sack, they manage to adjust it with a grace.   Most of them, however, wear a large woollen cloth, made with broad stripes of brown, grey, and white; which mantle is their covering by day, and their bed at night.

Besides these men who cross the frontier for the purposes of trade, there are many Spanish families residing in Pau, who have been compelled, from the state of their country, or from the nature of their own political sentiments, to seek refuge there; many who are reduced from a high station in society to live in comparative poverty, and others of the same rank who make a scanty livelihood by giving lessons in their own language.

But to return to our journey to Nay.   I had anticipated a pleasant ride along the banks of the river, at the foot of the vine-tufted hills; but we

G

122   SUMMER AND WINTER

found, to our disappointment, that the road led us along a complete flat, and was hemmed in by high walls or houses, which form, through this populous district, an almost continued line of villages, extending to the town of Nay, before entering which, we crossed the Gave by a long wooden bridge, supported on piles of stone.

This little town, still remarkable for the industry of its inhabitants, was once a place of very considerable trade in the manufacture and export of woollen goods, of the robes worn by the priests, of the brown cloth caps of the country, and of *bonnets Grecs*, destined for the coiffures of the orientals; but chiefly of flannels, twenty thousand pieces of which it is said to have exported annually before the revolution. Little trace of this flourishing state of things is now remaining, except in the groups of women and children, who ply their busy needles in knitting flat bonnets of thick worsted, which look extremely durable. There is, however, a manufactory of excellent flour, which supplies the neighbouring districts. To us, the whole place, almost overshadowed as it is by the neighbouring mountains, wore an aspect of stillness and gloom; for though the day was bright and clear, the long lines of colonnades, composed of rude and heavy masonry, under the shade of which the people were sitting at their work, gave a sombre and sepulchral character to the general appearance of the streets. Nor were our impressions rendered more agreeable by finding that we must dine in the bedroom of a dirty inn, the entrance of which was open to the stable, filled with horses, probably on their way to the fair.

Our object in visiting Nay, was chiefly that of seeing the Protestant minister stationed there, an interesting and excellent man, whose situation claims the sympathy of all whose best feelings are engaged in the cause to which he has devoted himself. He was originally destined for a Roman Catholic priest, and received his education preparatory to assuming this office. Subsequently, however, he, and several members of his family, became, about the same time, convinced of their error; and having openly espoused the Protestant faith, have ever since endured the persecution and contempt of their Roman Catholic neighbours; especially the minister, whose situation is such, that on one occasion, when he wished to hire a house for his family, not a single proprietor of the place would allow him one to live in. He was, therefore, under the necessity of purchasing such a habitation as his means were equal to; and though it is an old place, with only one little chimney,

G 2

and no glass window, it had, on the day we saw it,
an aspect of neatness and comfort far beyond that
of many nobler mansions.

In his office of Protestant minister, he now
receives annually from his little congregation, a
sum not exceeding £28, on which his family, consisting of a wife and eight children, are supported.
We had the privilege of seeing this worthy woman,
surrounded by her little flock; and truly their
contented cheerfulness, and their unmurmuring
resignation, are well calculated to teach a lesson
long to be remembered. The mother and the
oldest daughter, a sweet-looking girl of fifteen, and
in this country a little woman,—both wore the
common head-dress of the country, and were in all
respects dressed with the most unpretending simplicity. By way of adding to their slender means,
they employ themselves in many humble occupations, the mother often going out to wash and iron.
Would that some of the discontented wives and
daughters of other lands could have been with me,
and have seen their smiling faces, their humble
dress, their uncarpeted floors, with the general
aspect of order and neatness, which in this country
is the more to be admired, from its extreme
rarity.

After visiting the pastor's family, we went to

see his little church, or "temple," as the Protestant places of worship are called in France. We
had been told that it would be of no use leaving
tracts amongst the people of Nay; for some of our
friends who had done so, had seen, before they left
the place, the same parties amongst whom the
tracts had been distributed, throwing them into a
blazing fire, which they had lighted for the purpose of showing the visitors in what way their
gifts were esteemed. Such is the spirit prevailing
in the town where this faithful and undaunted
minister still continues to uphold the standard of
truth, "persecuted, but not forsaken,—cast down,
but not destroyed."

The town of Nay is beautifully situated, though
it has the appearance of being a little too closely
hemmed in between the river and the mountains
which rise immediately above it with peculiar grandeur. It was in pursuing our walk a little way
above the town, from a situation commanding an
extensive view of the fertile tract of country called
the "garden of Béarn," that our conductor pointed
out to us the ancient castle of Coarraze, more
interesting than all others associated with the
memory of Henry IV., from its having been the
scene of his youthful sports, as well as the situation
where he enjoyed the advantages of that rational

and vigorous training to which none but a noble-
minded mother like Jeanne d'Albret, would have
entrusted a princely son.

When first taken from the hands of his nurse,
he was committed to the care of Suzanne de Bourbon Busset, baroness de Miossens, a woman dis-
guished for her many virtues and high intelligence;
and in order to carry out with better effect the
system of education which the queen had adopted
for her son, he was sent, with his governess, to this
remote situation; where the purest air, the simplest diet, and the most natural exercise, could be
enjoyed without the interruption of courtly visitors,
or affairs of state. The directions of Jeanne d'Albret
were, that the future monarch should be trained
like a child of the mountaineers; and, faithful to
her important trust, the baroness exercised over
her pupil a discipline resembling that of a Spartan
mother. He was treated like the children of the
village, was clothed in the same dress, and par-
took of their enjoyments and their sports. His
food was often the same dry bread; he wore the
bonnet of the peasants, the same kind of woollen
vest,—trod the mountain paths with bare feet,—
fought not unfrequently with his little comrades,—
and excelled in many of their favourite games.
For many years of his life he knew no other

language than the patois of Béarn, and this knowledge contributed much in after life to endear him
to the people of this country. It is said of him,
that a bon-mot or a lively sally in his maternal
language, was one of the most powerful means of
influence he could employ over the young men
whom he led to the conquest of Paris; and whom,
by a happy repartee, couched in their native
tongue, he could beguile into forgetfulness of all
their fatigues.

Situated a little higher than the hamlet of
Coarraze, and about the distance of two leagues
from the village, is still shown a house, which
the prince was accustomed frequently to visit. It
was occupied by a family of labourers, of the
name of Gestas, now extinct. When the young
prince was obliged to quit Coarraze to return to
the chateau of Pau, he requested these friends
of his infancy to inform him in what he could
benefit them, or give them pleasure. They replied
with the true simplicity of peasants, that their
only ambition was to be allowed *to pay their tithe
in grain, and to preserve the straw.* What a happy
ignorance is betrayed by this reply, of what the
world beyond their mountains had to offer!

It is recorded, that long after Henry quitted
this castle, he was in the habit of returning to

visit his friends the Gestas, and to follow the chase
along the mountain paths which he knew so well.
In order to shorten the way, he was accustomed to
trace a narrow path along the side of a hill, which
still retains the name of the road of Henry IV.
Indeed, the same associations occur at almost every
step the traveller takes, so fond are the people of
the country of cherishing the remembrance of their
"good king."

Our ride from Nay that evening I shall not soon
forget.   The narrow road was literally thronged
with peasants returning from the fair, not intoxi
cated, but just so much excited as to induce them
to stand in our way, rather than to move out of it,
while the dust, without a breath of wind, rose in a
dense cloud, so that we could not see five yards
before us.   Out of this cloud the figures of men,
women, carts, oxen, and mules, came darkening upon
us, before we could be aware of them; like the
figures shown by a magic lantern, growing as they
came.   And when I add to this, that the horns of
the cattle are extremely wide—that the horses in
harness wear collars branching out at each side
into a wide frame, through the ends of which the
reins are drawn,—and that the mules, the only
malicious animals in the country, will often go considerably out of their way to kick at a passer by,—

the difficulties of our situation may be in some degree understood. Happily, we reached home without either doing or receiving any very serious mischief.

A few days after our journey to Nay, we set off again to the mountains, intending to visit Eaux Chaudes, and if possible to penetrate as far as the Pic du Midi de Pau. We were a party of three, were to travel on horseback, and having this time a journey of twenty-five miles before us, into an unknown land, it was necessary to be stirring early in the day. When I first looked out, it was upon one of those grey mornings which might be either rainy or fair; and I confess the length of the ride, and the accounts we heard about the frequent changes of the weather, and other accidents amongst the mountains, to say nothing of the wolves and bears, made me almost wish I could see a few drops of rain upon the stones, to justify my giving the matter up. No such appearance, however, could I discover; and my companions, who were in high spirits, having announced that the horses were at the door, I went down, prepared to put the best face I could upon the undertaking.

Nor was my effort greater than the occasion demanded, when I looked at the horses. I have

130   SUMMER AND WINTER

said that the horses commonly used in Pau are all
bad; but as the people are not very willing to let
them out for so long a journey, ours, instead of
being the best, were the worst amongst the bad.
Mine had been bought at the fair the day before,
and was guiltless of ever having tasted corn. It had
shaggy feet that swept the ground, and a long tail
dwindling off to a single hair, besides being of a
sandy colour. They were all, according to the custom of the country, wrapped about their heads and
necks with a quantity of tackling; for when you
expect to stop at any place, you must take with
you the fastening for your horse, there being no
such things in the stables; you must also look
well to it, that what you take is not exchanged for
trapping of a worse description, leaving you to
make good the loss to the owner of the horse.

The morning, as I said before, was grey and
cloudy; but as we rode along, the vapours rolled
away from one snowy peak and then another, and
as my steed carried me much better than I had
expected, the day seemed to promise much enjoyment. Our route as far as Louvie has been
already described. On arriving at this place, we
were joined by another party of our friends; and,
having this time made our bargain beforehand,
and the trout also condescending to be caught, we

made a plentiful breakfast, after the fashion of the country, beginning with bread, wine, trout, potatoes fried in fat, a mess of boiled cabbage mixed with lard, then eggs and bacon, and lastly, coffee. After such a breakfast, no wonder that the French constitution is sustained by only one more meal during the day.

About noon the party separated, our friends returning to Pau, and we pursuing our journey to Eaux Chaudes. I had then a travelling bag strapped to the side of my horse; and as none of these animals have anything worth the name of shoulder, I had every minute to stretch out a heavy riding whip at arm's length, in order to keep mine going at any pace more rapid, or more easy, than the native trot.

As we advanced towards the mountains, the scene became more bold, precipitous, and wild; but still our road lay along a lovely valley, where it was curious to see the various agricultural operations that were going on. In one place, especially, where the valley swells into a wide plain, the whole population of a small town appeared to be at work. There must have been at least three hundred people, with a proportion of little bullocks, carts, and harrows. The labourers, as usual, were chiefly women; and here they seemed to be a distinct race, wearing a very different costume from that of Pau. They were all dressed in coarse black cloth, with their heads tied up in little red hoods; but they had brilliant and blooming complexions, and all wore around their necks a ribbon or cord, from which was suspended a glittering cross of gilt, or tinsel, while their jet black hair hung loosely about their necks. It was curious, too, in one of the villages of this valley, where from all appearance one would suppose that no head, either of man, woman, or child, was ever shorn of its honours, to see a board against one of the houses, on which was advertised the owner's capability to cut hair "according to the latest taste."

The women above described, were employed chiefly in filling sacks with manure, which they carried on their heads, and then spread upon the land. Some of them also were harrowing, while others were sowing broad cast, with the seed in their aprons.

The afternoon was beautifully clear, and the declining sun displayed to advantage the many mountain peaks, on the north side perfectly white with snow, while to the south they were clothed with vegetation almost to the highest pinnacles. It was one of my amusements to trace out amongst these mountain wilds the many little scraps of cultivation which told of the industry of man; and occasionally to see at some far height, which it might seem to require a day's journey to ascend, a wide plain, on which we could discover the sloping roofs of cottages, and the long winding paths from one of these mountain hamlets to another.

At the extremity of the plain through which our route lay, and along the side of the same river which waters that of Louvie, we saw before us apparently nothing but inaccessible heights, or masses of rock, which no human foot could climb. It was through one of these masses, that the road we had to pass had been cut, and here was the frightful gorge of which we had so often heard, leading into the narrow defile of Eaux Chaudes. As we walked up the hill which leads to this opening, we often stopped to look back upon the bold outlines of those we were leaving, and which form the noble barrier of the valley of Ossau, through which the river winds its serpentine way until lost in the distance. On approaching the highest part of the hill we were climbing, a stormy sort of wind rushed past us, and we soon found ourselves in a narrow gorge, or cleft, through which upon the new world that opened before us, we looked down bewildered and amazed. There was the roar of rushing waters, too; and at a far depth beneath us, lashing its way amongst precipitous rocks, was a river, apparently of emerald water, and silver foam, which at the depth of four hundred feet below this gorge, hurries and buries itself in a boiling caldron, enclosed by rocks of the darkest purple and brown.

It is said of a traveller, that in looking into this gulf, he exclaimed, "Beautiful horror!" And the impression of awe seems to have been general, for here, at the turn of the road, where it begins to descend, with this precipice on one side, and a perpendicular wall of solid rock on the other, a little chapel, or place of prayer, has been erected, containing an image of the Virgin, whose protection the traveller is supposed to need in pursuing his course further down the valley.

The narrow defile we were now entering, is called the valley of Gabas, and derives its name from a little village, which is the last on this route before you enter Spain. The word valley, however, conveys little idea of the situation or the scene; for the mountains on either side are so near, and yet so majestic, that I soon became dizzy with looking perpetually on a perpendicular, instead of a horizontal surface; and yet they leave space for a road by the side of the torrent, so regular and smooth, that it might skirt a gentleman's park.

These mountains are of different structures of limestone, sometimes displaying blocks of the most beautiful marble, and clothed with a luxuriant drapery of boxwood and fern,—not boxwood as we see it in our English gardens, but wild and feathery, and often growing to an amazing size. Above these, on the far heights, were fields of snow, their whiteness broken here and there by forests of black pine, which made a fierce and bristling outline, at once cold, and desolate, and majestic.

Here, too, we could trace the most miraculous-looking paths, appearing and disappearing amongst the crags, to tread which, one would suppose that man must be more than human. Yet here is occasionally heard, breaking the solemn silence, the echo of falling timber, and even the voices of the woodcutters; while you see the smoke of the charcoal burning, where it seems that the wild goat or the wolf alone could exist. And the labour of these woodcutters would certainly be useless, were it not for the precipices down which they pitch their timber and boxwood, of which you frequently see the violent course they have taken in descending.

From these airy heights the aching sight turns
gladly to the beautiful river which foams below
the traveller's feet.   Whether it is the marble
bed over which it flows, or the tinge of the
boxwood, that gives it a peculiar hue, I am
unable to say; but its waters, though clear as
crystal, are of the most brilliant blue and green,
perpetually broken into foam, so feathery and
white, as to form an almost magical contrast with
the sombre colours of their rocky bed.   Not only
in the bed of the torrent, but along the sides of
the mountains, the rocks are tinged with the richest
purple and brown, while higher still, when the
sunshine is full upon them, they glow into every
tint of orange and yellow, crowned with moss and
verdure of the brightest green.

Along this defile we wound our way, past the
foot of one mountain, and then another, each rising
like a mighty barrier, bolder and wilder than the
last, until we came at once upon a little group of
well-built houses, which we knew to be Eaux
Chaudes, for "other dwelling there was none."
After making our bargain at the inn, for beds and
meals, all which have to be disputed down to the
lowest sous, we hastened out; for three good hours
of the day were yet left, and they were not to be
wasted.   Below the hotel, and beside the baths,

which are said to be excellent, is a narrow bridge across the river, from which we entered upon a most enchanting path, spacious, and safe for the wanderer's foot, yet almost buried amongst box and brushwood, and often diverted from its regular course by masses of rock, as well as by the stems of venerable oak, and branches of lighter beech which stretch towards the stream. This path led us to a rustic bridge, consisting of a single arch, rudely formed of unhewn stone, and stretching over a foaming waterfall, which looks every moment as if it would precipitate the little bridge into the bed of the river, towards which it hastens at a vast depth below.

Close to this bridge is one of those little watermills which at once attest their primitive origin, and the little progress of civilization amongst the Pyrenees. They are to be found in all parts of the mountains, and often in the most picturesque situations, by the side of foaming torrents, whose impetuous power bears no proportion to the humble structures by their side. They are small square buildings of unhewn stone, seldom more than ten feet from one gable to the other, while one opening for a door, another for a window, and an arch beneath, are all the distinctive features they present. It is said of the little mill at Eaux

138   SUMMER AND WINTER

Chaudes, which so many travellers have had the
good taste to sketch, that it once afforded shelter
to Henry IV. and his sister Catherine from the
terrors of a thunder-storm, which in this mountainous region are extremely violent.

Following the path which leads over the bridge,
and past the mill, we found it took a zigzag
course, and thus it cheated us up to a vast height,
from whence we looked down upon some of those
pitching places for the timber already described.
We were at a loss to imagine why so good a path
had been constructed in such a place, but found at
length that it terminated in a green and cultivated
plain of great extent, open to the morning sun,
and sheltered from the north, where a village was
situated, with some farming establishments of considerable importance.

On descending from this height, we heard far
beneath us, down the side of the mountain, the
tinkling bells of the herds returning to their home
for the night; and we soon saw the stately leader
of a flock of goats, peering at us past a bush of
boxwood, before he thought it prudent to conduct
his followers to an interview with such strange
intruders.   Accompanying the goats was a beautiful shepherd boy, in the same costume as the
older peasants, his blooming complexion contrast-

ing well with the flowing curls of his jet black hair. A little lower down we met the sheep returning by the same path; and last of all the cows, each flock conducted by these mountain youths, bearing on their shoulders a quantity of the green branches of the box for their evening fire.

It was scarcely possible to grow tired in such a scene; but the shades of evening warned us that it would be wise to husband our remaining strength for the morrow. We therefore returned to the hotel, where seated by the glow of a bright wood fire, we enjoyed our supper of eggs and bacon; and though the women who waited upon us spoke nothing but patois, and could not by any possibility be made to understand either spoons or salt, we retired to rest contented with our fare, and thankful for the enjoyment which the first day of our excursion had afforded.

We had already learned that it would be impossible to prosecute our journey to the Pic, the way being quite impassable for the snow; and as the weather had become much colder, and there were threatenings of a farther change, we had decided upon returning to Pau the following day. In the morning, when I first looked out, the scene was certainly rather appalling, for over the edge of the opposite mountain, down to the tops of the

140   SUMMER AND WINTER

houses, the mists were pouring, like the steam of
some mighty caldron, while a cold sleet was falling
on the ground.   It proved, however, to be nothing
to hinder our enjoyment; and we walked for three
hours on the road to Gabas, well pleased to see the
mountains in their more grand and gloomy aspect.
It was a scene entirely new to all the party.   The
rocks and ravines looked literally black beneath
the clouds, which were not so dense, but that one
mighty peak after another stood out, and seemed
to frown upon us, as if to overawe the daring steps
that would intrude upon their awful solitudes.
The valley, too, becomes much more sterile and
wild as you proceed, while the stream increases
in beauty as its course grows more rapid and
violent, becoming, as you ascend, a succession of
cascades, sometimes interrupted by enormous rocks,
at the foot of which it seems to sleep in quiet,
before hurrying down into the foaming basin below.

Besides this beautiful river, there are innumerable waterfalls down the slope of the mountains
on either side, sometimes curling smoothly over an
immense surface of solid rock, and then dashing
themselves into light and feathery spray, against
the crags that interrupt their descent.   Sometimes
on turning round a jutting crag, you are startled
by a hollow roar, and on looking up a dark defile

which suddenly opens before you, you see a mighty torrent, the course of which no human foot has ever tracked; or gliding down beside you, whispering and murmuring as it goes, you see a silver thread extending from the clouds, and far above that another, narrower and brighter still, from trackless fields of snow.

It may easily be supposed that we had no exclamation,—no adequate response of the full heart, for such a scene; and it is worthy of remark, that one of my companions, who has seen as much as most travellers of the loveliest aspects of nature, and who possesses besides, a more than common share of the quick perception of an artist, mingled with the deep enthusiasm of a poet, exclaimed more than once, "I have never seen any thing like this!" He afterwards explained, that though his memory was filled with pictures which no time could efface, of the verdant, sunny, aërial, and almost heavenly aspect of the isles of the Pacific, he had never seen before such a combination of fertility and gorgeous colouring, with the hoary grandeur, the massiveness, and the sublimity which we found here. How is it that our artists, who have gone far to trample down the verdure of all other beautiful places, should have left the Pyrenees comparatively unexplored?

142   SUMMER AND WINTER

The day was far advanced before we were willing to recollect that we must retrace our way to Pau before night; but as the weather still looked unfavourable, we deemed it best to return; and perhaps if the whole truth was told, were not sorry to exchange the sharp mountain air, the lifeless solitudes, and above all the comfortless abodes of Eaux Chaudes, for the milder atmosphere and the more social intercourse of Pau.

CHAPTER VI.

EARLY HISTORY OF THE TOWN AND CHATEAU OF
PAU—SOVEREIGNS OF NAVARRE—HENRY II. AND
MARGUERITE DE VALOIS—JEANNE D'ALBRET—
CRADLE AND BIRTH-PLACE OF HENRY IV.—ESTAB-
LISHMENT OF PROTESTANTISM IN BEARN—CATHE-
RINE OF NAVARRE—HENRY IV.—BERNADOTTE—
TRACES OF THE REVOLUTION—ILLUSTRIOUS VISIT-
ORS AT PAU.

HISTORIANS are not exactly agreed respecting
the origin of the town and chateau of Pau. It is
the opinion of many, that the latter was built as a
place of defence against the incursions of the
Saracens from Spain; while others, perhaps with
equal probability, attribute the commencement of
the town to the following cause. The inhabitants
of the valley d'Ossau, the rightful proprietors of
an extent of still uncultivated land lying northward of Pau, were accustomed to come down
from the mountains with their flocks, and crossing
the Gave at this place, used to drive them to feed
for the winter, in the wide wastes of the Pont

144   SUMMER AND WINTER

Long. It is but reasonable to suppose that the
woods and waters of the sheltered valley which
lies immediately at the foot of the castle, would
offer them a tempting retreat from the storms of
their mountains on one side, and the comparatively
barren desert on the other; and that they would
thus be induced to erect temporary habitations,
where they could meet for the exchange of their
simple merchandise, and where they could also
talk over their affairs.   And if the primitive occupants of the soil possessed the same gift of speech
as their descendants, it would be no trifling gratification to have a place of general rendezvous for
such a purpose.

With regard to the origin of the chateau, it is
also said, that the Counts of Morlaas, inhabiting a
district bordering upon the Pont Long, were in
the habit of repairing to the valley of the Gave,
then thickly covered with wood, for the purpose of
enjoying the pleasures of the chase; and that the
edifice which eventually became the chateau, was
at first a sort of house of pleasance, or place of rest
for these heroes, after the fatigues of the chase.

Without presuming to say which of these sup-
positions is the most correct, or even the most probable, it is sufficiently evident that the chateau has
been ·built at separate times, some portions of its

architecture differing very materially in structure and design from others. Nor does there remain the least doubt that one part of the chateau, a high square tower of enormous strength and magnitude, was erected by Gaston Phœbus X., one of the Counts of Foix, a part of whose name, with the addition of *me fe*, still remaining inscribed in gothic characters at the side of the arms of the house of Foix, upon the outside wall of this tower.

It was the same Gaston de Foix of whom Froissart speaks so often as one of his favourite heroes; a man who was no less noble in his bearing, than daring in his exploits; equally celebrated for his learning, and for the munificence of his gifts, yet possessing the enviable art of keeping his coffers filled, without oppressing his people. It is said of him, that his love of literature and poetry was scarcely surpassed by his passion for good cheer, and for the pleasures of the chase. His *meute*, or pack, consisted of 16,000 dogs; and it was in one of his excursions amongst the mountains, in chase of the wolves and the bears, that he first discovered the apparently miraculous virtues of the Eaux Bonnes, in memory of which discovery, he gave the name of the Montagne de Trésor to one of the lofty summits which overlook the source of these waters.

H

146   SUMMER AND WINTER

There is also another portion of the chateau, which was erected by Gaston XI., whose name has been rendered illustrious by the circumstances which followed his marriage with the daughter of the king of Navarre and Aragon. As a recompense for his valour and fidelity in assisting his father-in-law to subdue his rebellious subjects, he received the noble gift of the sovereignty of Navarre, by which means, his own provinces of Bearn and Foix were united under the name of these kingdoms. In the year 1460, he established himself at Pau, and neglecting nothing which belonged to the dignity of a king, enlarged and embellished the chateau, at the same time surrounding it with beautiful gardens, of which a part is still preserved under the name of the Parc.

This royal gift, however, remained not long in the hands of the princes of Bearn, for in the year 1512, Jean d'Albret II., then sovereign of Navarre, was excommunicated by Pope Julius II. as an adherent to the council of Pisa, his kingdom being declared forfeited, and offered to the first who would seize it. Of this licence, Ferdinand of Spain gladly availed himself, taking possession of High Navarre, or the portion which lay south of the Pyrenees, and leaving to the excommunicated Jean that portion only which lay to the north, and which is now recognised under the name Bearn.

These circumstances were not calculated to bias the king of Navarre in favour of the Church of Rome; but it was not until the reign of Henry d'Al bret II., when Luther's opinions became generally promulgated, that any open opposition was shown.

In the year 1527, this prince was united by marriage to Marguerite of Valois, sister of Francis I. king of France, a princess justly described as being "learned and polite, beautiful, soft, and as compassionate as *spirituelle*." Beyond this, it has been said of her with equal fidelity, that she "forgot no one service, neglected no one talent, and despised no one virtue."

Henry II. of Navarre, in the cultivation of his mind and manners, appears to have been not unsuitably matched with this admirable woman. Nor is it improbable that her feelings with regard to this connexion might have received a favourable bias, from the circumstance of Henry having been taken prisoner at the battle of Pavia, while fighting by the side of her brother.

It was during the reign of Henry and Marguerite, whose court was alternately held at Pau, and at the castle of Barbaste near Nerac, that the history of the chateau became marked by a different and

a more classic character than it had known before.
Justly distinguished as Marguerite was, for every
accomplishment which adorned her age, as well as
for more solid acquirements, which brought within
the circle of her society some of the most learned
men of her own and other nations; the character
of her consort was scarcely less admired for his
chivalry, and his devotion to the fine arts, which
entitled him to be called the Francis I. of Bearn.
Both are said to have brought from the French
court, then the most brilliant in Europe, a degree
of taste and refinement of which the despoiled
and dilapidated chateau of Pau still retains some
traces.   Amongst the many artists and men of
genius whom their liberality rewarded, and their
society drew around them, they invited from Spain
some Arabs, renowned for their skill in architecture; from which circumstance it is probable the
chateau has derived something of its Moorish
aspect.

   In all its higher and holier attributes, the character of Marguerite far surpassed that of her
consort.   Surrounded in early youth by all the
allurements of the French court, she had been
perhaps, in some measure preserved from its temptations by her love of study; and that her mind

was even then impressed with the worthlessness of all inferior objects of ambition, appears more than probable, from her having in her seventeenth year, adopted for her device a marigold bending to the sun, with this motto in Latin,— " Not following lower things."

Her first marriage in 1509, with the Duke d'Alençon, had not been a happy one, and she appears then more especially, to have given her mind to religious meditation, and her time to serious pursuits ; amongst which, her talents as an authoress were called into frequent exercise. Even our own Queen Elizabeth thought it not unbecoming her dignity to translate into English a work from the pen of Marguerite of Valois, which was printed in the year 1548, under the title of " A godlie meditation of a Christian soule."

In her second marriage with Henry d'Albret, Marguerite was still unfortunate ; for though his relish for the refinements of life might bear some proportion to her own, his religious impressions were of a very inferior order, and being ten years younger than herself, he was consequently exposed to all the temptations of youth, at the time when she was becoming gradually estranged from the gaieties of the world, and indeed from all earthly things.   His bias in favour of the reformed religion, was also of a widely different nature from hers; for while he was easily prevailed upon by the king of France to renounce these opinions altogether, and finally to espouse those of the Roman Catholics; his queen was enabled to maintain to the last, her zealous and faithful adherence to the true doctrines of Christianity, extending her patronage and protection to some of the most able and pious men of the protestant persuasion; enduring patiently, not only opprobrium, but cruelty and persecution as a Christian and a woman.

Amongst the many trials it was her portion to endure, none fell more heavily than the master-stroke of ingratitude inflicted by her brother, whose short-sighted policy induced him to deprive his sister of the society of her only child, in the fear that her mother's influence might be the means of turning her mind from the tenets of the Romish faith.   Jeanne d'Albret, daughter of Henry and Marguerite of Navarre, was born in the chateau of Pau, on the 7th of February, 1528.   At a very early age she was removed to the French court, and when only twelve years old, was married in a compulsory manner to the Duke of Cleves; on which occasion the poor child was so loaded with ornaments as to be unable to walk, and the constable of France was consequently obliged to carry the bride in his arms, from her carriage to the church.

Bitterly as Marguerite must have felt this privation, her attachment to her brother was such, that not until his death in 1547, did her gentle spirit sink under its accumulated sorrows. Retiring to a little village in Angouleme, she there joined a religious community of females, over whom she presided; but afterwards, having removed to the chateau d'Odos near Tarbes, she is said to have caught a severe cold while watching a comet, and at this place she died, December 25, 1549.

It has been recorded with some satisfaction by the Roman Catholic writers, that in her dying moments she kissed a crucifix that was held before her. I cannot better remark upon this fact, than in the beautiful language of a writer who has done much to render justice to the memory of this admirable woman. " She who had embraced the cross in early life, and had so long borne it by patient endurance, might, surely, while in the agony of leaving one world, and in the earnest expectation of entering another, have kissed a crucifix without any superstitious feeling. The materialism of religion could have had but little influence over the dying senses of a Christian like the queen of Navarre, who, while her paralytic hands grasped a crucifix, sufficiently declared the sort of feeling with which she viewed it, by thrice exclaiming as she expired, Jesus ! Jesus ! Jesus !"*

The king of Navarre, whose influence over the temporal affairs of his people was uniformly beneficial, died six years after his queen, and was interred at Lescar. He was succeeded in the sovereignty of the kingdom, by his daughter Jeanne. It was perhaps, well for this princess, that while gifted with the talents of her mother, she possessed a loftier and more commanding spirit, at once adapted to the support of her influence as a queen, and to the peculiar exigencies of the times in which she lived. Her ill-assorted marriage with the Duke of Cleves having been dissolved by a dispensation from the Pope, another was contracted in 1548 with Antoine de Bourbon, Duke of Vendome, a man whose weak and vacillating character was but ill calculated to support the prompt and judicious conduct of the queen.

On Jeanne d'Albret's accession to the throne, she and her consort took the usual oaths according to the forms of the Roman Catholic church, to the discipline of which they then conformed ; and two days after this ceremony, an address was presented to the new sovereigns from their estates of Bearn,

* Notices of the Reformation in Bearn.

stating that a new sect had lately sprung up, infected with heresy, and earnestly calling upon them to direct the bishops to search out these sectaries, in order that every means might be used for bringing to light, and finally putting down the offenders. In answer to this address, the king and queen expressed their desire to extirpate heresy, wherever it might exist in their dominions; and orders were published for so dealing with the prelates, as to incite them to greater zeal in the work of extirpation. Yet, notwithstanding this apparent severity, no effective measures appear to have been taken.

In the mean time, Jeanne d'Albret, who had been educated in the Roman Catholic faith, and who, in addition to her youth and beauty, possessed great shrewdness of wit, with a liveliness of temperament, which before her residence in Bearn, is said to have led her to a dance, rather than to a sermon, was now brought into contact with many of the persecuted protestants, amongst whom the memory of her mother was cherished with the tenderest affection; and besides that beautiful exemplification of the Christian character left to her in her mother's writings and example, she had the additional influence of her mother's friends, as a living testimony of the purer doctrines of the reformed religion.

H 3

154   SUMMER AND WINTER

The heart of Jeanne d'Albret was not callous to these impressions. While her vacillating husband appeared for a time to be convinced by the arguments of those around him ; the nobler-minded queen, when once her heart had been made the subject of deeper convictions, *conferring not with flesh and blood,* declared herself openly, and decidedly, to be on the side of the reformed doctrines ; and from that time the little court of Bearn became a place of refuge for the oppressed protestants, both of France and Germany, who richly repaid her hospitality by disseminating the seeds of religious truth amongst her people.

But I pretend not to give a history of the progress of the Reformation, as it subsequently extended in these provinces. This has already been done by abler hands than mine, yet the subject is one, which makes it difficult to remember, that my appropriate task confines me to a narrower and an humbler sphere. Already I should be afraid of having wandered too far out of this sphere, but that it may surely be permitted to a woman, to linger over associations with which all that is noble and exalted in her own sex, has been so intimately connected. A few more brief notices of the life of Jeanne d'Albret, will suffice for all I dare add on this momentous and fertile theme.

The stranger who visits the chateau of Pau, is shown the very chamber where Henry IV., then the only child of the queen of Navarre, first saw the light, on the 13th December, 1553. From thence he is led to another apartment, where, arranged with a degree of gorgeous splendour, but little in keeping with the massive and venerable character of the chateau, is the cradle in which the infant monarch was nursed. It consists of one entire tortoise-shell; and not the least remarkable part of its history, is the fact, that when during the reign of terror, the furious populace rushed upon the palace, determined to destroy every vestige of royalty, it was secretly conveyed out of their reach, and its place supplied by the generosity of a gentleman of Pau, who happening to have one of the same kind amongst his collection of curiosities, suffered his own to be sacrificed, and afterwards restored the real treasure.

From the state room in which this cradle is preserved, you walk out upon a balcony in front of the building, which commands a magnificent view of the river, the valley, and the mountains. But a far more interesting subject of contemplation to me, than even this elegant salon, of which our conductor appeared to think so much, was a little tower at the south-west corner of the chateau,

which was used by the queen as her private study.
That which is called her apartment, in this tower,
is small and unadorned, but it commands a view
combining all that is beautiful and grand in nature,
and which may well be supposed to have refreshed
her harassed mind, amidst the troubles and disap-
pointments she was destined to endure.   The
window to the southward looks directly upon the
whole range of the Pyrenees, while from that, as
well as one of the others, you see the winding
river sweeping past the foot of the old castle, the
bridge, the smiling plain, the vine-clad hills; and,
sloping off towards the point where the sun goes
down in such golden splendour, the rich foliage,
deep shadows, and lofty stems of the trees which
adorn the Parc.   But above all to a mother's heart,
this tower possessed the advantage of another view,
towards the little village of Bilheres, where her
infant son was nursed.

Was it in this chamber that undaunted resolution
of the queen was formed, which prompted the
utterance of those memorable words recorded by
Beza,—"that sooner than ever again go to mass,
or suffer her kingdom or her child to do so, she
would if it were possible, cast them into the depths
of the sea to hinder it?"   Or where did the scene
take place which the Cardinal Ferrara states that

he witnessed, when the queen with passionate tenderness clasped the young prince in her arms, and uttered a long and earnest exhortation to him, never to attend mass in any way whatever; adding, that if he disobeyed her in that, she would disinherit him, and no longer consider herself his mother?"

I have already spoken of the church of St. Martin, situated but a few paces from the chateau. It was here, on Easter-day, 1560, after the death of her husband, that Jeanne d'Albret received the communion according to the rites of the reformed church. This public avowal of her sentiments, was followed, as might have been expected, by the sentence of excommunication from the court of Rome, as well as by a declaration of the forfeiture of the crown, and absolution of her subjects from their oaths of allegiance. Throughout the whole of the conflict which she subsequently maintained against the enemies of truth, we find in the history of this noble-hearted queen, a series of trials and difficulties that would have subdued a spirit not peculiarly and providentially fitted for the support of the just and righteous cause she had espoused. Alone in the midst of powerful foes, her little kingdom hemmed in by envious nations, often betrayed by those from whom she hoped for aid, and not even supported by her son, in

158   SUMMER AND WINTER

the cause that was nearest her heart,—in the midst
of all these discouragements, her soul remained
undaunted, for she knew in whom she trusted.
With the noble daring of an upright mind, scarcely
equalled in the history of woman, she was thus
enabled to throw back the sophistries of priestcraft,
to meet with unshaken fortitude every fresh reverse
of fortune, to detect and baffle treachery, and,
what was more noble,—to forgive.

It is creditable to our queen Elizabeth, that she
more than once, at the solicitation of Jeanne d'Albret, sent sums of money and arms to aid her in
her difficulties; though not before the queen of
Navarre had given up her own personal property,
even her jewels, to meet the necessities of her
people, at the time when they were assailed by
hostile armies.

In the year 1572, Jeanne d'Albret had so far
succeeded in the great object of her life, that of
establishing the reformed religion in her kingdom,
as to have a decree acknowledged and registered
by the estates of Bearn, in which both firmness
and judgment are admirably displayed. After the
publication of this decree, the queen felt more at
liberty to leave her court at Pau, and accepting the
invitation of Gaillart, bishop of Chartres, who had
embraced the reformed religion, she became a

guest at his palace. On this journey the queen met her son at Blois, where the French court was then held; and on the 4th of June, 1572, she arrived at Paris. She was then in her forty-fourth year, and not considered to be in a declining state of health, though severely tried and harassed by the many conflicts she had so nobly sustained; yet five days after this time, her death is recorded to have taken place, not without strong suspicions attaching to the party of Catherine de Medicis, of having accelerated her passage to the grave by the means of poison.

Two months after the death of his mother, Henry of Navarre was united in marriage to Marguerite of Valois, sister to the king of France; and six days after this ceremony, the massacre of St. Bartholomew took place, in which Henry himself had once been doomed as one of the victims.

Jeanne d'Albret left an only daughter, Catherine, whose character was justly held in such esteem by her brother, that when called away from his court of Navarre, he left her sole regent of his kingdom; and such was the influence of this princess over the people of Bearn, that when in want of sums of money to aid her brother in his political career, she had only to send amongst them a simple billet signed with her hand, to obtain the necessary supplies.   Like her mother and queen Marguerite, she was gifted with superior talents, and a high degree of taste for the fine arts, particularly for poetry and music, in both which she excelled.

There is now no trace, beyond mere record, remaining of a beautiful retreat, erected by Jeanne d'Albret for this princess, to which she was accustomed to retire for the purpose of pursuing her studies.   It was situated near to what is now the Parc, and is said to have been adorned in the style of a temple dedicated to the muses.

Possessing so many excellences, and holding so exalted a position, it was to be expected that an alliance with this princess would be an object of much speculation in those scheming and politic times.   Amongst the many proposals submitted to her choice, queen Elizabeth would gladly have claimed her hand for the young king of Scotland, and, as a bribe to render this connexion more desirable, offered the promise of succession to the throne of England.   The heart of the princess, however, with a perverseness not altogether unprecedented, either in public or private history, yielded to no persuasion but that of a man whose religious faith was different from her own, and who was neither approved by her near connexions, nor by the people of Bearn, who were accustomed to consider themselves as possessing the right of influence over the domestic relations of their sovereigns.

In consequence of the failure of the scheme, by which the favoured lover, the Count de Soissons, had expected to accomplish his marriage with the princess at Pau, Catherine resigned the regency of the kingdom of Navarre, and after joining her brother, was subsequently induced by him to give her hand in marriage to the Duke of Lorraine and Bar. From this family she is said to have suffered much persecution, on account of her religious faith. All endeavours to induce her to renounce the faith in which she had been educated, however, proved eventually fruitless. She died under strong suspicion of having been poisoned, with these memorable words upon her lips, " Were there no other reason, I could never belong to a religion which would teach me to believe that my mother was damned."

The history of Henry IV., with the many important circumstances which distinguished his short but eventful career, are too well known to form a subject for the pen of a mere traveller. His residence at Pau as the sovereign of Navarre, appears to have been marked by no fact so powerfully as by the hold he obtained upon the affections

162   SUMMER AND WINTER

of his people, to which many circumstances connected with his early life no doubt contributed.
Over a remote people like the Bearnaise, no fact
could exercise a more powerful influence than that
of having fostered in the bosom of their country so
great a monarch as he afterwards became; while
his early education amongst them as a peasant boy,
—his love of rural sports,—his frank and cheerful
bearing, so much in keeping with the good-
humoured people themselves,—with the partiality
he ever retained for his native country, and the
well-remembered saying of his, when he assumed
the sovereignty of France, that he gave France
to Bearn, rather than Bearn to France,—are circumstances sufficiently powerful of themselves to
account for the proud affection with which they
still speak of him as the " best of kings."

There is in the chateau a full-length statue of
this prince, said to be an excellent likeness, and no
less valuable as a specimen of art.   At present,
however, it is secured from the inspection of the
public, the whole place being under repairs, and so
filled with workmen, that we could see but little of
the interior of the building.   It is highly creditable
to the present king of France, that he is laying out
considerable sums of money in restoring the chateau to a habitable state; but whether the repairs,

many of which are effected by the addition of white marble, will ever sufficiently harmonize with the rude and massive architecture of the rest of the building, is a question which I must leave to the discussion of future visitors.

In connexion with this edifice, and the death of Henry IV., a singular fact is told; that, while other buildings, and many lofty trees in the immediate neighbourhood, have been injured or struck down by lightning, the chateau itself was never struck but once, and that was on the memorable day when the king was assassinated.

Amongst other memorials of the great men of whom Pau may justly be allowed to boast, we were accustomed to see the following inscription on a marble tablet fixed into the wall of a house, not many paces from our residence :—

CHARLES JEAN BERNADOTTE,

ROI DE SUEDE,

APPELÉ AU TRONE

PAR LE VŒU UNANIME DES SUÉDOIS,

EST NÉ DANS CETTE MAISON,

LE 26 JANVIER, 1763.

This tablet might speak volumes in itself upon the incalculable course of human affairs. For when we think of the comparative obscurity of his

164   SUMMER AND WINTER

birth, the remoteness of his native place from the
scene of his subsequent glory, and the sunny world
around the cradle of the infant king, we are led to
suppose that few circumstances could have appeared more improbable to those who watched
over the Bearnais infant, than that he should ever
be placed upon the throne of Sweden.

The military career of Bernadotte is already a
matter of history: but it does not detract from his
glory, that with the same prudence and right
feeling which uphold his influence on the throne,
he continues to extend to the relatives he has left
behind him in his native land, such tokens of remembrance as are best calculated to increase their
happiness. Instead of drawing them away from
the sphere of comfort and respectability to which
they have been accustomed, or disturbing the even
tenor of their lives by ambitious hopes, too often
and too fatally deceived, his benevolence flows
back to the place of his birth, through various
channels, less ostentatious, it is true, but far more
calculated to benefit the friends of his early years.

Amongst many other circumstances equally
illustrative of the unsophisticated good feeling of
Bernadotte, we have been told, that he writes
every year to the father of a gentleman in Pau, a
letter of pure friendship, reminding him of the days

when they were boys at the same school together. It need hardly be said, in what esteem are held such tokens of remembrance, from a man of whom Buonaparte used to say, that he had a French head, with the heart of a Roman.

It is a fact worthy of notice, that of the two kings to whom Pau has given birth, Henry IV. and Bernadotte, one renounced the Protestant faith to obtain the crown of France, lightly observing, that " Paris was well worth a mass,"—and the other, two hundred years later, renounced the Roman Catholic religion, and became a Protestant in obtaining the crown of Sweden.

Distant as Pau is from the capital, and peaceful as the aspect of the surrounding country now appears, it is not difficult to perceive in walking along the streets of this town, that it must have shared in no ordinary degree in the conflicts by which the internal prosperity of France has been so often, and so frightfully destroyed. At the corners of many of the streets you still see one, two, and even three names displaced to make way for others. It needs no farther history to tell to what dates belong the following, which I have selected from many others of the same character: Rue Buonaparte, now Rue Royale, Rue Revolu-

166 SUMMER AND WINTER

tionnaire, Rue Libre, Rue des Bayonettes, Rue et Place Egalité, &c.

Nor are such the only traces that remain to tell the bloody history of those times. Many families still remain to lament the victims of barbarity torn from their social circle; and there are some dwelling in comparative obscurity, who before the revolution held a distinguished rank amongst their fellow-citizens. One case of this description has afforded us peculiar interest. It is that of a venerable countess, now occupying a small apartment beside the gateway of a noble mansion, once her hereditary home. In the courtyard of this house several members of her family were executed, and she herself was afterwards sentenced to the pillory, for receiving a letter from her son. But such was the esteem in which she was held, that while thus exposed, not a single passenger was seen in the street, every shop was closed, and no individual was found to look upon what had been vainly intended as her disgrace.

Another remarkable illustration of the strength of public feeling is found in the case of Madame Caudan, who suffered the sentence of death during the same eventful times. Such had been the piety and benevolence of this lady, that the poor people of Pau with one accord petitioned for her life; and so powerful was the popular feeling in her favour, that it was impossible to find, amongst the inhabitants of her native place, a man so hardened as to execute the sentence pronounced against her. Under these peculiar circumstances an executioner was brought from Tarbes, but even he was so affected by the description given him of her character, that he preserved from the property upon her person, which fell to him by right, a valuable relic in gold, which he afterwards restored to her afflicted family.

Thus we meet at almost every step with memorials of the great national events with which the history of France abounds; and the record of illustrious visitors who have paused in their career of interest or ambition, to enjoy the refreshment of this delightful climate, forms perhaps not the least important feature in the annals of the place.

One of the most brilliant of these occasions was when that imperious and artful woman, Catherine de Medicis, with her son, Charles IX., came to visit Pau, to fill the old chateau with her splendid and courtly train, and to startle the wondering Bearnaise people with a display of fanciful costumes, of sports and pastimes, such as they had never witnessed before. It may well be imagined what were the feelings of Jeanne d'Albret on this

168   SUMMER AND WINTER

occasion, especially when Catherine insisted upon
taking back with her to the court of France the
young prince Henry, with whom she professed to
be much pleased. But Jeanne is said to have
concealed her feelings with her accustomed fortitude, and to have done the honours of her court to
her gay and royal guests, in all respects as became
the dignity of a queen.

But the most important visitation which the
annals of the place record, was the eventful
entrance of Louis XIII. into the capital of the
ancient domain of his family, on the 15th of
October, 1620. On this occasion, it is said,
there was no testimony of joy on the part of his
subjects, but rather the sullen submission of a van-
quished people; for he had come to destroy the
ancient court and dynasty of Navarre, by uniting
it to that of France; and what was more, to re-
establish a religion, against which the people of
Bearn had for so many years been struggling as
against a common enemy—an enemy not temporal, but eternal.

It was then that the church of St. Martin, where
Jeanne d'Albret had received the communion, and
established the Protestant worship, was ordered by
this prince to be purified from its pollutions by the
accustomed ceremonies, the king himself attending

the celebration of mass, and joining in a solemn procession which paraded through the streets of the town, with a lighted taper in his hand. After which, he demanded an oath of fealty from his subjects; and thus ratified the means he had adopted to overthrow the laws and the institutions of the last fifty years.

CHAPTER VII.

LATENESS OF THE SPRING—ENGLISH COTTON SPINNER
AT JURANCON—VISIT TO A MAISON DE CAMPAGNE—
PONT LONG—COMPARISON OF ENGLISH AND FRENCH
COTTAGES — LESCAR — COMMENCEMENT OF WARM
WEATHER—FRENCH FROGS.

HAD we formed an idea of the beauty of spring
weather in the south of France, at all proportioned to that of winter, we should have been
grievously disappointed. But every one told us,
that before the commencement of spring, or rather
summer—for in this climate there appears to be
no spring—we must have a rainy season, not
unfrequently accompanied with severe cold; and
as these rains were unusually late, the progress of
vegetation was in the same degree retarded. I find
it recorded in my journal of the 30th of March,
that we had only had rain three times since
the beginning of February, and never sufficient
to moisten the ground. We had also about this
time sufficient experience of the peculiar effect of

cold in this climate, which, even when much less severe than in England, is probably more felt from its succeeding to a degree of heat unknown there in the winter season. At all events, it produced upon us so uncomfortable a smarting of the skin, accompanied with such chapped hands and chil-blains, that we ceased to wonder at the coarse, dry, and withered complexions of the old women, and began to apprehend a very speedy approximation to their appearance in ourselves.

Impatient as we had previously been to take up our abode amongst the mountains, we were now convinced that our friends had been right, when they told us there was no trusting to their sunny aspect before the month of May, at the very earliest; and we therefore took the opportunity of visiting other scenes of interest in the neigh-bourhood of Pau, amongst which I must not forget one of a very humble and unobstrusive nature. It was the residence of John Haydock, a "canny" old Englishman, who had been a cotton-spinner at Blackburn in Lancashire, and who, having estab-lished himself at Rouen during the peace of Amiens, has been a resident in France ever since. His business, it is said, answered sufficiently well for him at Rouen ; but family considerations inducing him to leave that place, he bought a little property

I 2

172   SUMMER AND WINTER

by the side of a beautiful stream at Jurançon, in the vain hope of establishing a cotton mill upon its banks. He is a most ingenious man, and an excellent mechanic; but there being no trade in this place, all his curious inventions, of which he has a great number, are of little use; and it is to be feared his circumstances are sinking rather low. He has, however, a comfortable cottage, and a luxuriant garden, of which he is very proud.

While watching his cheerful, honest, English face, and listening to his Lancashire dialect, as pure as if he had left Blackburn but a week ago, it brought back to my memory many a well-remembered scene; and when he showed us his gooseberry bushes, here very rare, amongst his vines and peaches, and told us they bore a "terrible sight of fruit," I could hardly believe I was so distant from some of the English cottage gardens which I had known in early life.

The workshop of this ingenious man is a real curiosity. Amongst a variety of his own inventions, and other specimens of art, he showed us some stamps of his own making for printing Spanish cards, by which he was obtaining a trifling profit; and though a strange occupation for an English cotton-spinner, it was evident from the elegance of their design, that the man was fitted for a higher fate than to dwindle out his days in poverty. His wife, who is a Roman Catholic, says that he keeps his Bible hid on a shelf, lest it should be discovered by the priests; and that every Sunday afternoon he locks himself in his bedroom to read it alone.

There is much in the situation of this man to interest the English residents at Pau. The walk to his dwelling occupies but half an hour, and its position is one of the most picturesque in the neighbourhood. It stands at the foot of a range of steep hills, whose sides are covered with vineyards, and on the banks of one of those fertilizing streams which supply the air with freshness, and the earth with verdure.

Near to the dwelling of John Haydock, is a space of ground entirely shaded by the finest oaks in the neighbourhood. This scene strongly reminded me of one in Ivanhoe, from its being the place where the swineherd of the village drives the numerous and noisy animals committed to his care. All the animals in Bearn, however, and these are by no means exceptions to the rule, appear to be good-humoured, docile, and generally well-disposed. Even the pigs are so easily disciplined, that the herdsman has only to sound his horn in the morning, and forth they come from

174   SUMMER AND WINTER

every cottage, far and near, the whole swinish
population of the village joining themselves into
one troop, which, without any farther trouble, is
conducted wherever the herdsman chooses to take
them.   In the evening he sounds another blast
upon his large cow's horn, when the multitude is
again assembled from whatever distance they may
have strayed, and pouring through the streets and
lanes of the village like a torrent—for the French
pigs are almost as swift as greyhounds, they gather
up the garbage from the doors, and having made a
general clearance, retreat to their separate domi-
ciles for the night.

Magnificent and beautiful as the view of the
Pyrenees unquestionably is from the Parc, the
Place Royale, and many other parts of Pau, there
are positions on the neighbouring hills, from whence
they appear to still greater advantage, the view
from these being less interrupted by intervening
heights.   One of these favourite points of observation is about the distance of an hour or
two hours' walk from Pau, on the summit of the
hills which rise southwestward of Jurançon, from
whence the whole range is seen, with the addition
of many stretching to the east and the west, which
are not visible from a lower elevation.

Another favourite view is from a range of hills running eastward of these; and this eminence is approached by a road which leads through the little village of Gelos, about a mile to the left of Jurançon. Humble as this village appears, it boasts its noble chateau, once a monastery, and now a handsome and regular building, which had the honour, in the year 1808, to receive as its illustrious guests, the Emperor Napoleon, and Josephine, then on their way to Bayonne.

A little beyond the village of Gelos, is the entrance of a beautiful valley, which seems peculiarly formed for solitude and repose. A road winds through it amid the welcome shade of spreading oaks, and along the banks of a crystal stream. Meadows of the brightest green slope down to the water; while higher up, the sides of the steep hills are hung with vineyards, and higher still, they are clothed with the rich foliage of lofty trees, amongst which are situated some of the most delightful habitations to be found in this neighbourhood.

It would be an act of ingratitude to forget, that half-way up the slope of one of these verdant hills, is the residence of one of the most hospitable gentlemen in France, or any other country; at

176   SUMMER AND WINTER

whose house, a little later in the spring, we spent
one of the brightest of many sunny days.   Seated
for some hours by the side of a cool fountain,
under the shade of a spreading tree, we then looked
down into the green valley, and watched the vine-
dressers at work in his vineyards; certainly without
envying the poor women who sometimes climbed
up the hill to come and quench their thirst at the
fountain.   Though picturesque in the distance,
they looked miserable creatures on a nearer view,
—their dress, on account of the excessive heat,
reduced to little more than one garment, and their
haggard features shaded from the sun by coarse
straw hats, with broad brims, which are usually
worn by the women when working in the fields in
hot weather.

Our kind host, after he had regaled us with a
dinner so plentiful, so excellent, and politely
pressed in such profusion upon our plates, that the
bare remembrance of it was enough to assuage
the keenest appetite for some time afterwards,
would not suffer us to leave his house until we had
taken tea in the true English style, though we had
previously had the most excellent coffee, served in
the French fashion, immediately after dinner.
Our tea, though certainly unnecessary, was well
worth having, for the picturesque effect of taking

it in the open air, on a terrace from whence we looked down upon the valley, while the sun was setting, and all things gradually sinking into that stillness which so often, amongst these hills and mountains, leaves nothing to be heard but the distant flow of rushing water, that "natural music" of the Pyrenees.

From this lovely spot we walked a little higher up the hill to another property, belonging to the same family, which commands the finest general view of Pau. And here, while we gazed first to the mountains, which were gradually fading from the purple of sunset to the cold blue look of death, then to the winding river, the sloping gardens on the opposite side, the long line of handsome buildings above them, the old chateau, and the tufted foliage of the Parc, still evening came upon us—so still, that I have often wondered how the imaginations of the people should have conjured up amongst their superstitions, any so turbulent and restless as that of the huntsman priest.

Yet so it is; and they tell to this day of a naughty priest, who loved the chase at least as well as he loved the duties of his proper calling. This priest, they say, had once entered the church, and was about to officiate on some solemn occasion, when, having been told that a wild animal was

I 3

in the neighbourhood, away he went, called up his dogs, and set off in full chase. The marvel of the story, and its moral too, is that he has never since been allowed to stop; but often on a fine still evening, when the sun is setting, his figure may be seen, scouring along the horizon, while his pack of dogs follow after him in full cry. I can only say it has never been my chance to hear them.

Extending for many miles to the east and north-east of Pau, is an uncultivated district, called the Pont Long, over which the people of the valley d'Ossau have from time immemorial exercised the right of possession; and so jealous have they ever been of any infraction of this right, that during the reign of Henry II., when he had enclosed a portion of the ground for a park, they took the liberty of striking down the walls he had erected, considering such appropriation an invasion of their rights. Many curious records remain of permission having been solicited by individuals of distinction about the court, for their cattle or horses to feed upon this land. The same jealous feeling may in some measure account for its remaining so long in its present dreary and uncultivated state, many attempts to improve it having been rewarded with the same unceremonious treatment.

It has also been considered by many as

incapable of cultivation; but this fact is sufficiently disproved by the condition of the little village of Uzein, situated like a green island in the centre of this desert. This village is said to owe its present prosperity to the efforts of a curé, who incited the people of the place to extraordinary exertions in the improvement of the land, which now remunerates them by producing some of the most beautiful maize in Bearn.

Though the aspect of this waste is by no means inviting, it is almost entirely screened from the town by intervening farms and cultivated plots of ground, but chiefly by extensive woods of oak, which are tracked in almost every direction by broad green paths, affording a delightful retreat for those whose element is not amongst the public and fashionable promenades. Here the botanist may range at will, fearless of deranging the order of a fence; and here, too, the artist may sit and sketch, without the stranger's curious eye to gaze upon his book. Nor need he wander far in search of subjects worthy of his pencil, for every object is a picture, from the old farmhouse with its sloping thatch and pointed gable, to the mud cottage, the stunted oak, and the stone well.

I scarcely think, that in any country the common buildings can be more picturesque than they are in

France; they have so many gables, and balconies, and points that catch the light, and irregularities of every description, with such deep shadows under their projecting roofs; to say nothing of the broken doors, the ruined walls, and often the rich colouring of their mossy thatch.   Yet after all, they are only pictures for the canvas.   There is no poetry,—if I might be allowed the expression, I should rather say, no moral in their aspect, since it fails to carry the mind of the beholder onward to any train of thought, beyond what is excited by mere form and colour.

The case is widely different with all that is picturesque in our native land.   An English cottage, for example, if one of the most respectable order, has its well-stocked orchard, its neat garden hedge, its old porch, its woodbine climbing to the roof, its bright windows, its clean stone step; and all these remind us of the family affection, the order, the comfort, and the simplicity within.   But if, on the other hand, it is one of the wretched hovels which, even in England may occasionally be found, we are reminded with equal force of what must be the degradation of character, the privation, the suffering, of an English family, before their condition could have come to this.

Of the effect produced by contemplating a neat

and comfortable looking cottage in France, I am
not prepared to speak, having never seen one.
But the aspect of disorder and dilapidation which
so many of the dwellings present, certainly excites
little feeling beyond a desire to make a picture of
it, and simply for this reason, because it is accompanied by no mental suffering. Seated at the doors
of these hovels, amongst heaps of filth and garbage,
companions to the swine they fed, and knowing no
ambition beyond the hope of feeding them in the
most profitable manner, the French peasants are
perfectly contented, for their requirements are so
few, they scarcely know the feeling of want; and
being neither ashamed of disorder, nor annoyed
by filth, they are conscious of no degradation.
They labour cheerfully because they have always
been accustomed to do so, and because the spot of
ground they cultivate is their own. If they have
two oxen for their team, a skeleton of a horse to
ride to market, a couple of fowls, or a dozen eggs
to sell, a bedstead, an armoire, and three crazy
chairs, with an iron saucepan, and an earthen pot
to make their soup, they may fairly be said to be
as rich as their neighbours, and that is happiness
enough for them. Thus we see them almost invariably when young, with fresh, healthy, good-
humoured, cheerful faces; and what is creditable

182   SUMMER AND WINTER

both to youth and age, always in decent clothing, suited to the simple and unambitious lives they lead.

Nor are the farm-houses, or perhaps I ought to say, the dwellings of the peasants of a higher order, less picturesque. The barn and the dwelling-house are sometimes under the same roof, and that is frequently composed of close thatch, on one side sloping almost down to the ground. On the other you see the entrance through a sort of cattle yard, strewn thickly with dead fern, which is used for litter. Around this yard are the mud walls, high gables, and sloping roofs of other buildings, with wide folding-doors, and open hay-lofts, and sheds, and all manner of receptacles, often kept from falling by props of timber, or the simple unhewn stems of trees; while broken carts, and rails, and rubbish, lie about in every direction. In many cases this scene of confusion is partially concealed by a high wall, the entrance through which is one of remarkably picturesque effect, being a high gateway with wide folding-doors, over which is built a light slated roof, with something of a Chinese curve, supported at each end either by pillars, or by higher portions of the wall. Nor ought I to forget the pretty little hen-house, either forming part of the human dwelling, or standing by itself in the yard, with its facing and door of lattice-work, which is generally the only thing that looks neat, about the whole concern.

Houses of this description are extremely numerous in the environs of Pau; and when you see them standing by the side of a green lane, beneath the shadow of venerable oaks, with an old woman spinning at the door, a peasant man with his blue frock and Bearnais bonnet, leading home his beautiful cattle, or a bare-footed girl, coming in with her basket on her head; and over the whole scene —over the green of the surrounding fields, the foliage of the trees, the thatch of the farm-house, and the bloom of the peasant girl, the sunset glow of a southern clime, you scarcely need go farther, in search of all the painter can require for the display of his richest colouring, and the happiest exercise of his skill.

The stranger in Pau will certainly not have done justice to the memorials of antiquity which the environs of this place afford, unless he visits Lescar, a small but ancient town, situated about four miles from Pau, to the right of the Bayonne road, and seen, when looking westward from the Parc, in a conspicuous situation on the southern slope of a tract of high ground, which terminates abruptly in the valley of the Gave.

184   SUMMER AND WINTER

This little town, which is said to be of Roman origin, was once the capital of Bearn. Its crowning objects of importance, its old church and castle, stand on a steep hill, or rather distinct eminence, separated from the high ground extending to the north, by a narrow but deep ravine, which has some appearance of having been excavated for the purpose of rendering the castle more secure.

The church of Lescar, like many in this neighbourhood, is said to have owed its origin to the remorse of a distinguished nobleman, who, in the year 980 endowed the edifice, in the hope of thereby expiating the crime of murder, which he had committed. It afterwards became the principal cathedral church of Bearn, and had the honour of numbering amongst its bishops, three men who were subsequently advanced to the dignity of cardinals. Among the many princely benefactors who enriched this edifice with their costly gifts, Gaston III. appears to have been the most munificent. At the time when he flourished, a very extensive traffic, entirely monopolized by the Saracens, was carried on with the east by the way of Oleron and Jaca; and the relation between his territories and the frontier of Spain, thus afforded him the means of appropriating his choice of the rich merchandise which passed that way, and of which, the incense used in churches formed no inconsiderable part.

The church of Lescar deserves to be visited with feelings of no trifling interest, from its having been the place of burial of so many of the sovereigns of Bearn, amongst whose names are those of Marguerite of Valois, and her husband Henry II. Beyond these associations, however, neither the town nor the church offers many attractions to those who expect to find the vestiges of former splendour. The latter is a lofty, spacious, and venerable building; but except for some beautiful specimens of Norman architecture at the eastern extremity, and some curiously carved oak within, it retains but few traces of the riches it once possessed, or the elegance with which it is said to have been adorned.

Still I must say, I either felt, or fancied myself to be feeling, that there was something of silent majesty within its venerable walls, perhaps rendered more impressive to us, from passing immediately out of the brilliant sunshine into the deep gloom of its stately aisles, where we trod at every step upon tombstones, on which were inscribed dates of the sixteenth, fifteenth, and fourteenth centuries. Nor were the words upon these tombs effaced, except in

186   SUMMER AND WINTER

a very few instances, and we could distinctly read the earnest appeal to the passer by, that he would offer up a prayer for the soul of the departed.

Amongst other tombs, there is one of a celebrated musician, buried here in 1678, who had for the space of thirty-six years, exercised his gift with all assiduity, in the service of this church; and all who read the inscription, are requested to pray for his soul, "that after having assisted at the music of this world, it may be received amongst the happy, to assist at the celestial music through all eternity."

While lingering over the marble tombstones, and meditating upon the ancient splendour of this church, we were much struck with the contrast presented by the figures of two young Bearnaise women, who came to offer their devotions, by kneeling before the picture of every saint with which the walls are adorned, counting a bead, and repeating a prayer to each. One of them especially, in her simple peasant's costume, was a far lovelier picture than any of the saints to whom she bowed, and the manner in which she performed her genuflexions, was graceful beyond description. I should have been sorry to suspect her attitude was studied, but what was there in the cold and senseless service she was rendering, to call her thoughts away from the mere form and aspect of devotion ?

Not many paces from the north side of the church, and extending a considerable distance from east to west, is a line of ancient walls and towers, the remains of a castle or fortress, which must have been a place of great strength and magnitude. Indeed the whole town presents a singular picture of antiquity, being almost entirely composed of high towers, curious arches, and massive walls; with a portcullis leading to the castle, and supported on one side by a lofty square tower, which looks as if it might have been strong enough to defy the world. There is an enemy, however, whose assaults this massive masonry has not been able to resist, and what might still have refused to yield to force, has been overcome by the insidious encroachments of decay. At the very foot of this high tower, there lies a solid mass of masonry, so thick, that in its fall it has not been shattered, but remains partially buried in the soil, and overgrown with weeds, amongst which, however, may be seen the smooth surface of what was once the inner wall, and a large portion of the roof.

At the foot of the steep hill on which this fortress is built, the southern descent from which to the valley of the Gave is almost precipitous, stands a large and regular building, formerly a Barnabite college, established by Henry IV. in the hope of spreading amongst his people of Bearn, the doctrines of the religion he had himself embraced. This building was subsequently converted into a cotton manufactory, but it is now unoccupied, and presents a gloomy and forlorn appearance.

On returning from Lescar to Pau, we pass, on the left side of the road, and situate at the foot of the hills, which are here clothed with vines, the village of Bilhere, where Henry IV. passed his infant years, before being committed to the charge of the Baroness de Miossens. The house in which he was nursed, is still shown with affectionate pride by the people, by whom also, it was long held so sacred, as to be regarded as a place of refuge, where those who were attainted for crime, might fly from pursuit. On a stone in one of the walls, is seen an escutcheon with the arms of Bearn, —two cows yoked together, and these words underneath,—*Sauvegarde du roi.*

The rainy season to which I have before alluded, set in at Pau, about the beginning of April; and before the twenty-fifth of that month, the whole world around us seemed to have undergone a change, more resembling some of the descriptions in a fairy tale, than any thing I had ever really witnessed. The sky was without a cloud, the thermometer at 71° in the shade, and all vegetation bursting into green. There had not, until this time, been so much difference as might have been expected, between the state of vegetation here and in England. But in the course of a single week, the corn fields, which, owing to excessive drought, had remained nearly in the same state for two months, were bearing wheat a yard in height. The orchards suddenly became white with blossoms, lilacs burst forth into full bloom, and all things assumed the same aspect they do with us about the end of May, or the middle of June. It became impossible then, to walk out in the glare of day with any comfort; but the evenings were delicious, and the windows in all the houses being protected by green shutters, so that the air can be admitted, while the sunshine is shut out, we found no difficulty in keeping tolerably cool, while remaining quietly within.

The poetical associations with which the first coming of spring are invariably connected, are not in this climate without their interruptions; for no sooner does the warm sun burst forth after the spring rains, than innumerable multitudes of frogs, with voices of such volume and compass as almost

to defy belief, begin every evening to croak in all
the pools and ditches in the neighbourhood of Pau.
About this time, too, we were invited to dine with
some kind friends, to partake of no less a delicacy
than a dish of these monsters !

I had always thought that an English frog might
rest upon my plate a good while, before I should
be able to bring myself to eat it; but to hear the
noise of these creatures, it would seem to be an act
of magnanimity indeed, to make a meal of them.
The first time I heard them, I was amazed, and
horrified.   It is no exaggeration to say, that when
in full play on each side of the road, two persons
cannot hear each other talk.   It is not the duck-
like "quake"-ing of our English frogs, but a sort
of rattle or ruttle that beggars all description.   An
idea of its loudness may possibly be formed, when
I say that the friends with whom we dined, lived at
least half a mile from the principal scene of action,
and yet they not only heard them through their
doors and windows, but when these are closed, the
sound came distinctly down the chimneys.

I knew the legs of these animals alone were
eaten, but I had expected to see them brought
upon the table floating in sauce or gravy, and
fortified myself accordingly against all persuasion to eat them.   When, however, I saw them as

small as shrimps, quite dry, delicate, and crisp, I did at last make the experiment, and had I never heard them croak, should probably have thought them a great delicacy. We had subsequently an opportunity of partaking of other epicurean dainties, held in high esteem among the French; amongst which were the delicious ortolans, and ducks' livers of enormous size, produced by the disgusting process of over-feeding.

The rapid and extreme change in the state of the atmosphere, which had been the means of clothing the world around us in such unimaginable freshness and beauty, was not without its inconveniences and discomforts. Though our rooms could be kept tolerably cool by the exclusion of a great portion of the light, there were occasions when we were compelled to walk out, and then the ground seemed actually to scorch our feet as we trod upon it. Besides which, those delicious refreshments for the table, green gooseberries and rhubarb, the French have nothing to supply the want of; and oil, and lard, and thick gravies, and garlic, whatever they may be in the winter, are intolerable in the summer. It was on one of these days, that our servant brought me, by way of treat, a bowl of the favourite soup of the country. I cannot say that the flavour was objectionable, but it was a compound of cabbage

192   SUMMER AND WINTER

and other vegetables, boiled together, mixed with
lard, and apparently beaten to a sort of pulp.
In our evening meal we were unfortunate too.
When we sat down to tea, the milk and the butter
seemed to have exchanged qualities, for, owing to
the excessive heat, the milk came out in a body,
while the butter had become liquid.   I had then
an opportunity of understanding how the sour milk
of Africa should be considered so great a delicacy;
for when changed in this rapid manner, it has the
flavour of the finest curd, and is really excellent.

One luckless day in particular, all the milk in
the town was spoiled, and we were obliged to have
recourse to sheep's milk, which I should only
venture to recommend to those who are fond of a
strong taste of mutton.   That of goats is much
better, and more frequently used; herds of these
beautiful animals being driven to the town every
day, for the purpose of being milked.

I have spoken of the Parc as being one of the
most delightful of promenades, even in the winter;
but when the trees are in full leaf, it presents a
scene almost like enchantment;—on one side the
deep shadow of the trees, amongst which their
stately stems are gleaming; on the other, their
feathery branches forming a canopy over head;
while the fresh cool river still murmurs over its

gravelly bed below.   Here we used to wander at the close of day, and when returning through the town, it was to us a novel and curious sight, to see the public rooms and cafés thrown open, while all the poorer class of people sat in groups around their doors, as late as ten, looking as if the night was a greater luxury to them than the day.   We had then excellent street music too, for the first time,—some Italians with their harps, and a band of Germans with their wild-sounding horns.   Indeed the whole aspect and character of the place was so changed, that we seemed in the space of a few days, to have been transported into a different region of the world.

It was, of course, our wish to set off immediately for the mountains, and we made arrangements for that purpose, though still told that the weather was not to be trusted.   We had ourselves observed, that each day towards the afternoon, a slight breeze sprang up, accompanied with dark clouds; and this change in the atmosphere was followed by thunderstorms, accompanied with so much cold and rain, that in the course of another week we all felt as if winter had come again.

K

194   SUMMER AND WINTER

CHAPTER VIII.

JOURNEY TO EAUX BONNES — CASCADES — MOUNTAIN
SHEPHERD — HINTS ON THE SUBJECT OF SKETCHING
— CULTIVATION OF THE VALLEY D'OSSAU — PYRE-
NEAN BOTANIST — EAUX CHAUDES — GABAS — AU-
BERGE IN THE MOUNTAINS — THUNDER STORM.

In consequence of the frequent changes in the
weather, which in this climate are far more extreme than in ours, we were not able to take our
departure for the mountains, before the end of
May.   Even then our journey was performed
under no favourable auspices, for we had a
drizzling rain all the way; but as the family of
friends, with whom we had been most intimate
during our residence in Pau, were going to take
up their abode at Eaux Bonnes for the summer,
we felt the less inclination to remain behind.

It was still a month earlier than the commencement of the fashionable season; but as we passed
through the old town of Lauruns, situated at the
foot of the mountain through which is the steep

and rocky pass to Eaux Chaudes, there were symptoms of eager anticipation on many a hard-worn countenance; and urgent were the solicitations of those who flocked round our carriage, to be allowed to supply us with bread or milk, or any other kind of provisions which their humble means might afford.

At a short distance from this village, the road, which until reaching this place is the same as to Eaux Chaudes, instead of ascending to the gorge, makes a turn to the left; and though the acclivity is not very steep, it is so long and wearisome, that in compassion to our horses, we walked all the way, a distance of more than three miles. We were joined on the road by many of the women of the country, who eagerly asked if we came from Paris, that being the highest recommendation a visitor to these mountains can possibly possess, in the opinion of the country people. These women, like all we had noticed in the valley of Ossau, appeared to be of an Amazonian race, tall, up-right, agile, well-formed, and with rich glowing complexions,—their dress most frequently a close jacket of thick blue cloth, with a short petticoat of the same material, extremely wide, and drawn together in a prodigious number of close plaits at the waist. Over their heads they wore a scarlet,

K 2

and sometimes a dark blue capulet, now that the weather had become warmer, often disposed upon the head in deep thick folds, so as to give an air of majesty to the face and the whole figure.

On arriving at Eaux Bonnes, we found it was a little town in miniature, consisting of one good street, and this composed almost entirely of spacious and handsome hotels and lodging-houses, with a neat chapel at the highest extremity of the village. Its appearance, with regard to situation, is that of being what is commonly called, at the world's end; or, in other words, at the end of the only road by which it is approached. It is no thoroughfare, but stands in a sort of basin, amongst the mountains, which rise almost perpendicularly from the houses, leaving no other opening than on the north-west side. It might, perhaps, be owing to the dullness of the day, which prevented our seeing the loftiest peaks of the mountains, and cast a sombre hue over every object; but I certainly was disappointed in the first aspect of Eaux Bonnes. The cleanliness and comfort of our apartments, the excellence of the provisions, and the general civility with which we were treated, were, however, far beyond my expectations, and such as it would have been unreasonable indeed not to have been more than satisfied with.

On the following morning, the mists had cleared away; not a cloud was in the sky; and having heard, that of the many waterfalls which constitute the chief attraction of the scenery of Eaux Bonnes, one at the distance of three miles was the most beautiful, we engaged a guide to accompany us, and set out on our morning's ramble. Our guide was one of those useful and communicative companions who are acquainted with all the phenomena of nature in these mountain scenes, and who delight to tell how far they can leap, and how high they can climb,—to what craggy peaks they have followed the wild goat,—from which frightful precipice they have rescued the unwary stranger,—and in how many hair-breadth escapes they have taken the boldest and most prominent part.

Like all the men of this country, he had jet black hair, cut close on the top of his head, and falling on his neck behind in long flowing curls. He wore the flat brown cap so much like the Scottish bonnet, a close red woollen jacket, with a handsome crimson sash tied round his body, brown small-clothes, and brown worsted stockings of his own knitting, which seemed from their excellent fit to be a continuation of the nether garments. They were finished at the foot in the fashion of the country, with a sort of frill or

198   SUMMER AND WINTER

fringe, which hangs over the top of the shoe, and
sets off the form of the ancle to great advantage.
He was altogether one of the most compact and
picturesque figures I ever saw; and he seemed to
take a peculiar pleasure in placing himself in conspicuous situations, where the agility of his move-
ments, and the contour of his form, would be
most likely to be seen and admired.

We had not walked far this morning without
being convinced, that a stranger can form but a
very imperfect idea of the beauties of Eaux
Bonnes, from a short stay, or a limited view of
the place.   Indeed, you can scarcely walk a dozen
yards from your door, in any direction, except
to the *Jardin Anglais*, without treading on what
appears almost enchanted ground, so rich is the
foliage with which the trees are clothed,—so brilliant the green of the many grassy knolls which
start into view,—so pure and white the foam of the
crystal stream in its rocky bed,—and so varied the
innumerable paths which track the sides of the
hills in every possible direction, sometimes passing
under the deep shadow of overhanging rocks—
sometimes winding round the knotted stems of
ancient and majestic trees—sometimes forming a
sudden angle on a steep promontory, that juts out
from the side of a mountain, where a foaming

torrent rolls at a far depth below—and sometimes leading to a sheltered spot by the side of a magnificent waterfall, where you may stand in perfect safety, listening to the ceaseless roar, and watching the strife of waters in the gulf beneath.

It was about the hour of noon when we set out on our excursion, first tracing some of these cool and enchanting walks, but soon emerging into the broad glare of sunshine, which blazed upon the southern side of the hill along which we passed. The ground was literally smoking and steaming after three days of rain; and as we wound our way amongst the green bushes, and over the emerald turf, a kind of hot breath, like that from a baker's oven, rose into our faces. I began then to question very seriously how it would be possible to exist through the summer in this climate; but I soon found there were ameliorations to the excessive heat, with which I had not previously been acquainted. The shade, for instance, where we find it, is so deep—so refreshing: in the hottest weather, there is generally a breeze towards the evening; but above all, the air is so light and pure, and the atmosphere altogether so invigorating, that you are neither so depressed by fatigue, nor so annoyed by inconveniences, as in the heavier climate of England.

Still there is something rather startling in the general state of things, when, as on this day, the rocks and stones are literally too hot to sit down upon; and when we see them, as we have frequently after a gentle rain, and even when the sun has not been upon them for hours, sending up a white steam, which we were at first at a loss to account for.

Our guide conducted us along a most circuitous route, by turns towards every point of the compass, either to enhance the value of his own services, or to afford him a better opportunity of expatiating upon the different mountain peaks which rose in abrupt and majestic masses over the nearer hills, whose sides we were skirting. Amongst these the Pic de Ger is always the most conspicuous, whether seen from Pau, or from the immediate neighbourhood of Eaux Bonnes. It was then partially covered with snow; but it always retains the same character—majestic, bleak, and rugged; and when the structure of its rocks is visible, it may be distinguished by a singular tint approaching to rose colour. This mountain rises south-east of Eaux Bonnes. More to the eastward is another, of singular and majestic form, which we had often observed from Pau, and remarked particularly for its jagged and saw-like summit, one portion of which seems from that distance as if it had been struck off by some mighty giant, and left with its high sharp spire, pointing upward to the sky. It is called the Col de Tortes, from a curious formation of the rocks which form its surface. On the morning of our walk to the waterfall, it rose before us in all its majesty, this mighty cleft immediately opposite to the valley along which we passed; and while we gazed upon its craggy heights, at that time partially covered with snow, our guide informed us that between those two awful-looking forks, or pinnacles, was a road by which travellers sometimes passed to Cauterets.

From the south side of a high hill, along which our guide had very unnecessarily taken us, we turned to wander over green meadows, towards the bed of the stream which winds its way along the valley, and amongst the pleasant promenades of Eaux Bonnes. All was here so calm and peaceful, that no idea could be formed of the proximity of a cascade, until we came at once to a deep ravine, where a hollow roar announced the tumult of the pent-up waters, and we saw a silvery column more than seventy feet in height, pitching over the side of a perpendicular mass of dark rock, into a foaming caldron, from whence it works its way through a deep and narrow passage, closed in from

K 3

the sunshine by walls of solid rock on either side,
fringed over at the summit with light and graceful
foliage.   In this narrow bed, the stream seems to
foam itself to rest, for it is seen in the distance
still winding its way past one projection of rock
and then another, until it becomes blue, and calm,
and peaceful as it was before; while through the
same narrow opening, may be seen the distant
mountains clothed in all the aërial colouring of the
clouds above.

From this beautiful scene, we returned by a
nearer way across the fields, weary, but not disappointed, and sat down to the table d'hote at our
hotel; where, at this early stage of the season, we
were only joined by one visitor besides our own
party.

The cascade we had seen, and which is certainly
the most beautiful in the neighbourhood of Eaux
Bonnes, is called the cascade of the Gros-Hêtre,
from a majestic beech recently cut down, which
stood by the side of the falling water, and bent
over the abyss.   There is another cascade much
more frequently visited, from its proximity to
Eaux Bonnes, and to this we went on the following day, crossing the stream at the bottom of
the valley, and climbing the adjoining hill, in
order to see it to greater advantage from a

position almost immediately opposite the village. The side of the hill over which we rambled is composed of a succession of tufted knolls, their sloping sides forming pastures of the most brilliant green, for herds of mountain sheep, as white as the snows of their native wilds. Here, too, was the shadow of lofty and umbrageous trees; for the vicinity of Eaux Bonnes is remarkable for the richness and redundancy of its foliage, perhaps superior to that of any other part of the Pyrenees.

On a verdant bank where the brilliant sunshine fell amongst these trees, lay an old shepherd of the mountains, alternately watching his happy flock, and reading a little well-worn book, which he held in his hand. He was evidently ill, and the damp ground was a couch but little suited to the nature of his disease; for like many of those who lead this pastoral life, he appeared to be suffering from symptoms of consumption, occasioned most probably by constant exposure to the extreme changes of the weather. On entering into conversation with him, Mr. Ellis found that he was reading a book of prayers and devotional exercises, of course adapted to the creed of his own church; and that he was calmly, and apparently without regret, anticipating the close of his earthly pilgrimage,

204   SUMMER AND WINTER

which he knew to be near; while at the same
time he appeared not to be neglecting, in his
solitary hours, the contemplation of a world to
come.   How gladly would we have left in his hand
a book of better instruction, and of higher consola-
tion than the one he possessed! but we were at
that time unprovided with the means.   All we
were able to do was to endeavour, briefly and
imperfectly, to direct his thoughts to the only true
foundation of hope in this life, and happiness in
the life to come.   Since this time, measures have
happily been taken for supplying copies of the
Holy Scriptures to all who may be found willing
to receive them, in this and the neighbouring
valley.

Before leaving Pau for the mountains, I had
been so convinced that a few rude sketches to
take home with me, would be preferable to no
vestige whatever of the scenes I was about to visit,
that I determined, amidst many discouragements,
to make the attempt; and from the pleasure I
have received from my own small measure of
success, would earnestly recommend others to do
the same.   It is true that without a strong determination to surmount difficulties, the weather will
always be found too hot, or too cold—the subject
too large, or too small—the paper, or the colours,

of the wrong kind; and above all,—as every idler tells you, the time too short. I have no velvet couch, no silken canopy, no magical means of transmitting pictures upon paper, to propose to my countrywomen who may visit the Pyrenees; but I do know that with a tolerable portion of health, and strong determination, much may be done to gratify the friends who remain at home, as well as to preserve memorials of scenes which few of us, perhaps, will ever be permitted to behold again.

I write thus by way of encouragement to the young, because it is amongst them I have so often heard the complaint, that they cannot draw from nature,—that they have never drawn without a master; and because I feel sure, that something must be wrong in the system of instruction pursued in our schools, if, after years of expensive lessons, after also attaining a degree of excellence in the art of copying almost equal to that of the master himself, numbers of young ladies loiter up and down the promenades of Pau, wishing the lovely aspect of the scenes around them could be transmitted to their albums, yet never, even at the solicitation of their parents, or the entreaties of their friends, being induced to attempt even so much as a sketch. Of course, I make exceptions in these remarks, of those whose health is delicate;

for I am well aware that such necessary exposure to the climate as sketching requires, must be attended with some risk.

Before leaving Eaux Bonnes, I was induced to make one of my first attempts, though I confess the situation kindly chosen for me offered the greatest amongst many discouragements, for this was no other than the cascade of the Gros Hêtre; and, remembering the almost awful solitude of the place, as well as the slippery nature of the declivity by which it is approached, where there is no other footing than loose stones and dead leaves, sloping " sheer down into the abyss," I felt a little strange about the undertaking, and talked about the distance, and the clouds betokening rain, and many other objections, without betraying my real one—that I was afraid.

Mr. Ellis, however, well assured there was no real danger, and wholly unacquainted with my fears, was not to be diverted from his object, and we both set out, carrying a little basket with colours, and all things requisite; and after tracing the course of the stream, climbing the green knolls, and passing the little shepherds' huts so thickly scattered along the smiling valleys, we reached again what was to be the scene of my presumptuous undertaking. I have always maintained, that in a certain degree of danger there is a vague feeling of enjoyment; and though I have seldom felt more nervous than on this occasion, I have seldom passed a pleasanter day. With some difficulty I had been persuaded to descend half-way down the declivity by the side of the torrent, so near, that the spray sometimes annoyed me a good deal. Here, on shelving stones, and slender twigs of box, my companion placed a piece of rotten wood, which gave way with my first attempt to sit down; but he built the fabric up again, and though my feet were only supported by leaves and loose fragments, and the foaming caldron was immediately below me, I not only arranged all my drawing apparatus around me, but remained so fixed for the space of three hours, in which time I had completed a very humble representation of the scene.

I confess there were moments when my courage nearly failed me; and if I had not been equally afraid to scramble up or down, I might have quitted my post, particularly when left to myself, the place seemed altogether so intensely lonely. It seemed to me as if in that great turmoil of the waters, there must be some mysterious power that would arise from the abyss, and make itself visible to my outward senses. Once or twice, the

wind having changed for a moment, the sound
of the torrent changed with it, the spray flying off
in a different direction; and then it was that I
would most gladly have heard a human voice in
my solitude.   All this while, however, I was in no
sort of danger, beyond that which my imagination
conjured up; unless it was the danger of being
startled by the approach of the French gentleman,
our companion at table, who came with one of
his friends to the brink of the cascade, for the
simple purpose of passing the time by throwing
stones into the bed of the torrent.   Happily,
however, I had heard their voices, and that of
Mr. Ellis, as they approached.

In the mean time, Mr. Ellis had enjoyed a
refreshing bath in the stream above, where it
flows under a thick canopy of spreading trees,
hemmed in by projecting rocks.   We were not
aware at that time, that his exploit was considered
one of extreme danger by the country people, who
never bathe in the water from the melting snow,
nor even drink it, where it can be avoided, be-
lieving it to be the cause of those frightful goitres,
which disfigure nearly the whole population of some
of the valleys. Those of the valley d'Ossau however,
are, for the most part, exempt from this disease.

They are, in fact, a much finer race of people

than their neighbours to the eastward, from whom they are separated by a barrier of mountains, impassable to the ordinary traveller, except through the giant cleft I have already described. The peasants of the valley d'Ossau, as in other parts of the Pyrenees, are almost all proprietors of little plots of ground, which they cultivate with great industry, in order that the produce of their short summer may be sufficient for their maintenance through the winter months. Maize is their chief article of consumption, and when the flour of this valuable grain is boiled either with milk or water, it makes an excellent and wholesome porridge, very superior to that which is made from oatmeal in the north of England. The maize is sown in the month of May, and gathered later in the autumn than any other grain, yielding a harvest of much greater quantity, in proportion to the seed originally sown, besides supplying, with its leaves and stalks, excellent food and litter for the cattle.

The population of the valley d'Ossau is about 16,000, a large proportion of which are herdsmen or pastors, who, during the summer months, live entirely amongst the distant heights of the mountains, to which they conduct their numerous flocks, and remain with them until the snows of autumn

force them to descend.   This valley has its natural
boundary of sterile mountains, hemming it in to
the east and the west, and sometimes reducing it
to a very narrow compass.   Southward it extends
beyond the Pic du Midi, to the frontiers of
Spain, while to the northward it lays claim to a
considerable tract of country north and north-east
of Pau.   Of this extent of ground but a very small
proportion is cultivated, and that in such a manner
as barely to meet the wants of the occupants,
who are consequently but little acquainted with
the luxuries and refinements of life.   The influx
of strangers, year by year increasing, appears to
have introduced no improvement in their domestic
habits, or the mode of cultivating their land; and
the supply of provisions for the visitors is consequently limited to the mere necessaries of life; nor
are these to be obtained except by paying a somewhat exorbitant price.   With the same facilities
for enjoyment,—the same advantages in the restoration of health,—scenery which never tires,—and
a climate which of itself is enough to constitute
enjoyment,—what a country this might become, if
the peasants could be inspired with a little praise-
worthy ambition, and at the same time retain
their simplicity !

Already, however, the first seeds of a new order of things are beginning to take root, where one would least wish to find them. Their characteristic costume, so admirably suited to their mountain wilds, is becoming gradually supplanted by articles of dress more commonly used in other countries, though on their fête days, and all grand occasions, they still wear the habiliments peculiar to their own valley. Amongst the amusements of Eaux Bonnes, it is a favourite one with the visitors to watch the games of these hardy and athletic people, whose accustomed sports are so much in keeping with the peculiar kind of life they lead. Hunting the izard, a kind of wild goat, or chamois, which frequents the high mountains, is one in which they are extremely expert; and not less fond of conducting the adventurous stranger who may wish to trust himself to their guidance, in pursuit of these animals. Of their exploits with the bears, too, great wonders are told, though this latter amusement becomes a much more serious affair; and the descent of these animals amongst their flocks is attended with very serious loss.

Their favourite games are almost universally such as require an uncommon display of agility and strength. I will mention only two. One is a race up the steep side of a mountain, to obtain, not the wreath, but the branches of victory, which at the summit of the hill are awarded to the most swift of foot. Another is a little more extraordinary, and requires caution as well as speed. It consists in having eighty eggs laid on the ground, in the street of Eaux Bonnes, at the distance of one foot from each other. It is then decided by lot what shepherd shall gather these eggs into his basket, without breaking one, during the time that the remaining number of youths can run from Eaux Bonnes to the nearest village, and back again. This distance is so well proportioned to the time required for gathering the eggs, that the two parties are said seldom to vary more than a minute; but the chance is, that, as time advances, the man who gathers the eggs will throw them in too quickly, and thus defeat his own ends.

The amusements which prevail amongst the visitors at Eaux Bonnes, are of a very different order. Within the salons a miniature Paris exists; and the balls, and other evening entertainments, are said to be scarcely rivalled by those of the most fashionable cities. Our friends, who remained there, and whose habits were as domestic and as exclusive as our own, found it not difficult, however, to hold themselves distinct from this kind of society; though I still think that the number of fashionable loungers must in some measure detract from the enjoyment of mountain scenery.

It is pitiful in all these places to see what they call the Jardin Anglais. But even this might have its use, in operating as a wholesome warning against some of our own futile imitations of what is French.

Our friends, Mr. and Mrs. W——, whom we left at Eaux Bonnes, enjoyed the enviable advantage of botanical taste, and considerable knowledge of plants, which of all sources of amusement, is, to an invalid so circumstanced, perhaps the most desirable. Walking, even in the loveliest scenery, becomes irksome, if exercise is the only object; but the botanist is beguiled onwards with a never-ceasing fascination, yet so leisurely as to prevent fatigue; and when his strength is unequal to excursions of higher attainment, he can find beauties in the humblest path.

From its immense variety of walks, neither too difficult, nor too much exposed to the sun, Eaux Bonnes is perhaps the most eligible residence for a botanist, of all the places of resort amongst the Pyrenees. Here too, he may enjoy the advantage of conversing with a man of that order of natural

214　　SUMMER AND WINTER

genius, which is scarcely met with more than once in the course of an ordinary life.

Pierrine Gaston, a native of the little village of Beost in Ossau, a man of respectable but humble parentage, was brought up to the life of a shepherd. He obtained while at school, as most of the peasant men of this neighbourhood do, a sufficient knowledge of the French language for the common purposes of life. In familiar conversation, he and his family still speak the patois of the country. While following the occupation of tending his sheep amongst the mountains, he amused himself with the collection and examination of plants, and first became distinguished by his knowledge of their medicinal properties. Not satisfied with this, he obtained an old work of Linnæus on botany, and in order to understand it, purchased a Latin dictionary, which he found on a book-stall at Pau, for the price of nine sous. With these scanty means he commenced his botanical career. He was then thirty years of age, he is now thirty-nine, and has in his possession a valuable collection of plants, amounting to three thousand specimens, accurately designated according to their class and order. All who seek his acquaintance from a real interest in this science, find him an intelligent and agreeable companion, combining all the delightful simplicity of his unsophisticated life, with the dignity of native genius, and the politeness of a true gentleman.

Nor are his talents confined to this branch of study alone. He is a very skilful musician, and when our friends visited him, which they did at his paternal home, where his venerable parents are still living, they saw a kind of harp, and a violin, with other musical instruments of his own making. His residence is a large farm-house, such as is usually occupied by cultivators of the soil whose circumstances are easy, and comparatively affluent. His house and premises appeared to be well stocked with servants and cattle, and on one occasion when our friends visited him, they saw in the yard the process going on, by which horses are made to tread out the corn, by being driven about in a yard where it is strewn.

In returning this visit, Pierrine Gaston drank tea with our friends at Eaux Bonnes, when he remarked with great simplicity, that he had never tasted tea but once before, on which occasion he had eaten it dry. We had afterwards the pleasure of meeting him at their house, and a great treat it was, for his appearance in every respect, equals the idea one would form of such a character. His figure is above six feet in height, thin, agile, and admirably formed. His jet black hair, which hangs in loose

216　　　SUMMER AND WINTER

curls upon his shoulders, is cut close in front, and
this he told us was the custom of the country, because of the habit the peasants have, of carrying
immense bundles of hay and straw upon their
heads, and the necessity there is for them to see
straight before them.　He wore that day, a short
blue jacket, with a handsome sash of crimson silk
tied round his body.　But his majestic brown cap,
which he kept on even in the house, from a habit
he had acquired in consequence of the keenness of
the mountain air, was the most striking part of his
costume, and harmonized with his appearance
better than any other could have done, by casting
a deep shadow over the thoughtful expression of his
interesting face.　His countenance was entirely one
of the valley d'Ossau : his nose slightly aquiline, his
eyes quick and intelligent, his eyebrows clearly pen-
cilled and a good deal arched, and his regular, white
teeth, the most beautiful I ever saw.　His move-
ments, which were as rapid as expressive, were at
once dignified and graceful; but the most extraordinary feature in his behaviour was, that seeing
the floor half covered with a carpet, he could on
no account be induced to tread upon that part,
until he had taken off his shoes, which he placed
under a chair, and resumed when he went away.

On this occasion also, he appeared to be very

much in the dark with regard to our manner of taking tea, for when the lady of the house asked him in the morning if he would come and drink tea with them in the evening, he thanked her and refused, saying he had already taken some that day. When the cup was placed before him in the evening, he plunged into it a large piece of bread, and as soon as it was emptied, at once returned it to the tray, and rose up to go away. What a pleasure I thought it would be, to show to such a man all that is worth seeing in our own country; yet if that would endanger his simplicity, far better that he·should remain where he is, unacquainted with the world which lies beyond his native mountains.

Eaux Bonnes is not a place for distant views, nor yet for that sublime and majestic scenery which is found in many other parts of the Pyrenees; but for a protracted residence it is said to be more agreeable than any, and certainly combines the beauties of all, on a miniature scale. Having satisfied our curiosity with exploring its immediate neighbourhood, we directed our course again to Eaux Chaudes, and set out to walk to that place, a distance of about five miles, one beautiful morning when the weather was less intensely hot than it had previously been, owing to the gathering of dark clouds which betokened rain.

L

At a little distance from the entrance of the gorge, I climbed up a ridge of rocks, and amused myself with sketching a view of the valley d'Ossau, which from this point appears to peculiar advantage; the mountains with their rocky summits rising like mighty barriers on either side, the blue river, winding its serpentine course along the valley; and immediately to the left, as if guarding the pass, a majestic mass of richly-coloured rocks, presenting every variety of tint, from the deepest purple, to the brightest yellow, and the liveliest green.   I was delightfully situated, except that troops of wild-looking Spaniards rather startled me as they wound their way along the path at my feet, driving their mules through the rocky gorge, from which I was distant only about a hundred yards.   A peasant woman too, of no very pleasing aspect, came and put all sorts of puzzling questions to me about my husband, and condoled with me in so sympathising a manner on the misery of being left alone, that I was quite afraid she meant to spend the day with me.

The people here, however, are remarkably civil and inoffensive, and you may wander or repose in perfect peace and safety amongst their rocks and hills, provided you do not mind a group of little girls coming to peep over your work, giggling and running away, and then peeping again, with their bright black eyes, shaded by their little red hoods. A shepherd-boy, too, will often come and throw himself down on the grass beside you, watching the progress of your pencil; and they are all, when young, such beautiful creatures, that the only objection to their presence is, you are tempted to look at them instead of the landscape. The men are a fine race, and the pastoral life they lead, gives them a simplicity, accompanied with a habit of observation, which raises them far above what is either gross or vulgar. But the youths, half men and half boys, are the most beautiful specimens of human nature I have ever seen; and if I were to select a subject for a painter, as a personification of glowing health and buoyant youth, chastened by the simplicity of an unambitious and inoffensive life, it would be one of the shepherd boys of the valley d'Ossau. Would that the women were of the same grade, but even the little girls make one sad to think of the hard fate to which they are destined, and the women make one sadder still, to see to what condition they are reduced. It is always said in relation to their occupations, that use is every thing, and that hard labour is no hardship to women who are inured to it from childhood; but I cannot be made to believe, that ever the

L 2

bodily functions of women are such as fit them for
this excessive toil; and while expending their youth
and their strength in labour which ought to be performed by men, they must necessarily neglect those
happier and more delicate offices of domestic life,
which even in the humblest station ought to be their
province.

The clouds, which had looked threatening all the
morning, began, at last, to roll up the valley in dark
and heavy masses, while peals of distant thunder
warned me that it was high time to make the best
of my way to a place of shelter.   The purple and
singularly coloured mountain before me, with its
head wrapped in clouds, looked absolutely black
below, and the dark ravines which plough its
rugged sides, assumed the appearance of deep
gulfs, or yawning caverns.   With all nature growing
every moment more gloomy around me, I turned
alone into the narrow pass, where the blast which
precedes a storm, was already sweeping through.
I was able, however, to reach Eaux Chaudes
before the rain fell heavily, and turning again
into the little inn where we had first made our
acquaintance with mountain fare, I was much
struck with the difference of accommodation between this place and Eaux Bonnes.

Notwithstanding this difference, however, I must

always give the preference to Eaux Chaudes; if for no other reason, because it is a place without pretension. It asserts no claim to distinction, for any thing but what it really is; in short, it is not *Parisian.* It is a noble mountain pass, connecting France with Spain; and if its waters are healing, and its baths superb, they rest upon their own merits, unsolicitous to assume any other.

With regard to the medicinal properties of these, as well as other waters in the Pyrenees, I shall not presume to offer any remarks. A partial statement of their merits would be of little use, and a more lengthened one would most probably be erroneous. There are descriptions of their chemical properties, with opinions as to their general use, in most of the guide books which relate to these places; but beyond this, there is at each of the celebrated springs, a medical gentleman, appointed and paid by government, whose advice it is extremely desirable to take, before making any use of the waters, many lamentable consequences having accrued from individuals having used them without proper caution. Those whose partialities lean to the advice of an English doctor, may obtain all requisite information on the subject, from one, who, with his amiable family, has for several years been a resident at Pau, and who has made

222   SUMMER AND WINTER

himself intimately acquainted with the properties
and the use of these waters.   They will also find,
that he has the happy art of blending all the kindness of friendship with the solicitude of a medical
adviser.

A thunder-storm in the Pyrenees is seldom
succeeded, as in England, by brighter skies and
lovelier weather than before; but on the contrary,
it is almost invariably followed by a continuation of
cold and heavy rain.   It was so on our arrival at
Eaux Chaudes, nor was it until the afternoon of the
following day, that we could venture out.   Even
then the mountain tops were still enveloped in
thick clouds; but time with us was too precious to
be wasted, and we set off with some friends from
England, whom we had happily met with at our
inn, to trace the mountain road farther up the
valley leading to the Pic du Midi de Pau.

The road from Eaux Chaudes to Gabas, the last
French village on that route, is justly considered
one of the most sublime and beautiful amongst the
Pyrenees.   Even while the mountains were partially concealed, we were so beguiled by the grandeur and novelty of the scene, as to be led on from
one point of eminence to another, until at last,
finding ourselves too distant to return to dinner,
we determined to proceed to Gabas, the road to

which is one continued ascent of seven or eight
miles, so steep, as to be considered no trifling
undertaking with a carriage.

Lovely and enchanting as the first part of our
excursion had been, the last mile was wild and
dreary in the extreme. We had ascended so high,
that the mists were rolling around us, while all
along the precipitous defile, the wreck of shattered
pines and timber, blocking up the course of the
torrents, indicated the prevalence of frightful storms
in these desolate regions.

A livelier scene was presented by the flocks and
herds which thronged the path on their way to the
pasturage of the mountains, each little company of
shepherds seldom consisting of more than three or
four, driving along with them a single horse, laden
with all their domestic apparatus for at least three
months. Amongst these articles, we saw invariably
a large brass pan or caldron, and a few other vessels
for making their cheese; but for luxury, or even
for comfort, there was nothing. In many instances
the shepherds themselves carry on their backs every
article for their summer use; while their flocks are
always accompanied by goats, which furnish a supply
of milk for them and their mountain dogs.

At Gabas is an establishment of government
officers, for the purpose of protecting the revenue

which France derives from the traffic with Spain.
It is stated that 15,000 mules pass annually along
this route, into Spain. Had we set out, as many
visitors do, from Eaux Chaudes, for the purpose of
reaching the Pic du Midi, we should have been
stopped at this place for our passports. Our object,
however, was merely to obtain refreshment, and
the single auberge in the wretched-looking village,
half filled as it was with Spaniards and Bearnais
shepherds, whose flocks were browsing round the
door, presented no cheering promise of the entertainment to be found within.

We entered this auberge through a stable, where
the mules were feeding, and were ushered into a
low but spacious chamber over the stable. This
apartment was lighted only by one small window
and a blazing wood fire in a snug recess, beside
which were seated on a long bench, men, women,
and children, evidently travellers; but where from,
or where to, it was impossible to imagine, from
their extraordinary costume, rendered still more
striking by the red glare of the blazing fire.

It was worth walking to Gabas, to see the tall,
majestic-looking woman who cooked our dinner,
with her crimson hood folded almost in the style of
a turban round her head, her short full petticoat
of massive folds, her close cloth jacket, and the

glittering cross that hung suspended from her neck; while other figures of inferior importance, though scarcely less striking, moved about with their long white capulets, giving them a mysterious and ghost-like appearance. Strange, wild-looking men, too, who might have been banditti from the other side of the frontier, were seen emerging from dark recesses, or standing about in those majestic attitudes which the Spaniards always assume. It was a scene, altogether, never to be forgotten; and even when we entered a more private chamber, there lay the black velvet conical hats of Spain, the sandals, and woollen mantles worn by travellers of that country; with a vast variety of things, that looked not only foreign, but suspicious, to our unaccustomed eyes.

Although the outward aspect of the place was so unpromising, it was soon evident that many a weary traveller had halted at that house of entertainment; and we read at once, in the aspect of the cook, and the magnitude of her culinary apparatus, that we had nothing to fear. And so it proved; for her dinner, to appetites sharpened by the mountain air, was excellent. The cloth had been spread for us in a little chamber, and here we had as usual, the same abundant supply of clean table napkins, and silver forks. Our first dish was an

226   SUMMER AND WINTER

omelette, and the first I ever liked; then followed
trout, which is almost always abundant amongst the
mountains; then a leg, or rather hind quarter of
salted goose, well boiled; and what else I really
forget, but I know we were so refreshed, as to set
out on our walk back to Eaux Chaudes, with considerable elasticity and vigour.

Late as it was when we arrived, we had sufficient
daylight by the way, to see the evening milking of
the goats, which the shepherds had driven together
for that purpose; and never do these picturesque
animals look more beautiful, than when the drowsy
hour of twilight comes on, and they sink to sleep
amongst the bushes of box and fern, or stretch
their limbs for the last time before reposing for the
night, on some bank of green moss, or promontory
of grey stone.

The brilliance of the following day revealed so
many wonders, which the mists of the preceding
one had hidden from our eyes, that we were determined to retrace our steps along the road to
Gabas, where we found that the scene was rendered
almost entirely new to us, by the sunshine of a
cloudless sky. We had taken the precaution this
morning, to deposit in a basket, the remainder of
an overabundant breakfast; for in France there
prevails a very convenient notion, that all which

remains on the table of an inn, even the sugar and the dessert, is the property of the traveller. We were consequently independent of time and place, and had nothing to do but spend the day as the inclination of the moment might dictate. It proved, however, to be a day of that intense and peculiar kind of heat, when the sunshine seems to cling to you like a hot garment, and once or twice in the lowest part of the valley, we almost despaired of reaching a celebrated point of view, at the distance of five miles. Yet the variety, the beauty, and the grandeur of the scene, were such as to beguile us almost unconsciously, up the long and steep ascent. Behind us were bold barriers of mountain, their outlines intersecting each other as they shut in the track along the gorge; to the right were inaccessible heights, their hoary summits clothed with pine, and their rugged sides broken into thousands of dark defiles, down many of which impetuous steams were pouring, till they joined the foaming waters of the river, which ran immediately at our left. Over the bed of this river, the richest and most graceful foliage was drooping, amongst which were seen, jutting out into the sunshine, enormous blocks of richly-coloured slate and marble, sometimes at a prodigious height, forming a long line of perpendicular or overhanging walls; while these

again, fringed with foliage, formed the foundation
of another, and then another still, until the mighty
fabric seemed as if erected to support the skies.

Beyond these shelving and woody heights, was
a higher mountain, distinct and of peculiar formation, almost entirely bare up to its bold summit,
with neither tree, nor shepherd's dwelling, nor
pasturage even for the wild goat; yet even more
irregular in its form, and brilliant in its colouring,
than those more richly clothed.   Beyond this,
and separated only by a deep gorge, was another,
presenting a still greater contrast—massive, dark,
and solemn.   Above its towering pinnacles, two
eagles were floating, wheeling their flight, which
Byron has called "happy," because "highest into
heaven," without a flutter; for this is the distinction, and a noble and characteristic one it is, between this and other birds, that the eagle soars
without ever fluttering its wings.

And then below us all the while, far down in a
deep still valley, the blue stream was sweeping
amongst verdant meadows, or foaming along its
pent-up passage through the rocks; while shepherds' cottages were scattered here and there upon
its banks, with one small village and its rustic
bridge, the central point, from whence diverged
innumerable mountain paths.

But how shall I describe the fairy work of nature, immediately around our feet, in all the tempting ways we traversed? The crevices of the rocks sometimes made purple with the deep-coloured gentian, and starting out beneath the boldest masses, a flower resembling a violet, which is altogether the most beautiful specimen of flower, and stalk, and leaves, which the imagination can conceive; with a thousand others, equally new, though none so beautiful as this; for not only the earth, but the apparently sterile rocks, on a nearer examination, seem to teem with vegetable life. Besides the flowers, the trees and shrubs, to me always the most welcome and beautiful of all the treasures of nature, though certainly less majestic in their foliage, and less sombre in shadow here, than in England, are yet more wild and free, and consequently more picturesque. Over the bed of the roaring torrent, you sometimes see the most elegant branches of the birch, drooping like those of the weeping willow. The beech is the tree which grows most luxuriantly on the sides of the hills, while in higher regions, the venerable oak is often seen stretching its green boughs across some dark ravine; and higher still, the gloomy pine, not unfrequently twisted and riven, or torn from its hold by the violence of the winter storms.

230   SUMMER AND WINTER

But a very imperfect idea of this scenery would be formed, without picturing those innumerable green slopes and tufted knolls, to which the painter's art is so unequal; and it is chiefly these peculiar spots which give so much of their Arcadian character to the Pyrenees. In the sunshine of the climate, these green islands of the wilderness seem to glow with every tint, from green to gold; while down their verdant sides is often seen the long slanting shadow of tall trees, or those of the shepherd and his peaceful flock. I know not how this character of the scenery has appeared to others, but to me it has seemed but little stretch of the imagination, to suppose it was amongst such scenes, that our first parents held their innocent and happy communion with angels, before a leaf had faded in paradise, or the springs of human life had been tainted by disease.

Loitering along through this region of beauty, we reached at last the eminence, where the road making a sudden bend, you come at once in sight of the Pic du Midi, rearing its cloven crest at the extremity of the defile. Here, on looking back, we perceived that dark clouds were gathering behind us; but taking courage from the shepherds, who told us the rain would not fall for some time yet, we sat down to rest by the side of the road, with the stream, which is here almost overhung by pines, roaring at the bottom of a tremendous ravine beneath our feet. The clouds now became blacker; and a distant roll of thunder in the direction of Eaux Chaudes, reminded us that we had five long miles to walk, with the probability of meeting the storm by the way. We therefore resumed our route, and found that a gusty wind had already begun to whirl the dust and the dead leaves in ominous circles along our path. But still our steps were arrested as if by enchantment; for, turning back from the brow of the hill, a scene presented itself never to be forgotten. All the vivid lights were gone. The stream lay at the bottom of the dark valley, like a bed of white foam, the trees seemed to shiver and rustle with an instinctive sort of terror; and the great mountains, in the morning so clear and bright, were turned into huge masses of blackness and gloom; while the gorge in the distance, through which we had to pass, was completely filled with dark rolling clouds. The rain soon began to fall in torrents; the lightning flashed before us; and the thunder peals became louder and louder; while their lengthened echoes, mingling with the roar of the torrent, seemed to roll back from side to side in the narrow and now darkened ravine.

The road by this time had become like a river;
yet we reached our hotel in perfect safety, and
rose the next morning with considerable regret, to
think our stay at Eaux Chaudes had reached its
utmost limit. We did not leave, however, before
Mr. Ellis had found an opportunity of exploring
the grotto, which is justly considered as one of the
greatest wonders of this place. It is situated
nearly at the summit of a mountain, in the wall
of richly-coloured slate, which I have described
as rising amongst terraces of foliage, immediately
to our left, when we walked to Gabas. Within the
hollow of the grotto, a cascade is heard to pour its
hidden waters, which a little lower down the side
of the hill, emerge from their obscurity, and form
one of those beautiful waterfalls with which the
sides of the valleys are diversified.

I have said that there is a mountain pass over
the Col de Tortes to Cauterets, thus affording the
means of communication with other parts of the
Pyrenees most frequently visited. To me, however, it appeared far preferable to pursue our tour
to these places, by returning along the more easy
and ordinary route to Pau. We therefore left our
hotel by diligence, and though we travelled in a
pouring rain, had no occasion to regret the choice

we had made; for we afterwards learned, from one of the friends we left at Eaux Bonnes, who made the experiment of the mountain pass, that it was difficult and fatiguing in the extreme.

CHAPTER IX.

JOURNEY TO ARGELEZ—HOTELS IN THE PYRENEES—
MOUNTAIN PASS FROM PIERREFITTE TO LUZ—
VALLEY OF LUZ—ST. SAUVEUR—GAVARNIE—PAS-
SAGE OF THE TOURMALET, AND ARRIVAL AT
BAGNERES DE BIGORRE.

ON the 13th of June we again left Pau, with
the intention of prosecuting our tour through the
mountains. The morning was beautiful, and as
on this occasion we were a party of three, a saddle
horse, and a light open conveyance, had been
engaged to take us as far as Argelez, in the day.
To accomplish this journey, however, it was necessary to be early on the road, which was also rendered still more desirable by the excessive heat of
the weather. At five o'clock I looked out, and saw
beneath our window the carriage which was to
convey us a day's journey on our route; and which
it required some ingenuity to identify with the
many encomiums its owner had bestowed upon it
the previous day. It was innocent of paint, except

that a sort of behind part, which stood out to a considerable distance, like a large box, was a bright sky blue. The reins and traces were of rope; and when the driver, a large broad-shouldered man, seated himself before us on the board at our feet, with his legs hanging down beneath the tail of the horse, and set off in the usual French style, with whoop, and slash, and rattle, over the stones of Pau, we were not sorry to think it was too early in the morning for us to be likely to meet with any of our acquaintance there.

Early as it was, the washers by the bridge leading to Bizanos, were all at their accustomed work; for theirs is an occupation which knows no cessation, either for the summer's heat, or the winter's cold. They seldom wash in the Gave, or in any stream from melted snow; but this little river, the Ousse, which flows from the nearer hills, and joins the Gave, at the bridge of Pau, is said to be more favourable for their employment; and I have seen as many as six and twenty women in one continued line, washing in its waters, besides a great many other groups in different stations on its banks; while the whole village of Bizanos,—its fields and hedges, and much of the surrounding plains, were white with the linen bleaching in the sun. The great mystery is, how these poor women can continue their operations through the severest winter weather. I have seen them standing barefoot in the water, when the snow was on the ground, and a sharp north-east wind blowing; their aprons and petticoats literally dripping; and no refreshment during the whole day, but dry bread, onions, and sour wine. Yet they sat down in groups upon the ground, while they ate this pitiful repast, and chatted, and laughed with as much apparent enjoyment, as half-a-dozen English washerwomen over their lengthened tea, with the bright blaze of a kitchen fire sending its comfort to their hearts all the while.

It was the loveliest hour of morning as we passed these familiar groups, now somewhat more in their element; for the bright sun was upon them, and the mountains to our right were just looking so as to make one's heart ache to be leaving them behind. Well has the language of poetry spoken of " making friends with mountains." It would be difficult to describe in what manner this mysterious friendship steals upon us; yet few persons, I imagine, have dwelt long in the neighbourhood of mountains, without having felt its power.

As the day advanced, it became one of the hottest we had yet experienced; and, our route lying entirely along the course of the valley, we had the full benefit of the sun, without a breath of wind. Our first halting place was at Betharam, where there is a bridge over the Gave de Pau, so beautiful, that almost every one who visits this place brings away a sketch of it. It consists of one simple arch; but the festoons of ivy with which it is adorned, constitute its chief merit, as a subject for the painter.

The sanctuary of Notre Dame, at Betharam, is a place of great celebrity amongst the devotees, who make an annual pilgrimage to this place in the month of August. Many miracles are said to have been wrought here; and the pilgrims who flock hither in great numbers, seldom return without having purchased some of the trinkets which are always exposed for sale beside the door of the church. They consist of rosaries, crosses, rings, and amulets: all having been blessed at some shrine, and some of them even by his Holiness himself. The church is a handsome and venerable edifice, with a good deal of curious and ornamental sculpture and masonry about the principal entrance. But the wonder and admiration of the country people, is perhaps more excited by a succession of little chapels, or stations, placed at every point of a zigzag path leading up the side of an adjoining hill, in each of which is displayed a group of figures, carved in wood, as large as life, and painted in all the colours of the rainbow, representing different scenes connected with the crucifixion of our Saviour—all as hideous and grotesque as it would be possible to make them. Yet here we saw a poor woman counting her beads, and looking as serious and devout as if she had been treading the ground of the real Calvary, the name by which this place is known.

On leaving Betharam, we passed over the beautiful bridge, and from that point entered the department of the High Pyrenees. Our course now lay along a richly cultivated valley, with the cool river running immediately on our right, while on our left, reflecting the intense heat of the afternoon sun, was a range of little vine-covered hills, just high enough to prevent a breath of air reaching us from that quarter. We were really in distress, but there was no help for it. Such was our situation, that even when we got out to walk up the hot hills, it was some relief to be in action; for I have always found that in sitting still with nothing to do, the heat is most intolerable.

At the distance of about twenty miles from Pau, we came in sight of the curious and ancient castle of Lourdes, which, when seen from this position, has a most striking and imposing effect. It is built on the summit of a bold mass of rock, entirely without verdure on that side, and so situated as to appear to be guarding the mountain pass to the valley of Lavedon and Argelez. We expected to stop here; but our conductor persisted in going on to Argelez, eight miles farther: he therefore flogged his reluctant horse through the town; after leaving which, we again crossed the Gave, and entered upon the scene so justly celebrated for its beauty, and preferred by most travellers to all others in the Pyrenees—the valley of Argelez.

It is indeed a paradise, but so entirely composed of rich corn-fields, verdant woods, and mountains towering to the sky, that to succeed in any detailed description of it, would be impossible. We were also a little too warm to be able to do it justice, even in our own appreciation of its merits; for there is a degree of heat that melts down one's enthusiasm. Besides which, I was suffering great anxiety on account of Mr. Ellis, whose exposure to the intense rays of the sun, in his precarious state of health, was attended with real danger; and the event sufficiently proved his inability to sustain it without serious consequences. I am the more particular in mentioning these circumstances, because I feel convinced, that none but those who

are in robust health, or at all events, who are
unaccustomed to painful affections of the head,
can really enjoy a hurried tour through the Pyrenees, during the heat of summer; and that without
great care, such an excursion must be attended
with danger.   Our conductor through the valley
of Argelez, was one of that numerous class of
Frenchmen, who, rather than say they do not
know, will answer your questions in any manner
that occurs to them, no matter how improbable, or
how far removed from the truth.   He, like ourselves, had never travelled that route before; yet
whenever we asked him the name of a place, he
called it something which suited his fancy at the
moment, and sometimes gave it the name of
another place which we knew to be twenty miles
off.   Argelez, the place we were most anxious to
reach, was the only one he confessed he did not
know; though he only acknowledged his ignorance
so far as to say, that he did not at that moment
recollect the name; and we should certainly have
driven through it, weary as we were, had we
not asked a boy in the street what place we had
come to.

I have seldom been more disappointed, than on
reaching this dirty little town, in the midst of so

beautiful a valley. The thing one most longs for, after such a journey, is plenty of water for a good refreshing wash. But this is seldom to be met with at the inns in this part of France; and that of Argelez was more than usually deficient. We were shown into an apartment, half sitting and half bed-room, with a floor black and filthy, on which it was loathsome even to tread; and such a mockery of washing apparatus—a little basin, into which one could not plunge more than one hand at once, without sending all the water out; and, as is universally the case in France, no soap. Where to recline for rest was the next consideration; for there were chairs of every shape and kind, except what belonged to cleanliness and comfort: yet with all this, there were such gay and even elegant hangings to the beds and windows, that it was necessary to keep perpetually gazing upwards to escape disgust. How much would one be willing to give, under such circumstances, for a re-freshing wholesome cup of tea! This luxury, however, is rarely to be had, and seldom in such weather even a draught of milk in the after part of the day. Trout and eggs are the only palatable things one meets with. The rest is all stewed meat, or vegetables fried in lard; and the former

M

is often covered up with thick sauce of the consistency of treacle, and sometimes I have seen it equally thick, and green.

For the people at the inn, I must say, they did their best to make us comfortable; and after making a tolerable meal of eggs and trout, we walked out in the cool of the evening—if cool it might be called. By the light of a cloudless moon, we traced a woody path along the side of the hill which rises immediately behind the town; and a beautiful sight it was, to see the mountains, some silvered over with the moon's soft radiance, and others reposing in the deepest shadow. While my companions sat down to rest, I wandered alone by the side of a chestnut wood; and such was the clearness of the moonlight, and the dryness of the soft still air, that I should scarcely have recollected night was coming on, but for a troop of wild and witch-like women, with their mules laden with charcoal, who asked me if I was not afraid.

The usual route, in making the tour on which we had set out, is to go from Argelez to Pierre-fitte, a distance of about four miles, and from thence to Cauterets. This had been our original intention; but Mr. Ellis having already suffered so much from the excessive heat, we felt at a loss how to dispose of ourselves, and longed for nothing so much as a place where we could be cool and quiet.

Hoping to escape the full power of the sun, we set out early to walk to Pierrefitte, on the following morning; but the heat was even then so great in the valley, that I was obliged to stop under almost every tree, to enjoy a transient respite from its burning rays. Yet it was impossible, even under such circumstances, to be insensible to the beauties of the scene; for the rustling corn, now nearly ripe, was waving by the side of the road,—the haymakers were busy at their work,—while troops of Spaniards were driving their mules along this route, which leads by the way of Gavarnie, into Spain.

When at last we arrived at Pierrefitte, we found the inn there little better than the one at Argelez, and the breakfast altogether most repulsive. The dish I chose was pigeon, trusting to the inoffensive nature of these birds. Here the birds, however, formed but a small proportion of the whole affair; for they were lean and small, yet stuffed out with a mixture of garlic, and other abominations, and floating in a sea of lard.

The day we spent at Pierrefitte was so intensely hot, that although I knew there was a splendid view from the side of the opposite hill, scarcely

244　　　SUMMER AND WINTER

rivalled by any in the Pyrenees, I dared not
venture one step from the door of the comfortless
inn, where we spent the remainder of the day,
until released from our prison, by the arrival,
about four o'clock, of the diligence for Luz, to
which place we had decided to proceed, in the
hope that it would afford the sort of peaceful
retreat we were so much in want of.

Almost immediately after leaving Pierrefitte,
we entered a mountain gorge, perhaps the most
sublime and astonishing of any amongst the Pyrenees. At the entrance of this pass, the road is
hemmed in between a perpendicular mass of bare
red rock, and the cool refreshing waters of the Gave,
flowing almost level with the path. This, however,
soon rises to such a height, that it becomes nothing less than appalling to look down into the
abyss, where the torrent, there foaming and impetuous, works its way between stupendous masses
of smooth black rock, sometimes shelving sheer
down, and at others projecting over the bed of the
roaring waters. The road which is hewn out of
this solid mass, winds sometimes at one side of the
chasm, and sometimes at the other; and the
different bridges of marble, by which it is crossed,
look most frightful for the ponderous diligence,
drawn by six horses, three abreast, which work

their zigzag way, often at a thundering pace, where the road is not broad enough for two carriages to pass, and the view intercepted every two or three yards, by enormous blocks of stone forming portions of the mountain, along whose side this wonderful way is cut.

Perhaps the most astonishing feature in this route, is that another road is now being constructed lower down in the chasm, and apparently hewn out almost under the old one. Some dreadful accidents have suggested the idea of this improvement; but it seemed to me, that nothing less than the genius of Buonaparte could have devised and carried into effect the work that is here begun. A better idea may be formed of its character and situation, when I add, that the first workmen employed upon it, had to be let down and suspended by ropes; and many of them spend the whole of every day, hammering and toiling on the sloping side of a precipice of smooth stone, from whence they look directly down into such a gulf, as I, at five times the distance, was unable to look at without horror. It was a melancholy spectacle, to see amongst the men thus employed, and who in the hottest part of the route were boring and blasting the solid iron stone, poor women assisting them by carrying their heavy tools; while in another part, where masonry was begun, they were carrying stones and mortar on their heads, and climbing barefoot up the stony path.

We were not sorry to find the road so steep that all were obliged to get out and walk; as by this means we could see better into the depth, where the blue waters of the stream were hurrying on their way; and beautiful was the little Eden which in one particular spot spreads out before the view, like a sort of waking dream; for the contrast in the scene appears almost too sudden to be real. It is where the mountains just leave space enough for a smooth green valley, through which the same river meanders for a while at perfect rest, between low green banks of velvet sward.

In the course of little more than an hour, we emerged entirely from the gorge into the valley, or basin, as it is often called, of Luz, as beautiful, though much less extensive than, the valley of Argelez. If the traveller has ever heard the little town of Luz described, he may know when he reaches it, by the many silvery streams which hasten through and past it, to join the river on the other side of the valley, immediately after it has swept past the foundation of the rocks on which is built the pretty little town of St. Sauveur, about the distance of a mile from Luz. Gave being the generic

name for rivers in this region of the world, it is
a better distinction to say, that this is the Gave de
Pau, which takes its rise from the cascades of Gavarnie, and sweeps, a prouder stream, past the foot
of the old chateau of Henry of Navarre, at Pau.

Our first view of the valley of Luz convinced us
that this was indeed the place of refreshment and
repose we were in search of. The calm of a lovely
evening was then spread over the scene; while the
fertility of its soil, the silvery flow of its thousand
streams, the summits—sometimes golden, and
sometimes purple—of the surrounding mountains,
with the innumerable villages, cottages, hanging
woods, and cultivated plots of ground, gave it an
aspect of grandeur, yet at the same time of plenty
and fertility, beyond what we had before beheld.

Nor must I forget, as unimportant in our circumstances, the unfailing kindness of good old
Madame Cazaux, a respectable widow lady, who
keeps the principal hotel in Luz. She may be
known by her honest and benevolent countenance,
her close white cap with long lappets and plain
black ribbon tied round it; but chiefly by her singular figure, presenting the outline of a substantial
cone, her waist being considerably broader than
her shoulders. It is a thousand pities her inn is
not a little cleaner; but one forgets the floors and

248   SUMMER AND WINTER

furniture in the good wholesome English dinners
she provides; and one forgives still more, because
she has a veritable kettle, and something like respectable tea.

Singular as the outline of this good lady's figure
may at first appear, it is less striking in France,
than it would be with us; because the ambition of
exhibiting a small waist, or even a waist at all,
seems never to have reached these people: and
the shapelessness of the female figure may perhaps
be one reason, why a shawl, both in hot weather
and cold, both for rich and poor, both in-doors
and out, when at rest, as well as when taking
exercise,—is considered so indispensable an article
of clothing. Even on Sundays, when better dressed
than usual, and often when the weather is intensely
hot, the French servant will mount her last new
shawl upon her old one; and in all departments of
their work, even cooking, they may be seen enveloped in their shawls.

On the evening of our arrival at Luz, we walked
to the top of a little hill, crowned with the ruins
of a hermitage, and jutting out into the valley,
so as to command a view, not only of the entrance
of the gorge through which we had passed, but
of the two other defiles which terminate in the
basin of Luz—that of Gavarnie, through which

flow the foaming waters of the Gave,—and that of Baréges, presenting a less lovely aspect, from the dreadful ravages to which it is subject, when the winter floods have swollen the wilder and more furious Bastan, whose torrent mingles with the Gave in the valley of Luz.

Well might the hermit, if such a being did ever really occupy the rudely constructed building on this little hill, have sought this situation for its beauty and repose.   Nothing I have ever seen and felt, or perhaps shall ever see and feel again, can surpass this lovely scene, for the perfect picture of peace presented by its evening aspect. If one requisite for the enjoyment of peace be a sense of security, we find it here, in the majestic mountains rising on every hand, some to the height of six or seven thousand feet above the level of the verdant plain or hollow, which lies before you, extending to the distance of about two miles in length, and one in breadth. If in order to calm the stirrings of anxiety and apprehension, which the accustomed habits of the world have rendered a second nature, it is necessary for our peace, that we should see around us the industry of man, facilitating the produce of a fruitful soil, we have it here in more than ordinary perfection ; for not only in the valley, but far up the sides of these majestic mountains,

M 3

250   SUMMER AND WINTER

at an altitude never reached by the cultivation of colder climes, are thousands of little barns and cottages, their white gables gleaming out from clumps of tufted wood; and villages, with their little rustic churches, sometimes half buried in the deep ravines; at others, standing out like fairy citadels, on the point of some bold promontory, which catches the beams of the declining sun. And then the rich deep woods with which some of the lateral hills are crowned, and the patches of different kinds of cultivation, extending to an almost miraculous height, all different in their tints, yet all blending into a beautiful mosaic, in perfect harmony with the colouring of a southern climate. If again, there is a craving in the human mind for something beyond what belongs to the bare notion of utility, a craving which perhaps destroys our peace more than all the actual necessities of life, for something to fill, and satisfy, and render perfect, the enjoyment of the spiritual part of our nature, we are surely brought nearest to it in a situation like this, when the mind is impressed with conceptions of the boundless power, and equally boundless beneficence of its Creator.

I am aware that this is not religion, and that the requirements of Christian duty may direct our steps to paths of a far different nature. I am aware, also, that difficult, or even ordinary and obscure as these paths may at first appear, He to whom all things are possible, may diffuse around them an attractiveness, and a beauty, as far surpassing all material excellence, as spiritual enjoyment is raised above that which belongs merely to the body; but I still think it has so pleased the Creator of the universe, to endow the mind of man with an intuitive sense of the loveliness and magnificence of nature—a sympathy which lets in the power of beauty, as it were a flood upon the soul: and I believe it is good that the spirit should be thus refreshed, and consistent with the wise purposes of God, that the hills, and the streams, and the verdant earth, and the fertility of the smiling landscape, with the calm of evening spread over it, should give us afresh to rejoice in his goodness, and to feel that there is such a thing as peace, even in this world, where the repose we are all in want of, is so often and so fatally destroyed by our own tumultuous passions.

Nor is it the smiling landscape below, or the sublime, untrodden heights of the mountains above, which constitute the sole interest of this view. The scene is diversified by many vestiges of antiquity, which carry back the thoughts to former times, and thus form a link of connexion between

the present and the past. One of these, a very
ancient ruin, said to be of Roman origin, stands on
an almost perpendicular mass of bold bare rock,
rising like an island in the green valley, and situated
as if to guard the entrance into that of the Bastan.
It is called the Fort of St. Marie; and not the
least interesting portion of its history is, that it
was once occupied by the English, led here by the
Black Prince when his court was at Bordeaux, and
much of this part of France was subject to his
sway. But the most perfect of the many ancient
buildings to be found in this neighbourhood, is a
large old church in the centre of the town of Luz,
formerly belonging to the Knights Templars, who
held rich possessions in this part of France. At
first this building, with its high surrounding wall of
massive architecture, strikes you as being more
like a prison than a church, and you are at a loss
to account for its turreted walls, high towers, loop
holes, and strongly defended windows; but all is
explained, when you learn that it belonged to those
proud warriors of the cross. While we trod the
ancient pavement, with a little girl to run before us
and chatter about the "jolie" chapel, with its altar
adorned with flowers, before which one solitary
peasant woman was kneeling, a strange contrast
was presented to our minds between its present

and its former state,—between its appropriation as a place of prayer by the simple peasantry of the valley of Luz, and its commanding position in the surrounding country, when the stately gown of its warrior priests, was accustomed to be worn above the armour that defied the world.

Here for the first time we saw that separate door let into a low part of the wall, by which alone the miserable Cagots were permitted to enter any of the churches. One cannot reside long amongst the Pyrenees, without hearing much of this singular and separate race of people, though they are seldom to be seen by the mere traveller, on account of their number being greatly decreased, and also because the remnants of their race occupy, with few exceptions, the most remote and inaccessible recesses of the mountains. That these people once constituted a numerous class, is sufficiently attested by many curious facts, while their isolated situation, cut off from all sympathy with the rest of mankind, is also evident from the abject and degraded state in which the residue of this wretched people is still found. It is said that they are below the average of human beings, both in their personal appearance and in their mental faculties,—abject, stupid, and little raised above the brute creation. Yet no instance has reached my knowledge, of their returning oppression with injury, or rewarding the injustice of years, with any of those momentary ebullitions of revenge, which belong to the history of almost every other class of despised or injured people.

It is impossible at the present day, to arrive at any authentic account of the origin of the Cagots, but that certainly appears the most probable, which supposes them to have been persons infected with leprosy, a disease imported into their country after the first crusade; and some writers even suppose that their name may have come from the word *gafo*, which in Spanish signifies leprous. This idea is also supported by the nature of the laws which were made for the purpose of separating them from the rest of the people; for besides the low door by which alone they were permitted to enter the churches, there was an edict of Gaston IV., by which particular houses in the most isolated situations, were assigned to their use; they were also excluded from all trades or occupations, except such as could be carried on in the open air, and were even forbidden to carry arms, and to walk barefoot in the streets or roads, under pain of having their feet bored through with hot iron. Of course they were not permitted to intermarry with the rest of the people; and one remnant of the contempt in which they were held, may still be found in the word cagot being applied as the lowest term of opprobrium amongst the country people.

St. Sauveur, the little Cheltenham of the Pyrenees, I have already said is situated about a mile from Luz, and you may walk there either by the green meadows and the hill of the hermitage, or by an excellent public road, leading to it by a marble bridge across the Gave. The town itself consists of a single street of well-built houses, standing on the edge of the ravine of the Gave, and in that direction which leads, by a road on the opposite side, to Gavarnie. It is chiefly the resort of nervous or fashionable invalids, who find its waters more mild, though I believe they are of the same nature as those of Baréges. It is, upon the whole, a more genteel residence than Luz, though to us it possessed fewer recommendations, there being no road through it, no view from it, and, according to report, nothing to be found in it, except the gossip of fashionable idlers, which, however, I cannot complain of, as the season of their arrival had not then commenced.

Both St. Sauveur and Luz possess the recommendation of being central points, from whence excursions can be made to many places of interest and attraction, lying at the distance of but one day's journey; so that you can set off early in

the morning, on sure-footed and well-practised
horses kept for the purpose, see as much as the eye
is capable of admiring, and the mind of enjoying
at once, and return in the evening to rest, at either
of these places.

The ascent of the Pic du Midi de Bigorre, is
an object of attainment at once the most difficult
and the most desirable from this situation.   Mr.
Ellis and I had promised ourselves the enjoyment
of the view from this mountain, which from its
peculiar position, standing out to the northward of
the general line of the Pyrenees, overlooks a vast
extent of country; including the fertile plains of
Bearn, of Gascony, and Languedoc.   We had here,
however, to remember, that we were travellers in
search of health, not merely of enjoyment; and as
the young friend who accompanied us took advantage of a beautifully clear morning to make the
ascent, we awaited the result of his experiment, in
order to be better able to judge of its practicability
for ourselves.   It was, perhaps, well that we did
so, though the day was most favourable, and
the path is said to be so good, that you can ride
even to the summit; but there was then so much
snow, that the party were obliged to dismount
and leave their horses.   They were five hours with
the burning sun upon their heads, and the reflec-

tion of the glaring snow in their faces; the effect
of which was sufficiently visible in the aspect they
presented on their return,—swollen, red, and some
of them almost black. They were the first travellers who had ascended that year, and the guides
were consequently obliged to make footsteps in the
snow for them to tread in. Our friend was well
satisfied that he had performed this exploit, but
the description he gave of the effect produced on
his head by the sunshine and the snow, rendered
us equally satisfied not to make the attempt; and
so much of our time had already been sauntered
away amongst the waterfalls and green shady walks
of Luz, that we could not find a day for ascending
the nearer mountain of Bergons, less difficult, but
also commanding a very extensive view.

Still, if the object of travel be to fill the mind
with the contemplation of what is great and glorious in the works of the Creator, and the heart
with feelings of contentment and repose, perhaps
we succeeded in this object as completely as we
could have done in any other way, by tracing out
the shady paths that wind around the sides of the
hills more immediately surrounding Luz, by watching the hay-makers at work in the valley, and by
resigning ourselves to the dreamy silence, and the
quiet beauty of these never-to-be-forgotten scenes.

258   SUMMER AND WINTER

I speak of the silence of this valley, for the perpetual murmur of its streams, is no interruption to
that soul-felt stillness, which the language of poetry
so often describes as silence.   It is well for those
who have youth and health to bear them on, or for
those whose object is to tell of the many points of
interest they have visited, to hurry on from place
to place, and crowd a world of images into the
recollection of a single day; but if the object is,
as I confess it has often been with me, to thank
God and be still, it is better to wander out alone,
or with one quiet companion, to trace the herdsman's path, to sit down when weary, to converse
with the peasants, to enter their cottages, to gather
wild flowers, and to watch, without excitement or
fatigue, the wonder-working process by which the
beauty of each day is developed by the morning
light, and folded back as it were, into the bosom of
nature, with the dewy fall of every night.

The circle of Gavarnie, the great world's wonder
of the Pyrenees, being within a few hours' journey
on horseback from Luz, and also being a less difficult excursion than that to the summit of the Pic
du Midi, the weather also being clear and beautiful
beyond description, we fixed our plans for visiting
it, and rose early on the appointed day, intending
to commence our journey before the heat of the

day. What then was our disappointment on looking out, to see the morning dark and drizzling,
with a north wind, and a cold hazy fog, like many
of our spring mornings on the north-east coast of
England. Our guide, however, assured us it
would clear away by the middle of the day, and
we mounted our horses, and set off in company
with a lady and gentleman from Normandy.

The almost unrivalled sublimity of the route
to Gavarnie, commences on leaving St. Sauveur.
The road then rises to a frightful height above the
black precipitous rocks which hem in the deep blue
waters of the Gave; while the road, dwindling to
a mere bridle path, winds through the defile with
dark threatening mountains almost overhanging
it on either side. In one place is a scene of
peculiar horror; and in consequence of the many
frightful accidents which have taken place in this
part of the road, a wall has been built to protect it
where it curves into a hollow of the mountain;
while all the way beneath it, to the torrent foaming
at a far depth below, is a sort of grooved descent,
down which, it seems almost as if to look, would be
to fall. It is told as one of the legendary wonders
of the place, that in this very spot the peasants of
the country once overcame a troop of Spanish
banditti, and hurled them headlong into the abyss;

and there is a rude tablet placed in the protecting wall, to commemorate the almost miraculous exertions of a priest, who on one occasion,
rushed down this awful descent, and nearly succeeded in saving the lives of two young men who
had missed their footing, and fallen from the road.
The stream, however, was too powerful, and both
were drowned.

The route to Gavarnie becomes wilder and more
sterile as you advance, abounding in cascades, the
most insignificant of which, surpass some of the
most celebrated in the neighbourhood of the
English lakes.   We passed one to our right, called
the Cascade of the Four Mills, and there, on the
bleak side of a mountain, without cultivation, without a tree, and apparently without a road, stood
four of those little, lowly, and primitive looking
mills, one above another, up the course of a magnificent waterfall, which looked as if, with some
freak of its fantastic spray, it might sweep them
all away at once.   Nothing is more striking in
passing along this defile, than the perfect solitude
which its aspect presents.   Few houses are to be
seen, few peasants, and scarcely any animals, either
domestic or wild.   The foaming Gave alone seems
to be instinct with life, and even that has all the
terrors of an awful death for those who may ven-

ture too near its rocky bed. The first time you cross the torrent, is by the bridge of Scia, built, like all the others we had passed, of marble. The descent to it is by a frightfully steep and zigzag path, which brings you at once upon this comparatively frail structure, thrown at an amazing height above the torrent, just where its waters are the most tumultuous, where enormous blocks of granite intercept its course, and where masses of shattered pine, and sometimes whole trees are seen, driven onward and dashed against the rocks by the fury of the pent-up stream, whose roar is like the bellowing of thunder.

It is a pity to have one's feelings of the sublime interrupted by the ridiculous; yet I cannot think of the bridge of Scia, without recalling a most romantic story in a French guide-book, where a tale is told of some fancied Lady Clara, who, seated by the side of this bridge, repeated the celebrated soliloquy of Hamlet, "To die—to sleep,"—and then cast herself into the gulf. The ridiculous of the story is, that the French writer, after describing the scene in the most affecting manner, gives the commencement of the soliloquy in the following words, "*Todie toslip.*" Might not this, with the many other embellishments of language of the same description, which one occasionally meets with, operate as a useful caution against the too frequent use, perhaps I might say abuse, of other languages than our own?

As the day of our excursion advanced, it made no progress towards improvement. Not one mountain peak was to be seen. Yet giving up the summits of the mountains, and that is unquestionably a great portion of the sublime, I confess I have often thought, that when the clouds are low, the precipitous ravines, the dark sides of the hills, and the masses of irregular and broken crag immediately around you, are seen to the greatest advantage. At all events, I journeyed on this day with my quiet pony, as much wrapped in admiration as I had ever been before, and perhaps more impressed with the shadowy gloom and deep majesty of the scenery around.

Before reaching the little village of Gedre, situated about half the way to the great circle, the valley becomes much wider, and cultivated fields, and human habitations, once more enliven the scene. At this village, opposite the auberge, or perhaps I ought to call it the hotel, both horses and guide make an equally determined stop. It seems to be an understood thing that you will descend, for crowds of bare-footed boys and girls are standing ready to dispute the honour, or rather the profit, of holding your horses. You are then conducted through the house, into a sort of garden at the back, to see a grotto, which, after all, is no grotto at all; but just a narrow passage of a torrent behind the house, where it has worked its way through a sort of rocky bed, which is quite open to the sky, and which presents nothing more rare or beautiful than you can find by yourself, along the course of any of the mountain streams. The only thing remarkable about it, is an enormous rock, which they show you as having been forced out of the bed of the torrent during one of the storms which work such terrible devastation in this valley.

Beyond Gedre all cultivation again ceases, and you enter a region not inappropriately denominated Chaos. No human habitation is now within the range of sight. The mountains on both sides are broken and precipitous, black and threatening, and look as if it had been in rage against each other, that, at no very distant period, they had hurled down their heavy burdens into the bed of the torrent at their feet. The masses which have fallen, are in some places mountains of themselves, sometimes so pitched upon the edge of others, as to leave a dark cavern below,—sometimes blocking up the way, so that the path winds around or beneath them,—and sometimes in the bed of the

torrent, so that the stream rushes foaming and
boiling with noisy wrath amongst the ruins by
which its course has been impeded.   It is scarcely
possible to look upon this scene without thinking of
Milton's description of the angels, who, in their
awful combat, seized on the mountains and hurled
them at each other.   Yet the most agitating sensation the scene inspires, is that with which you
look up, when it seems as if at least half the
remaining rocks, hanging suspended as it were
above your head, were on the point of making
another descent, and that before you can possibly
have time to pass.

   It was here, amongst this gloomy wilderness,
that we saw the richest profusion of that bright-
coloured rhododendron, which is called the rose of
Switzerland; and another feature in the scenery
struck us in this day's journey, which we had not
witnessed before.   From the elevation of the
mountains, and their consequent exposure to frequent damp and fog, the rocks, especially those
near to Gavarnie, are almost covered with a kind
of green and yellow moss, which blends so beautifully with the cold grey stone, and the pastures
below, as to form a sort of softening medium in
the picture, rendering the whole more beautiful
than pen or pencil can describe.

It seems strange to speak of pastures in such a region of desolation; yet no sooner have you emerged from Chaos, than in every spot where the rocks afford room for pasturage, not only flocks of sheep and goats were feeding, but nearer to the stream, meadows of high grass, rich with the colouring of innumerable flowers, were waving, even where the huts were so poor and so thinly scattered, that one wondered where could be the hands to secure the produce of the land.

In clear weather, a great part of the amphitheatre of Gavarnie is seen distinctly from Gèdre, but we went on, and on, the mists thickening around us as we attained a greater elevation; and nothing was to be seen in the distance but shadowy forms of mountains, and sheets of snow, gleaming white through the floating clouds. On reaching the little village of Gavarnie, a number of bare-footed women and girls run along with you for a distance of about three miles, to hold your horses when you alight. We had still another bridge to cross, which looked rather formidable to one accustomed only to ride along the safe and level roads of England, for it was composed only of four loose trunks of trees, without any protection on either side. Yet I had by this time attained to such a degree of confidence in my horse, that had it attempted to cross the river on

N

266   SUMMER AND WINTER

one, I should have believed it possible, though
I might have taken the precaution to dismount.
One of the bridges we had crossed before this, had,
I confess it, startled me a good deal. It was
broader and firmer, but at a much greater height,
and where the stream was rapid and tumultuous,
with no protection on either side. There came,
too, such a frightful blast when I was half way
over, that it seemed not unlikely to blow both my
horse and me into the torrent.

On arriving at the circle of Gavarnie, our guide,
who must have known all the way exactly how it
would be, exhibited every sign of surprise and disappointment, to find that we were still enveloped
in a cloud of mist, through which we could but
dimly discern the great waterfall, and saw nothing
of the high towers, two extraordinary rocks rising
from a mighty wall of marble, which crown the
summit of the central part of the amphitheatre.
We were indeed in a bleak, wet, uncomfortable
state, with nothing but beds of snow and white
mist before us, and a north wind and drifting rain
behind, looking into vacuity, and wondering what
we had come there to see. We amused ourselves,
however, with sauntering over the snow, which,
after the intense heat of the preceding day,

was attended with a strange, and to me novel sensation.

While engaged in this cheerless occupation, and when we had resigned every hope of beholding the wonderful spectacle we had come so far to see; to our inexpressible delight, the mists began to float away, the rain ceased, and though I cannot say that I have clearly seen the great circle of Gavarnie, yet I have seen, as in a passing dream, glimpses of the mighty rocks, the stupendous waterfall, with fields of snow, one above another, far up into the clouds, which afforded, I am strongly inclined to think, a more forcible impression of sublimity and awe, than I could have experienced under clearer and more sunny skies.

The circle of Gavarnie is so named from its being a sort of basin, enclosed on all sides but one; and at the time we saw it, the depth of the hollow was covered with a thick bed of snow. Of its perpendicular height an idea may be formed, by the great cascade, which falls over a surface of rock of fourteen hundred feet, thus forming the highest waterfall in Europe. On the first melting of the snows, and at the season when we beheld it, it is as magnificent in the volume of water which descends, as in its height. At the summit where

N 2

it rolls over the lofty precipice, two gigantic masses of rock stand forth, as if to guard its fall, which is not interrupted until the last quarter of the distance, where a bolder and darker mass separates the column of water, without the majestic line of the whole cascade being broken.

In order to form a correct idea of the beauty of the whole scene, it is necessary to imagine the rocks of the finest marble, streaked and variegated with every tint, from the deepest brown and purple, to the brightest yellow, sometimes varying even to rose colour. A perpendicular wall of this structure rises beyond the great waterfall; and down its side were precipitated twelve other waterfalls, while over its summit lay a vast field of snow: again another wall of marble, diversified with cascades, more faint and blue in the distance; and above all, the more majestic wall on which stand the two mighty rocks, called the towers of Marboré, crowned with eternal snows, and all formed of the most beautiful marble, fluted like the columns of a Grecian temple. The highest of these walls of marble rises at a perpendicular height of about one thousand feet above the amphitheatre, which is formed by the receding of the different beds of snow, in the form of a semicircle. To the right, the snows and the pinnacles of rock seem to mingle into a more chaotic mass; while, rising immediately from the bed of the hollow basin, are bold buttresses of the adjoining mountain, standing out like barriers to protect the whole; and over their perpendicular sides the most beautiful cascades were pouring, some of them like silver threads, making in all sixteen within the circle.

It is over this portion of the circle that the celebrated *Breche de Rolande* appears, a giant cleft in a solid wall of rock, about six hundred feet in height, said to have been made by the warrior from whom it derives its name, when he opened for himself a passage for his conquests over the Moors. Amongst the many wonders told of this more than mortal hero, he is said, after effecting this passage into Spain, to have reached, by one leap of his horse, the centre of the rocky defile, now called Chaos; and our guide actually stopped as we passed through it, to show us the mark of his horse's foot-print on the stone where he alighted.

The appearance of the circle of Gavarnie is very deceptive as to its actual extent. It seemed but a trifle to walk from where we stood at the entrance, to the base of the great waterfall; yet the guide told us it would take an hour to reach it: and I could the more readily believe him, when I re-

270   SUMMER AND WINTER

flected, that we could but just hear, from where we
stood, the hissing fall of that immense body of
water.   Later in the season, when the heats of
summer have prevailed with lengthened power,
this waterfall works for itself an archway, which
leaves a bridge of snow; and the waters then
form a sort of lake in the hollow of the circle, the
whole circumference of which is said to be about
ten miles.

We had not gazed long upon this wonderful
spectacle, when the atmosphere again became
thick and cloudy; and there seemed so little hope
of a clearer view, that we returned to the inn at
Gavarnie, not forgetting to station a boy to watch
and tell us if the mists cleared away, even for a
moment, during the time we dined.   He came
not, however, and we went after dinner to see a
little church at the outskirts of the village, situated
on the route which leads into Spain, by the
Porte de Gavarnie.   In this church are kept, as
curious relics, twelve skulls of the Knights Templars, who were beheaded at the time when their
order was proscribed.   They were taken, by a
little boy, out of a sort of corner cupboard, and
presented, in their decayed condition, a striking
picture of the impotence of human power, and the
transient nature of the glory of this world.

The settlement of our affairs with the landlady of the inn at Gavarnie, was a matter not easily accomplished; for it is in all such situations, where, from the remoteness of the place, and the length of the journey, the traveller has no other alternative than to take advantage of such accommodation as he may find, that the most unreasonable charges are made; and being generally made in the first instance as a sort of experiment, to try how much the stranger will give, a lengthened and most annoying altercation is the only means of escaping excessive imposition. The best method, and that which is always adopted by experienced travellers in this part of France, is to make a bargain beforehand for whatever may be required, and by no means to settle down in an apartment for the night, without first stipulating for its price.

Finding the arrangement of these affairs at Gavarnie was likely to be a very lengthened business, and being a little weary of the fatiguing motion of a horse, scrambling, as they must, along a great part of this route, over rough and slippery rocks, I set off to walk on the road back to Gèdre, and most thoroughly enjoyed my solitary ramble, notwithstanding my path was often interrupted by streams, or rather torrents, which it nearly baffled my ingenuity to cross. My way was as silent as it was solitary, for I met only one or two peasants, who condoled with me on being on foot and alone; a wild-looking Spaniard; and, amongst a mass of rocks, a perfect personification of Meg Merrilies— a tall, gaunt, but somewhat handsome woman, contending with a mule, apparently as wild and wilful as herself.

I had forgotten that the defile of shattered rocks was on the side of Gèdre nearest to Gavarnie: what then was my surprise to find that I was entering upon the awful region of Chaos alone at the close of the day, with no human habitation, no living creature within the reach of my sight, or the sound of my voice—nothing but the roaring torrent at my feet—nothing but the dark masses of rocks, their deep shadows and frowning summits around and above me. I need hardly say, that I loitered until the rest of the party came in sight, and then pursued my way at such a distance from them, that I could see them behind me winding round the point of every rock I passed.

On descending from Gavarnie to the more sheltered and lower regions of St. Sauveur and Luz, we found ourselves in a milder and clearer atmosphere; besides which, the weather had really changed; so that we had the mortification on looking back, to see the beams of the setting sun reflected in all their radiance on the snowy summits of some of the mountains we had left.

After the fatigues of this day, which were nothing less than ten hours' riding over roads which in many parts I should previously have thought it impossible for a horse to travel, yet over the whole of which mine had never made a false step,—I did not find myself on the following morning much disposed to retrace my steps. Mr. Ellis, however, was more enterprising; and the day being beautifully clear, he rode again to Gavarnie, and was amply rewarded by a perfect view of the whole amphitheatre, which first opened before him on turning round a hill, before arriving at Gèdre. It was a day which brought to light all the most delicate and exquisite colouring of the marble rocks, the blue course of the distant waterfalls, and the sublimest heights covered with trackless snow. Instead of the sombre shadows and majestic masses of undefined and gloomy rock which we had seen the day before, the whole was spread before him like the magnificent structure of some vast temple, where light and beauty were inconceivably blended with impressions of magnitude and space.

On the evening of this day we had fixed to leave Luz, intending to walk as far as Baréges, that we might be ready to cross the Tourmalet on the following morning, in company with the courier, who, during the summer season, conveys letters by this route, from Baréges to Bagnères de Bigorre.

Baréges is situated higher up in the mountains, at the distance of about two leagues from Luz. It was late in the evening when we took leave of our kind hostess, and turned into the valley of the Bastan, with the hope of reaching Baréges before nightfall. The first part of the road is a beautiful avenue of trees, with the ruins of St. Marie to the left, and smooth green meadows, sprinkled with cottages, sloping down to the side of the torrent which sweeps past the foot of the rock on which this ancient fort is built. With the last glow of sunset on the scene, we could form little idea of the region of desolation upon which we were entering; and as the twilight in this climate is of such short duration, that night comes on before you are aware of its approach, we soon found ourselves travelling by no other light than that of stars and glow-worms. We were, however, able to perceive that the valley, or gorge, had become narrower, less peopled, and that the torrent foamed over a more rocky and precipitous bed.

It is in this valley, more than any other of the Pyrenees, that the inhabitants have to dread the ravages, not only of the winter, but the summer storms. In vain has the ingenuity of man erected barriers against the devastating floods : every winter large portions of the road are washed away; and there are times when the loss of life and property in the neighbourhood of Baréges is most awful and tremendous.

It is perhaps at all times a gloomy place. The town is hemmed in between the threatening and angry Bastan on one side, and the steep side of a sterile mountain on the other; while the scantiness of vegetation all around, and the number of cripples, and other invalids, who throng the place, for the benefit of its far-famed baths, are sufficient of themselves to fill the mind with impressions of melancholy and distress.

The waters of Baréges are stronger than any other in the Pyrenees, and its baths are the resort of persons of all classes afflicted with rheumatism, gout, and other diseases; but above all, they are celebrated for the cure of gun-shot wounds. To soldiers thus afflicted the baths are administered gratis, and there are frequently not less than eight hundred in the place, with an equal number of visitors, amongst whom those of the poorest class, have appropriated exclusively to their use, a sort of subterranean bath, over which there is a public promenade. It is, perhaps, more necessary at

Baréges, than at any other place, that the baths
should be under government inspection, on account
of the insufficiency of their number to supply the
increasing demand.   Great regularity, however, is
practised in the adjustment of these matters, under
the direction of the medical inspectors appointed
and paid by government.

Owing to the steepness and length of the ascent,
it was nearly ten o'clock when we arrived at
Baréges, and we had consequently to experience
the usual advantage which is taken of travellers in
such circumstances. In the hotel where we stopped,
eight francs were asked for one bed; and it was not
until we had disputed half an hour with six women,
each trying to talk faster and louder than the rest,
that we succeeded in obtaining two beds for four
francs.

The next morning, a little after six, we mounted
our horses, to accompany the courier on a journey
of eight hours over the Tourmalet, by the way of
Grip, and the valley of Campan, to Bagnères de
Bigorre.   The morning was unusually clear, and
we then saw what a sterile and desolate scene
we had reached the previous night. Nothing, in
short, could form a greater contrast to the fertile
plain and happy-looking peasantry of Luz. Here
there was little to be seen on the bleak sides of

the mountains, but here and there a rude and miserable dwelling, with a scanty patch of cultivation; while the single street of the town was thronged with wounded soldiers, and cripples of almost every description.

The road is a perfect scramble on its first commencement, and nothing better than a mountain path all the way, though less slippery and dangerous than many we had travelled. For some time our way was the same as to the Pic du Midi, which reared its proud crest a little to our left, and of which the Tourmalet, six thousand feet in height, appears from that position to form a part. We soon left all trace of cultivation behind, finding no human habitation but those shepherds' huts, entirely deserted in the winter, which always made me think of the kraals of the Africans, being composed of six or eight low-roofed cottages, with sheds and yards for the cattle fenced in from the wolves and bears, which not unfrequently visit these solitudes.

On our right we passed the entrances of two of the most wild and dreary valleys of the Pyrenees, said to be the hiding-places of the Cagots,—those of Lienz and Escabous, one of which presents a frightful barrier to this passage in the winter, being the bed of a torrent little less furious and destructive

than the Bastan, into which it pours. The stream,
when we saw it, was small and insignificant; but
it had scooped for itself a deep shelving groove in
the side of the mountain, within which the path
was extremely narrow, and the descent immediately
below, both vast and steep.

About seven o'clock we met a party returning
from the Pic, who had been to see the sunrise on
its summit, and a magnificent sight they must
have had. One of them, a lady, was carried in a
kind of chair, with six bearers, allowing for three
changes. I cannot say I envied her; for if the
ascent is difficult on foot, how painful must it be
to be carried at this expense of human strength!
It is not more than seven years ago, that most of
the excursions we heard of, even that to Gavarnie,
which must be a distance of fifteen miles, were
made in this manner; and so light and sure is the
footing of these mountaineers, that they are capable
of bearing the traveller in this manner up to the
summits of mountains much more difficult of ascent
than the Pic du Midi.

Before reaching the summit of the Tourmalet,
the road, though neither rugged nor extremely
steep, becomes so wearisome by its continued zigzag course, that we dismounted, and walked a
considerable distance. We had now a range of

rocks, like giant battlements, on one side of us, and the snowy crags in the direction of the Pic on the other; but the mountain over which we passed was comparatively smooth and verdant all the way; so much so, that far above several patches of snow which still lay in the hollows, we could see flocks of sheep, and goats, and cattle, grazing on the green slopes amongst the scattered rocks.

On gaining the highest summit, we saw before us an altered scene. Greenness, and beauty, and fertility, with the mountains above Grip and Campan lovely and varied in their colouring, but far inferior in magnificence and grandeur to those we were leaving behind. On looking back, the long bold vista of the valley of the Bastan stretched in sight, the thousand pinnacles of its surrounding heights fiercely starting into the sky, as if to threaten the presumptuous traveller who might pass their trackless solitudes. Far in the distance we could still see the gentler outlines and the shadowy forms which had made the boundary of our horizon in the vale of Luz; and over all the sun was shining with that magnificence of splendour, which brings every crag, and cleft, and shelving precipice to light, and which, falling on the pathless snows, converts them into fields of glittering gems.

On descending the side of the Tourmalet to

Grip, the path, after winding for some distance
over a perfectly smooth sward, becomes extremely
rough and difficult; and Mr. Ellis's horse having
proved an exception to the general rule of safe-
footed animals, we were glad to find ourselves
approaching human habitations, hoping that the
village of Grip might not be far distant.   The
first of these was in the little hamlet of Trasme-
sagues, composed entirely of the cottages of herdsmen, whose chief support in these mountain habitations, is the milk of their own herds, and the
cheeses of their own manufacture.   The size of
this establishment is considerable, when we see all
its sheds, and yards, and roofs of huts, but little
elevated above the ground; and an idea of the
industry of its inhabitants, as well as their prosperity, was indicated by the number of beautifully
polished brass vessels for their milk, hung out in
the air, and glittering in the sun.

From this place we found it still a long and
weary descent to Grip, near which are three celebrated waterfalls, one of them scarcely rivalled
in beauty by any in the Pyrenees.   There is
also a magnificent view of the summit of the Pic,
and the adjoining mountains, from this side; but
they were soon lost as we descended, and we were
not sorry to shelter ourselves from the burning

rays of the sun, in the little inn at Grip, where an excellent breakfast, with the never-failing trout, refreshed us for the rest of our journey to Bagnères de Bigorre.

CHAPTER X.,

BAGNERES DE BIGORRE—MARBRORIE—VARIETIES OF
KNITTING—PRIORY OF ST. PAUL—EXCURSION TO
THE LAC BLEU—VISIT OF LAMARTINE TO BAG-
NERES — MOONLIGHT RAMBLES — EXCURSION TO
L'HERIS.

BAGNERES de Bigorre is a pretty little town,
and the only clean one I have seen in France.
How far in this respect it may bear an examination in detail, I am not able to say; but the many
limpid streams of crystal water that run along the
sides of its streets, the cheerful and pleasant aspect
of its houses, many of them ornamented with
festoons of vine, and the neat and industrious
character of its inhabitants, render its appearance
to a stranger more inviting than that of any other
town in the neighbourhood of the Pyrenees. It is
a place of delightful resort to the French, and
scarcely less so to the English whose habits have
assimilated with those of France, because it contains within itself during the season of the waters,

a little world of amusement and of fashion; because amongst its many beautiful promenades, there are few involving either difficulty or danger; and because it has a public place called *Les Coustous*, shaded by regular rows of trees, and surrounded by handsome shops and houses, where all kinds of marchands exhibit their tempting treasures, and where the many idlers whom illness or curiosity brings to the neighbourhood of the mountains, can loiter away their summer's evenings.

It has its *Frascati* too, comprising all that is Parisian on a miniature scale; where the amusements and the gaiety which reign throughout the season, are surpassed only by those of some of the principal cities of France.

All these, however, to some minds appear but ill-assorted with the grandeur of mountain scenery, and more especially with the different stages of bodily disease, under which a large proportion of these gay visitors are suffering.

Although the lively and modern appearance of Bagnères presents little which carries back the mind to past ages, it has, notwithstanding, many just claims to antiquity, and was evidently well known to the Romans, from the different inscriptions which have been found relating to its baths, and expressive of the thankfulness of these con-

querors of the world, for the benefit of its waters.
Its two chief points of modern distinction are, its
manufacture of the marble of the Pyrenees into the
most beautiful articles of household furniture, and its
knitting.   For the former there are three large establishments, well worth the attention of the stranger;
and if to purchase some of the most beautiful tables,
pedestals, mantel-pieces, slabs, or articles of a more
curious and merely ornamental nature, be an
object of desire, the proprietor engages to pay the
carriage of any such article to Bordeaux, and to
answer for its being safely shipped from that place.
Unskilled as I am in the nature and character of
marbles, I am unable to say which of the specimens we saw was the most valuable or rare.   All
were to me beautiful,—the price extremely reasonable, and the variety so great, that had I been a
purchaser, the difficulty would have been where to
choose.   The only perfectly white marble found in
the Pyrenees, and that which supplies much of the
statuary in the Gardens of Paris, as well as adorns
the chamber of the legislative assembly, is found at
a considerable distance from Bagnères, in the
valley d'Ossau.

The other manufacture to which I have alluded,
is of a much humbler nature, and is carried on by
the women of this place, to an almost incredible

degree of perfection. Whether it is from the beautiful texture of the Spanish wool, which is here easily obtained, or the native ingenuity of the people, I am unable to say; but certainly some of the shawls and scarfs of their knitting, are scarcely to be rivalled by the finest lace. Counterpanes, however, are the chief articles of trade, and these are light and gauzy, yet extremely durable, and made in all patterns, and of every colour. Besides which, they knit the most beautiful fancy aprons, mittens, bags, and indeed every article of dress, and many of ornament. It is true they are in some measure indebted to the bright colours of the wool, setting off their work to advantage, but their own skill deserves no small share of praise; for we see them seated at their doors, and even walking on the public roads, with the most disengaged and easy air imaginable; while a curious border of the richest flowers, or the flowing drapery of a graceful shawl, is growing between their fingers.

The situation of Bagnères is one which is generally considered as possessing many advantages, being a wide and fertile plain, extending on one side as far as Tarbes, and having the far-famed vale of Campan, with the vicinity of the mountains, on the other. It is also rich above all other towns of the Pyrenees, in lovely promenades; by which I mean those short excursions which can be enjoyed without fatigue.

One of these, and that which generally claims the first attention of the stranger, is the Camp de César, situated on a hill westward of Bagnères, and commanding a most extensive view, not only of the plain of Tarbes, and a vast tract of country beyond, but of a noble range of the neighbouring mountains; while Bagnères, with its pretty houses, its gardens, its shady walks, and woody slope rising behind the town, lies immediately beneath.

But it would be endless to tell of the many fertile valleys, old chateaux, and points of view which are visited from this place, and which doubtless owe some portion of their celebrity to the idleness or curiosity of the many visitors who throng the place, who, in some seasons, are said to have been as many as 8,000, and to whom anything in art or nature would be a welcome resource, if it furnished them with an excuse for a pic-nic, or an excursion. Indeed there is no place amongst the mountains, where any object to live for through the day, appears in such demand as at Bagnères. Perhaps I ought to make an exception of a single instance at Cauterets, which occurred under the shrewd observation of our botanical friend, when pursuing his researches in the neighbourhood of that place. He was a good deal annoyed by a sauntering man, who followed him with a drum, and while stooping for his plants, it was not the most agreeable accompaniment to have this man beating his drum close beside him. He asked him at last why he did so. *" Pour passer le temps,"* was the Frenchman's very characteristic reply.

Our arrival at Bagnères in the last week of June, was long before the commencement of the fashionable season, which is later here than elsewhere. We had been received with a true English welcome by an amiable family from Devonshire, whose acquaintance we had made at Pau. In their company we paid our first visit to the Priory now commonly called the Chateau de St. Paul, situated in the valley of Campan, about four miles from Bagnères.

This delightful situation was originally selected by the Abbé Torné, preacher to Louis XV., when renouncing his episcopal dignities, he fled from the vanities of the world, to terminate his days in this peaceful retreat. The many trees, some of majestic growth, which now surround the mansion, are said to have been planted by him; and the terraces shaded with stately poplars, which form so conspicuous a feature in the scene, are attributed to the Abbé's peculiar taste.   Nor was his talent for improvement confined to what was merely orna- mental.   The situation of St. Paul is one of the most tantalizing that can well be imagined to the cultivator of the soil.   Placed on a promontory of ground between two lovely rivers, the sound of whose refreshing waters may always be heard from this position, it was wholly destitute of water, until the ingenuity of the Abbé conducted from the summit of a neighbouring mountain, into his own grounds, a stream which never fails, and which, being let off by lateral branches, renews the green- ness and luxuriance of the grassy slopes which extend from the chateau to the valleys on either side.   Thus it presents the picture of an island of fertility and beauty, immediately behind which, rise the more sterile heights of a mountain, in some parts cultivated nearly to its summit, and in others broken into bold masses of grey rock; while farther still is a wide extent of dreary forest, once of stately pines, now almost entirely destroyed by fire.   Above this again, and towering to the skies, is the Pic du Midi, rearing its giant crest over the surrounding mountains.

Such is the noble back-ground of St. Paul.   At the foot of the eminence on which the chateau stands, is the road from Bagnères to Grip, and beyond that the verdant fields of the valley of Campan, watered by the beautiful river Adour, which runs through Bagnères to Bayonne, and which we had seen on the summit of the Tourmalet, in its infant state, just dropping from stone to stone, beneath a sheet of melting snow. If an idea should be formed by any one who had heard of the unrivalled beauties of the valley of Campan, from that part of it which lies between Bagnères and the village to which it owes its name, and which is situated within half a mile from St. Paul, it certainly would be attended with disappointment. At least it was so with me. The valley is fertile and *riante*, but flat and tame in comparison with those of Luz and Argelez, and the long range of mountains which form its eastern boundary, even with flowery L'heris amongst them, bear no comparison with many other ranges in the Pyrenees.

The valley of Lesponne, which opens into that of Campan immediately below St. Paul, is of a very different description. Here the surface of the ground presents every possible variety, from the greenest slope, to the boldest precipice of rock; from the gentlest undulations, to the most craggy heights; from the richest woods, to the most sterile wilds; and from the rugged outline of distant

o

mountains, to the pastoral scenery, the gardens,
the orchards, and the fruitful fields of the straggling
village on the banks of the stream, which, pouring
down from the waters of the Lac Bleu, flows
through this valley with a perpetual murmur, till
it joins the Adour at a short distance from St.
Paul.

The road from Bagnères to St. Paul is the most
attractive I have seen in France, because it winds
with the course of the river, and in many places is
delightfully shaded by trees.   It loses the rays of the
afternoon sun at an early hour of the day, in consequence of a high range of hills to the westward,
whose sides are clothed with the rich foliage of
chestnut woods.   About half the way, you pass the
old and ruinous monastery of Medous, much visited
by strangers, on account of its source of crystal
water which rises in the grounds, and which was
formerly celebrated for its miraculous power.

On the evening we first visited St. Paul, the sun
was just setting, and the mountains to the westward
of Lesponne were bathed in the richest tints of
purple and gold; except that Mont Aigu, a lofty
mountain higher up the valley, and remarkable for
its dark and sombre colouring, was already clothed
in the shadowy tints of evening.   Of all the habitations we had seen in France, St. Paul presented

the most welcome, the most inviting aspect. We approached through an avenue of plane trees, and found a long, spacious, but comparatively low building, literally embowered in trees, from between whose stately stems we looked down to the east and the west, into the two valleys I have described.

Nor was the interior of the chateau less attractive than its outward aspect. The most delightful blending of the elegance of France with the comfort of England, was to be found throughout. And the friends—but I must go no farther. It is enough to say, that with a delicacy which knows how to take into account the feelings of the obliged, as well as the pleasure of conferring an obligation, arrangements were afterwards made for our remaining in this delightful retreat through the rest of the summer months, and made in such a manner, as to render St. Paul in every respect the kind of home of which we were in need, and for which we might have sought in vain elsewhere.

The experience we had lately had of the effect of excessive heat upon the health of Mr. Ellis, convinced us that further travelling at this season was extremely undesirable. All the principal places of resort among the mountains, were crowded,

o 2

292   SUMMER AND WINTER

and consequently extremely expensive: Pau was
uninhabitable to northern constitutions on account
of its excessive heat; and the remote villages
which one fancies before seeing them must be so
pleasant at the foot of the mountains, require no
very particular inspection to be assured that no
English person could find a home in them.   But
St. Paul, even in the hottest weather, when a blaze
of sunshine fell around us, was always cool: from
its situation at the meeting of two valleys, it caught
the current of air from both; and the vicinity of
the mountains, with the constant flow of the two
rivers so near it, imparted a freshness to the air
more invigorating and more delightful than can
be described.

Indeed the difference of the atmosphere between
the mountains and the adjacent plains, is greater
than could be imagined, without a personal acquaintance with the peculiarities of the climate of
the Pyrenees.   In the valley of Campan, vegetation in the month of June, was little farther
advanced than it is in England at the same season.
The hay was not all gathered in, though that
appears less extraordinary, when one sees that the
people have to carry it all on their heads, and that
this is performed chiefly by women.   While the
cornfields were still green around St. Paul, we

heard that the harvest was all finished in the neighbourhood of Montauban, and even at Tarbes, a
distance of about fifteen miles, it was at least a
month earlier. The weather, which on our arrival
at Bagnères was intensely hot, assumed a more
variable character than that of which we complain
so much in England; for we seldom had more
than two or three days of heat, without its being
followed by thunder-storms, which in their turn
were succeeded by at least a week of cold; and
often when we could see through the opening in
the mountains to the northward, that the sunshine
was smiling on the plain of Tarbes, cold mists
were rolling over the hills around us; while the
atmosphere of St. Paul was certainly as cold
as we ever experienced in England during the
summer.

During our residence at St. Paul, we made many
excursions. One to the Lac Bleu was perhaps the
most memorable, from the singularity of the scenes
it afforded us an opportunity of beholding, and the
difficult ascent of the mountain beyond whose summit the lake is situated. We had heard much of
the Lac Bleu, but not being able to meet with any
one who had seen it, nor to learn any facts relating
to its distance or accessibility, we set out in a state
of happy ignorance of what we might meet with by

the way. As usual, the horses we had engaged at Bagnères, failed us at the appointed time, an evil which must always be calculated upon, and we were consequently several hours too late; for the mountain mists, which so frequently gather towards noon, by this delay had time to get the advance of us; but we jogged away at a brisk pace along the valley of Lesponne, too much occupied with its variety and beauty, to be very anxious how we might spend the remainder of the day.

In passing along this valley, Mont Aigu rears its dark summit immediately to the right; the forest of burnt pines forming part of a high range of mountains, runs to the left; and beyond these, the Pic du Midi towers high above them all. The air was then so clear, that we could have distinguished a goat on its topmost crag; and we could distinctly see a little hut of rude stones, erected there for the accommodation of two travellers, who spent several days on its summit, for the purpose of making scientific observations.

The valley, as we advanced, became wilder, the cottages less frequent, and cultivation more sparing, though the same beautiful stream still flowed beside our path. It seemed as if we were drawing near the end of the world—all was so still, and so shut in from human fellowship. At last no houses were to be seen, only those huts or kraals, built half in the ground, with low sloping roofs, for the shelter of the cattle,—but still the same stream, and a noble amphitheatre of mountains, amongst which we could not discover the least appearance of a passage. Our guide, however, conducted us across the stream, when we all rested on the green bank at the foot of a dark beech wood, through which we had to pass, and thus to make our way into another opening amongst the hills. The party persisted in mounting again, and trying the skill of their horses in threading the mazes of this thicket, which grew amongst large masses of slippery rock; but the ascent soon becoming alarmingly steep, and the rocks more precipitous, we thought it best to abandon our horses, and proceed the rest of the way on foot.

For some time after this our path was very pleasant. We entered upon a wide hollow valley, strewn with rocks which had fallen from the surrounding heights. The sun was shining without a cloud, though not without some of those insidious mists which already began to creep after us along the sides of the hills; but thus far they only seemed to add to the height and the sublimity of the craggy peaks above. Within the silent valley along which we trod, it seemed as if no human

296   SUMMER AND WINTER

foot had ever been before; yet even here was a
single shepherd's hut, most bleak and solitary, for
there was no tree in this vast wilderness, only shrubs
of rhododendron and beautiful wild flowers.

On our left there rose almost precipitously from
the plain, and towering at a far height into the
sky, vast ranges of those rocky piles so frequent in
the Pyrenees, and which constitute perhaps the
most striking feature in their scenery.   They consist of abrupt and broken crags, towering up in
peaky summits, often so cleft and shattered, as to
leave narrow gullies or ravines of enormous depth
between them.   They are composed of slaty rock
and marble, sometimes of the richest purple, tinged
with streaks of red and yellow.   The most beautiful aspect they present is when the brilliant sun-
light gleams in and amongst them, as it did this
day, glowing through their peaks and pillars, down
the sides of the mountain, where the grass lay,
even at that far height, like the richest velvet,—
where dark pines were growing, and where flocks
of sheep and goats were browsing in peace, looking
rather as if suspended against the side, than resting
on the mountain.

I am aware that description can do little towards
conveying an idea of such pictures, never to be
effaced from the memory of those who have beheld

them; for after all, it is from the atmosphere, the sunshine, the enchanting brilliancy of a southern climate, that the scenery of the Pyrenees is so rarely rivalled in its beauty.

To the right of the valley were the same lofty peaks, with a less precipitous ascent extending to them, yet still so steep and rugged, as to look, to my inexperienced eye, almost as inaccessible as the moon; and before us, a little to the right, the view was bounded by a torrent, which fell from an amazing height, and dashed its way through the hollow or basin below, down to the valley of Lesponne.

Immediately to the left of this cascade, the scene was lost in vapour; and for some time I was too much occupied to look up, with a violent throbbing in my head and temples, which on such occasions, while exposed to the blazing sunshine, was often very troublesome: when suddenly a shout from my companions aroused my attention, and I looked, and the mist had disappeared; and a mountain, the most sublime I ever beheld or imagined, appeared before us, apparently bending over our heads. It was probably the blending of the mist and the sunshine, which increased the extraordinary effect produced; for it appeared to be close upon us, yet reaching to the sky; and so clear and vivid was the blaze of light which fell upon its almost perpendicular surface, that every rock and cave, with all the blue slate and yellow marble, and green herbage on its vast extent of surface, looked as distinct as if reflected in a glass held up immediately before our eyes.

It was now time to commence our ascent to the right, and well it was that we all scrambled on in perfect ignorance of the distance or the difficulties of our way. All our past fatigues amongst the mountains had been mere pastime compared with this. I thought more than once, that I should have been obliged to give the matter up, and remain amongst the rhododendrons and coarse slippery grass; and had it not appeared still more difficult to get down again, than to get up, I might never have seen the Lac Bleu. The ascent was so steep, the grass so slippery, and the stones so loose and deceitful, that my only chance of safety seemed to be when I found the bed of some torrent, where the rocks were too large to give way.

In this manner we toiled on until four hours had elapsed from the time of leaving our horses: when joyful shouts, from the foremost of our party, announced that they had reached the lake; and, encouraged by their success, we soon found ourselves upon its banks. It is a basin, or tarn, in

a hollow at the top of a mountain, and surrounded by bare craggy peaks of the most curious
formation, within whose declivities the snow always
remains. The lake itself is an oval about two
miles in length. It is a solitary spot, with no
house, or tree, or living thing to be seen its vicinity, a stillness almost death-like reigning around.
It might be dreary, but for the rich warm colouring
of the rocks, the depth and stillness of the water,
and its intense blue, from whence it takes its
name. The surface is like an emerald sea; and
there is neither ripple, nor oar, nor shelving shore
where boat could be stranded, except in one particular spot, where we seated ourselves, and where
the torrent which had formed a sort of landmark
to us through the valley, pours down from the lake.

I never can forget the strangeness and the stillness of this place. We had time to give one
delighted survey of its beauties, and only one;
when a thin misty cloud, which had pursued us up
the mountain, overspread the whole; and though
it sometimes passed for a moment, so that we
could distinctly see a part, it grew thicker and
thicker, until we lost all the grand outlines of the
scene. Some of our party succeeded in reaching
a point from whence another lake can be seen, as
well as this, called the green lake; but this can

only be in fine weather. On the day of our
luckless exploit, we could see nothing but each
other, and that rather indistinctly.

Our guide, who really knew little about the
matter, had promised to take us by an easier way
back; and in spite of the fog, we at last set off
much refreshed by our dinner, and none of us
really the worse for our fatigue. In order to
pursue this new way, we crossed the stream, and
then turned round the side of the mountain immediately above the fall of the torrent, scrambling
along a path of jagged rock, so narrow as only to
admit of one foot being set down at once, with the
cascade thundering below us into a world of mist,
and a perpendicular rock immediately on our left.
This, however, was not the worst of our route; for
though the catching of our dress upon any of the
points of rock, might have precipitated us into the
bed of the torrent, by exercising a little care, there
was really no danger: but we soon after came to
hollows in the sides of the mountain, where beds
of snow and loose stones had slid down, and left no
footing. In one place, in particular, an immense
hollow, or groove of loose earth, almost perpendicular, with neither bush nor twig to lay hold of,
presented an obstacle which I thought it impossible
to surmount; nor was it until one of our party had

kindly made foot-prints in the slippery earth, that
I could attempt to pass. From the thickness of
the mist, too, our guide was often at a loss where
to lead us; while such was the deceitful nature of
the ground on which we trod, that often before one
foot had reached its place, the other had sent down
a whole bed of stones on which it had been resting, to thunder their way to the bottom of the
mountain.

Nor were these personal difficulties all we had
to excite uneasiness. A gentleman of our party,
who had gone in search of the Green Lake, had
lost his way in the mist; and though we had
called and waited for him a whole hour, he was
neither to be seen nor heard. He told us afterwards, when he had happily rejoined us in the
valley, that he had become completely bewildered
by the fog,—that when attempting to descend, he
had gone completely round a mountain, finding
nothing but impracticable precipices on every side;
but at last most providentially meeting with a
peasant, he was safely conducted by him to the
valley, where we all arrived in safety.

On reaching the hill side, where we had left our
horses, we found them all safe under the care of a
peasant, and were not sorry to mount them again;
for even the native trot was a luxury, after such

302   SUMMER AND WINTER

fatigue as we had experienced; and although the
cold mists were still around us, though not so
thickly as on the heights, we soon forgot both them
and our past difficulties, in the hospitable welcome
of St. Paul.

I find it noticed in my journal, that on the 4th
of August, the real summer of the Pyrenees had
set in; an observation which originated in there
having been four of five sunny days, without a
thunder-storm. The weather was then extremely
hot at Bagnères, but at St. Paul we still enjoyed
the green shades, the rustling breezes, and the
perpetual flow of fresh cool water. The moon was
then in the height of her beauty; and at night we
used to sit out upon the terrace looking towards
the valley of Lesponne, where her beams were the
brightest, until nearly ten o'clock. We used, in
short, almost to live in the open air; for the
rustling leaves of the tall poplars, the cool green
alleys where the wind swept through, and the deep
shadow of majestic trees, constituted the luxury,
and no trifling one it was, of our mountain life.
Delicacy forbids that I should say how much this
luxury was enhanced by association with those
elements of human character, which combine all
that is most distinguished and excellent in France,
with all that is most noble in the deeper tone of

feeling which belongs to our native land. The youngest members of the family, however, I must mention, because they were the two happiest, most amiable, and interesting children I ever knew; and never were our evening pictures so complete, as when our walks were enlivened by their gambols with one of the finest of the race of mountain dogs.

Notwithstanding the excessive heat of the weather, to which I have alluded, the skies were so clear, and the aspect of nature so inviting, that a party was again arranged for the Lac Bleu; and in order to see it to greater advantage, their plans were laid for setting out the evening before, and sleeping in a tent at the foot of the mountains. This party consisted of five ladies, seven gentlemen, four guides, and a donkey laden with provisions. Mr. Ellis accompanied them, his object being to make a sketch of the singularly formed mountains around the lake; and though I had determined to remain behind, I confess my resolution was somewhat shaken, when I saw them mounting their horses, and riding down the avenue, conducted by our kind and generous host, whose consideration for others, and habits of order and arrangement, often of the highest value on more important occasions, were never wanting when they could add to the comfort or enjoyment of his

friends.   Our view from the terrace commanded a
considerable extent of the lovely valley of Lesponne; and we stood and watched "them on their
winding way," the clear moon shining over their
path, and appearing to invite them on, towards
the mountains behind which she was about to set.

For us who remained at home it became the
duty for the evening, before retiring to rest, to
make the circuit of the little farm and premises,
to see that all was safe in the absence of the
master.   Between the hours of nine and ten, the
poor women were still at work in the fields; and
we met several of the peasants stealing barefoot
down the hills, with their load of corn upon their
heads, fastened up into an enormous sheaf, in the
middle of which the man's head was buried, the
ears of the corn being downwards round about
him.

The next evening our travellers returned, highly
delighted with their excursion; and what was very
tantalizing to me to hear, in consequence of their
having better guides, they had found a much more
practicable path.   They had not used their tent
for shelter during the night, but had lodged in a
less romantic manner, in a hay-loft over a barn,
and were thus enabled to reach the lake before the
sun had attained its greatest power.

We had not long been residents in the valley of
Campan, without discovering that, isolated as the
situation of St. Paul at first appears, it is not unfrequently the resort of the gay world from Bagnères,
from which town parties flock to every place that
is worth seeing, and many which are not, frequently stopping at the grounds of St. Paul, and
asking to see the chateau. In such a land of
visitors, it was to be expected that occasionally
some would arrive whose celebrity had previously
extended even to these mountains. Amongst this
number was the eastern traveller and poet Lamartine, of whose arrival at Bagnères we were acci-
dentally told, on the evening when this event was
to be celebrated by a serenade of mountain music.

Impelled by a natural curiosity to hear and see
all that is peculiar to such remote regions as the
Pyrenees, we set off late in the evening to walk to
Bagnères, and arrived just as the crowd was gathering about the door of the hotel, where the
musicians were already stationed. The moon had
not neglected the occasion, but rose above the tops
of the mountains, in the most poetic splendour.
The people—so unlike an English crowd—were
perfectly still; and when the music began, and
the poet and his party leaned forward from the
window, my thoughts went back to his strange

visit to that wonderful woman, Lady Hester Stanhope.

Never was a night more suited to a serenade. The music was good, the moonlight splendid. One of the poet's own pieces was sung, when he seemed to hang forward with peculiar interest. At last we had a song in patois, when the people could hold their peace no longer, but burst into fits of laughter, either at the wit, or the familiarity of their own tongue. But that which pleased me best, indeed the only thing we really went to hear, was one of the wild chants of the mountains, sung by three or four voices; and a fine spirit-stirring thing it was. We could only catch here and there a few words, but they were such as, in union with the air, brought vividly to mind, images and associations connected with the mountain winds, the sparkling torrents, the bounding goats, and all that belongs to the bold free life of a *"brave montagnard."*

When Lamartine concluded his speech to the people, there was scarcely so much as the clap of a hand to be heard; but their silence was infinitely more expressive on such a night; and I was much impressed with the fitness of the scene altogether for a poet's welcome.

The road from Bagnères to St. Paul is, of all I

have here seen, the best adapted for a moonlight walk; and never did it look more so than on this night. Unlike most French roads, it winds with the course of the river, which, always impetuous, swells into a broad stream, before it reaches Bagnères. The outline of the mountains was on this night as clear as at noon-day; the cottages in the villages which cluster along the valley, looked white in the moonlight; the shadows of the poplars across our path were dark, and tall, and majestic as the trees themselves; while the cool rustling of their leaves, and the rush of the glancing water, as we saw it sparkling between their stems, sent a freshness to the feelings, which in colder climates never can be so fully enjoyed.

It was early in the month of August, that we first perceived in the atmosphere of the mountains, that autumnal feeling, of which it is so difficult to say in what it consists. Scarcely a leaf had then changed its hue, the green maize was still waving in the sunshine; and yet there was something in the air, and in the general aspect of nature, which made the mind involuntarily recur to those September mornings, when the harvest fields of England are stripped of their yellow sheaves, and when the sportsman goes forth to range the woods with his delighted dogs. One symptom, too, of the approach of autumn, was the number of sheep which daily came down from their summer pasturage in the mountains, with their tinkling bells, some of them so loud, that we could hear them in the night as the flocks passed along the road.

We now began to find more enjoyment in our rambles, and to extend them to a greater distance amongst the neighbouring hills. On one of the first of these autumnal evenings, we set out about five o'clock, for a walk which had become a great favourite with Mr. Ellis. It was to the top of a ridge of hills, from whence we could distinctly see the Pic du Midi, the mountains around the Lac Bleu, and Mont Aigu immediately before us; while the valley of Lesponne with its carpet of verdure, lay far down beneath. This valley is remarkable for being flanked on one side by an almost perpendicular ridge of limestone rock. Crossing a crystal stream which always flowed with the same pure and rapid current, we ascended one of these ridges by a slanting path, which led us out at the summit upon a beautiful plain of green sward, as smooth as velvet, and tufted here and there with fern; the only spot I have ever seen amongst the Pyrenees, resembling an English common.

Before advancing many yards upon this soft green turf, we saw another valley, almost parallel with Lesponne, stretching more to the west, and lying as it were, almost at our feet. This valley, and the hills which slope down into it, are remarkable for the excellence of their cultivation. It is studded all over with orchards and cottages, but still more thickly with those low thatched barns, whose white gables gleam out from little tufts of trees, planted about them for shelter from the storms. At the bottom of the valley runs a rapid stream, while the sides of the opposite hills are so steep, and the space between so narrow, that the labourers, whose voices echoed from side to side, could distinctly hear each other call, and that at a great height up the mountains.

The hill, which we had set out with the purpose of ascending, lies between this valley and Lesponne. It is shaped like the roof of a house, and from its highest and most distant point, is a view which can scarcely be exceeded for its variety and beauty. It is, however, no pastime to attain this point, and by the time we reached the summit, the Pic du Midi had just caught the last golden rays of the setting sun. We had watched them fading away, first from one, and then another of the mountains of Campan, and now the huge dark mass of Mont Aigu seemed to lie like a sleeping monster before us, so black, that it was almost frightful; while far down at its

310   SUMMER AND WINTER

base, in the deep valley of Lesponne, the tinkling
of the sheep bells, the glimmering of the lights in
the cottage windows, the softened murmuring of
the Adour; and then, the full round moon rising
with a mellow light over all, in a few moments produced that magical transition from day to night,
which in these southern latitudes, is as startling as
beautiful.

The depth of the valley, and the height of the
mountains, now seemed doubled, by that mysterious mingling of light and shade, which spread
rapidly over the scene, until the full moon gained
the ascendancy; and while she sailed in solemn
pomp along the sky, huge pinnacles of rock gleamed
forth from their hiding-places; rich woods and
cultivated slopes caught the influence of her silvery
light; and not the least lovely portions of the scene,
the innumerable white gables of little rustic buildings, glanced out to view, each from its separate
bower of green foliage.

Such were not unfrequently our evening rambles.
Sometimes we spent the whole day amongst the
hills, and on one occasion in particular, I recollect
setting out on a clear, cool, fresh morning, when a
canopy of clouds still rested over the Pic du Midi
and Mont Aigu, while the hills on the opposite side
of the valley of Campan, were perfectly clear.

Our intention was to climb the range of mountains which bounded our view to the eastward, rising to a narrow rocky ridge, over which is seen the higher crest of L'heris, called from its beautiful spring flowers, the Garden of the Pyrenees.

Half-way up this range of hills, is a sort of land-mark beyond all cultivation, a long low hut for the accommodation of the shepherds who tend their flocks on these heights. At each end of the building, stand two tall poplars; and there is something in the solitary aspect of this rude dwelling, that tempts one to visit it, though few would be aware, until they reached the actual spot, either of the difficulties of the ascent, or the extent of view it commands. To the north is Bagnères, with the fertile plain of Tarbes beyond; to the west, the bleak summit of Mont Aigu, with the mountains of the Lac Bleu in the direction of Baréges; the Pic du Midi and the beautiful valley of Lesponne; with that of Campan and its murmuring Adour, at the foot of the mountain on which this hut is built.

From the opposite side of the valley, it is easy to distinguish the zigzag path which leads to the hut, but often as I have attempted, I never could find it on a nearer view; and the friends who followed us, and who were more fortunate, confessed they had been much beholden to a donkey which

312   SUMMER AND WINTER

was accustomed to ascend that way in fetching burdens of box-wood to the village of Campan. As usual, I worked my way in the bed of a dried-up stream, for I never feel so safe in a steep ascent, as when I have solid rocks to lay hold of. By the time we reached the hut, a brisk north wind had separated the clouds into distinct white masses, and nothing could be more invigorating than the whole scene. We found, however, on gaining the hut, that we were but half-way to the summit, and the sun being full upon us, the remainder of the way was sufficiently wearisome.

These hills, like most of the Pyrenees, are broken at the top and jagged into thousands of pinnacles, amongst which the shepherds drive their sheep and goats to find pasturage for the day. On one of the highest crags of this mountain, where he might well fancy himself monarch of all he surveyed, sat a solitary shepherd-boy, singing with all his might until the rocks echoed, I can hardly say with his melody; yet doubtless it was melody to him, in comparison with that silence which the French find it impossible to endure, because it reminds them of solitude.

Soon after entering the region of crags and pinnacles, we found ourselves standing on the sharp ridge of the mountain, as the traveller stands on the summit of Helvelyn, looking down into the lonely and melancholy tarn. Instead of this tarn, we looked down into a little bower of beauty, filled with beech wood, fern, and moss; so cool—for the sun could never enter there for more than an hour or two in the morning; while far away to the eastward, stretched a wide tract of country leading to Toulouse.

I have often noticed in this climate, the strange alternations of feeling one experiences in passing immediately from sunshine into shade; but I never felt it so forcibly as this day, on stepping a few paces down the eastern side of the mountain, where the cold and damp were like those of a sepulchre. There is much of this sensation to be felt even in passing amongst streets and houses; and when I, who was in perfect health, have not been able to bear it without a shudder, I have often wondered how it was endured by the many invalids who flock to these regions.

On this day I was glad to leave the chill and damp of the beech wood, for a higher path which led from one ridge to another, into a high grassy sort of plain, where the cattle driven up from Campan were feeding, where a few shepherd's huts were scattered, and where we seemed to be in a sort of green basin, one side of which was guarded

P

by the celebrated L'heris, which, whatever may be its flowery beauties in the spring, looks stern and sterile in the autumn, one side presenting a perpendicular surface of bare rock, on the green crest of which, I suppose, the flowers which attract so many travellers are gathered.

We found upon the grassy plain I have described, one of the happiest-looking groups I ever remember to have seen,—a party of village boys and women, who had been up to the woods to gather nuts, and were returning with their sacks full of treasure, and their hearts full of glee. At a fountain near which they had been resting on the grass before we disturbed them, some of the party went to drink, and, never at a loss for expedients, one of the women made a basin of her scarlet capulet, and drank out of it.

This pure stream, however, was not enough for me; for the keen mountain air, and the length of time we had been in ascending, had given me a craving for something more substantial. I asked one of the women, therefore, if she could procure me some bread and milk from one of the cowherds' huts; and away she ran, clattering over the rocks with her wooden shoes, until, finding them a hindrance to her progress, they were soon slipped off; while we sat down and watched her tracking her way amongst the masses of grey stone, until she reached the huts, which, from the rudeness of their structure, were scarcely distinguishable from the rest of the mountain, except from the gable form of their walls and roofs.

The woman soon returned with bread and milk enough for half a dozen people. Both were good, but the bread, of the coarsest kind ever eaten here, notwithstanding its sweetness, was so tough, that it enabled me to account for what had often puzzled me before, why the peasants of the Pyrenees lose their teeth so early, and apparently without any defect in the teeth themselves. I now suspect it arises from their eating almost continually, this dry tough bread, which literally draws their teeth, or forces them out without the common process of destruction.

On returning to the rocky ridge from whence we had first obtained a view to the eastward, we found our friends from St. Paul, who had just attained the summit, and who had suffered much from the heat of the afternoon sun having been full upon them as they wound round the hollow of the mountain. They were therefore glad to take advantage of the cool beech wood; and while standing with them, they pointed out to us the steep path by which travellers ascend from Bag-

316   SUMMER AND WINTER

nères to L'heris, and which winds along this woody
and sunless dell.   They explained to us also, what
is considered one of the wonders of Bagnères, a
curious kind of snare for catching wild pigeons,
situated not very distant from this place.   To us it
appeared nothing more than a regular row of lofty
trees on the ridge of a hill, but when the trap is in
operation, it consists of long poles fastened to these
trees at almost twice their height; and in little
baskets fixed at the top of these poles, are seated
men who have a perfect command over wide thin
nets, which are placed from tree to tree, so that
when they see the pigeons enter the snare, they
can draw the nets together by cords and pulleys,
and thus secure the birds.   It is said these men
make all speed to come down on the first awakening
of a wind, and no wonder.

When we turned from the summit of the mountain to descend, the sun was declining, and the
clouds, partially rolled away from the highest peaks
to the westward, left them covered with the hue
and the splendour of gold; particularly one mountain to the left, which we always called the fan
mountain, from its presenting a vast radiated surface, somewhat in the shape of a fan, and on this
afternoon, each ray, catching the colours of the
west, appeared to shine with a glory of its own.

There is something peculiarly delightful in descending a mountain, and just reaching its foot
as the shadows of evening steal on. On this day
we enjoyed such pleasure in perfection, for we
could hear the gentle murmuring of the Adour in
the valley below, while there was just light enough
left to see the glancing of its crystal waters. If to
such enjoyment we could more frequently add the
welcome of an English home, the world would be
too happy, and we should love it too well.

CHAPTER XI.

ADVANTAGES OF LIVING AT BAGNERES — FRENCH
BEGGING—JOURNEY TO CAUTERETS, AND VISIT TO
THE CASTLE OF LOURDES — SPANIARDS — PONT
D'ESPAGNE, AND THE LAC DE GAUBE — RETURN
BY WAY OF LUZ TO BAGNERES.

THE town of Bagnères possesses many advantages to English as well as French visitors, and it
is consequently the favourite resort of many
families, who find the heat of Pau too oppressive
for the summer months.   Amongst its highest
recommendations are the religious services of an
excellent French protestant minister from Tarbes,
who preaches every Sunday through the summer
season, to a congregation of from fifty to a hundred
persons, in a public room appropriated to that
purpose.   There are many occasions also, when
English service is held at Bagnères; for amongst
the numbers of clergymen who visit this country with
that peculiar affection of the throat which seems
to be increasingly attendant upon their labours at

home, it not unfrequently happens that some are still able to take the lighter duty of occasional services abroad; and the welcome with which these efforts are received by numerous congregations, testifies how much the absence of the accustomed means of religious instruction is felt abroad.

Would that the influence of the many English visitors who flock to this country, was commensurate in its good effects upon society, with their apparent interest in occasional religious observances.

We have been told on good authority, that there are residing in Paris, between fifteen and twenty thousand English; and in France altogether, including Paris, sixty thousand, and that their expenditure exceeds four millions sterling annually.

That this influx of English people does produce an impression on the minds of the French, favourable to the integrity and good faith of our country, is observable from the extraordinary manner in which the English are trusted in all money matters, by the tradespeople here; but there are other impressions received along with this, equally powerful, and perhaps equally just. The same gentleman, for instance, whose statement of the number of visitors I have just copied, in speaking of the English taste for strong wine observed, that our countrymen love the "wine which speaks to the throat;" and the mayor of Bagnères, during our residence in that neighbourhood, was heard to observe one day, that Bagnères would attract a greater number of English visitors than any other town in the Pyrenees, if he could ensure for them always a clergyman, and—beef, an article of consumption but rarely met with amongst the mountains.

The influence of fashionable visitors upon the habits of the people, is certainly more visible at Bagnères, than elsewhere in this part of France; and there is an air of greater coquetry amongst the young women, whose pretty head-dresses render them almost always attractive. Still, like the inhabitants of half-civilized countries, when they first assume the embellishments of artificial life, there ¡s a discrepancy in their personal adornments, as novel as it is amusing, to an English observer. I thought, for instance, when I had seen a woman without stockings, her bare foot adorned with neat sandals and smart shoes, that I had witnessed a somewhat extraordinary spectacle; but Mr. Ellis afterwards saw a much smarter person in Bagnères without stockings, while her feet were set off to still greater advantage by white satin slippers.

The country people too, in the valley of Campan, are of a very different order from those of the valley d'Ossau, probably owing to this district having been for a much longer time the resort of strangers. They are almost all beggars, either positively or indirectly; and time being the only thing of no value amongst them, they run after you with nosegays, and all sorts of things, to obtain a sous; while an offer to show you the grotto, is echoed from almost every hill side. I have seen a youth of seventeen, standing all day beside the gate of St. Paul, offering to all who passed by, a little rose-bud not bigger than a nut, and I have often been asked to see the grotto after dark in the evening.

Their direct beggary is annoying, but not impressive. The beggars by profession, begin as soon as you are in sight, with a monotonous drawl of set words, all pronounced on one key, and precisely the same to every passer by. Perhaps it is well for their own interest, that they generally ask you to give for the merit of the gift, or the prayers they promise to breathe for you, for certainly there is nothing in themselves to prompt it. How different have I often thought it was from the genuine eloquence of Irish beggary, which makes the heart ache so bitterly, that it would be almost a relief to give one's last sixpence! The begging in France is simply asking for money, while the beggar often looks all the time as comfortable and well fed as

322   SUMMER AND WINTER

yourself.   It is true they ask only for one sous, but
in the valley of Campan, when you have given
them that, they make no scruple to ask you for
another.   Nor is this only on the public roads.
There is scarcely any place so retired, but you
hear the pattering of little bare feet behind you,
then loud breathing which diffuses around you the
perfume of garlic, and as soon as you look round,
the demand is made, and persisted in for a length
of time proportioned to the ability of the supplicant
to keep pace with you.

Of the pleasant walks, many of them alone, which
I have taken in the neighbourhood of Campan,
this system of importunity has destroyed much of
my enjoyment.   There was also a disposition in
the people to talk with me, to pity me for being
alone, and to accommodate their pace to mine,
asking questions all the way, which rendered my
walks anything but solitary.   All this it may be
said, might have been both instructive and interesting, and to no one would it have been more
so than to me, but for their unintelligible patois.

This language, which is properly that of Bearn,
is a mixture of French and Spanish.   All public
documents were written in it until the reign of
Louis XIII.   It is about a century since a native
poet, Despourrins, born at Accous in the valley

d'Aspe, published a collection of songs and tales in this language, said to be extremely touching in their interest, and adapted to the feelings and habits of the people amongst whom he lived. These are extremely popular amongst the country people.

The range of the Bearnais patois is very limited. At Tarbes, only twenty-five miles east from Pau, a different idiom is spoken; and thirty miles to the westward, the Basque only is used. This last is entirely different from the various provincial patois of the south of France, and it might be a question of interest, whether from some points of similarity to the Arabic, it might not have been introduced by the refugee Moors, driven from Spain in the year 1492.

Few of the peasant women understand French beyond a few words, but it is rare to meet with a man who does not, though we have occasionally found a shepherd, who had no other means of making us answer to his importunate question of the hour of day, than by repeating the word *montre*. That the men understand the French language so much better than the women, is accounted for by the military services of the latter having drawn them so much more away from their rural homes.

A proposal having been made to us to accompany some young friends on a tour of three days to

Cauterets and the neighbourhood, and the weather being then sufficiently cool to prevent all danger from exposure to the sun, we set out for that place in the first week of September. We had then had a long series of wet days, and the morning of our journey looked anything but promising. However, we hoped for the best, and having the companionship of young and buoyant spirits, went cheerfully on our way, relieved by a canopy of clouds, from all apprehension of suffering from the heat.

For four or five miles, our route lay along the perfect flat extending from Bagnères to Tarbes. We then turned to the left, in a direction towards Pau, and travelled along a beautifully undulating line of hills, richly cultivated, and clothed with vines. Looking back from the highest of these to the mountains we were leaving, a splendid scene opened upon our view. The mists were then rolling away from the summits of the mountains, and the Pic du Midi, and Mont Aigu, rose out of their vapoury beds, majestic in their elevation, and clothed with that purple blackness, which neither pen nor pencil can describe. Upon the fleecy clouds which rolled down their sides, and along the valleys, the sun was then shining, and making them look like masses of molten silver; while far away to the left, stretched the mountains of Bagnères de

Luchon, many of them sheeted with snow which never melts.

As the day advanced, our hopes of fine weather advanced with it, though we had still some showers of drizzling rain, which after all, were more welcome to me than the heat I had experienced on my first journey through the valley of Argelez. We found that vegetation was here much more advanced, and more vigorous than at the foot of the mountains. There the Indian corn had not arrived at its full height, here it was already stripped of its leaves and tops, which are used as fodder for the cattle, leaving the naked plant nothing to do but nourish and perfect the ear. In the immediate neighbourhood of the mountains, vines are rarely cultivated; here they were stretching from bough to bough, often to the tops of tall trees, from which they hung in festoons of the most delicate and beautiful green.

On this journey we had an opportunity of visiting the castle of Lourdes, and from its highest tower looked out upon a lovely view, our guide taking especial care to specify the different chateaux to be seen from this eminence, amongst which is one belonging to the brother of Marshal Soult. At the foot of the eminence on which this castle stands, we again saw the Gave de Pau, flowing in a broad dark stream, with no ripple to disturb its surface, except at one particular spot, where there is a beautiful silvery fall.   It was really a relief, to see again a river that had some depth and stillness, for the Adour, and all the other streams we had lately seen, are in such a perpetual tumult and bustle, that I have sometimes longed to stretch over them an enchanted wand, to make them be still.

The castle of Lourdes has much in its history to render it an object of interest to the traveller, besides the aspect of strength and antiquity which it now presents.   The noon of its glory was in those chivalrous times when it belonged to the ancient warriors who ruled over their adjoining domain of Lavedon.   Subsequently it was converted into a state prison, and was appropriated to that purpose by Buonaparte, when in the year 1804, Lord Elgin was treacherously imprisoned within its walls.   Passing through the French territory on his return from Constantinople, to which court he had been British ambassador, he was arrested as a prisoner of war, and resided in the neighbourhood of Pau on his parole.   He was afterwards taken from his family, and kept in close confinement in this castle.   In the mean time, letters were written in Paris, and an agent sent down to attempt to implicate his lordship in a pretended conspiracy, for the purpose of sacrificing his life, or producing cause of complaint against the British government. But the sagacity, high-mindedness, and straight-forward conduct of Lord Elgin, baffled the subtlety of his enemies, and were the means, not only of preserving his own life, but of exemplifying a high degree of moral worth, as advantageous to the possessor as it was honourable to his country.

On leaving Lourdes, we entered again upon the route by which we had travelled from Pau to Argelez early in the summer; nor was it difficult to see what time had been doing since last we were there,—browning the hills, laying bare the rocks, scorching the grass, sending home the grain from the harvest field, mellowing the tints of the woods, and giving to the whole that peculiar richness of colouring, which is the certain prelude of decay.

The day now became beautiful. The clouds separated, revealing first one mountain peak, and then another; while along with the partial, but brilliant sunshine, came the refreshment of a breeze almost cold, from the north. In the valley of Argelez, that region of warmth and beauty, with a cool fresh breeze, I had little left to wish for, and nothing now to detract from my admiration of the glorious scene which lay before us; for

the extent and variety presented by this valley, are
far beyond any other in the Pyrenees, though there
may be little isolated spots, more perfectly Arcadian
in their loveliness.   Vistas of mountains were now
opening upon us in every direction, some near and
distinct, with the sunshine full upon them; others
stretching far away, and their shadowy forms seen
only through a purple haze; while the nearer hills,
glowing in all the golden hues of autumn, displayed their pastoral, and even park-like scenery,
the road sometimes winding through chestnut
woods, and sometimes almost overhung with the
vines that grew from tree to tree.

This valley is, more than any other in the Pyrenees, rich in the remains of former dignity.
Scarcely a green hill, or craggy mound, but has its
tower of ancient strength, now mouldering into
ruins, and strangely contrasting with the simple
comfort and humble toil of the now thriving peasantry, with their orchards laden with fruit, and
their vines already hanging out their rich clusters
in the sun.

Remembering but too well the inn at Argelez,
I was glad to hear our driver propose to go on to
Pierrefitte without stopping; and it was in this
part of the road, that the sublimest view opened
upon us—the mountain gorge leading to Cauterets

on the right, and the no less wild ravine to Luz on the left. High up the hill immediately to our right, and commanding a view of which the eye could never be weary, was the venerable Abbey of St. Savin, originally founded by Charlemagne, where the people tell you the princess Catherine of Navarre, sister to Henry IV. once took shelter, when driven from Cauterets by a furious storm. A little farther on the road to Pierrefitte, and on the same range of hills, is a large and handsome chateau, belonging to the family of Despourrins, the poet of the Pyrenees. It stands on a green eminence, almost embowered in beech wood, and if its interior answers to its exterior aspect, must be a delightful residence.

To the left of the valley opposite to Pierrefitte, is a bold mass of rock, apparently jutting out from the side of the adjoining mountain, on which stand the ruins of what must have originally been a castle of no ordinary size and strength. It belonged to the ancient counts of Lavedon, and was exchanged by them for some other property, with the counts of Bigorre. Beyond these, are many other ruins, all whose chivalrous, romantic, or religious history, would require volumes to record.

From Pierrefitte, the road was new to us all, and a wonderful one it is, ascending from the little

330   SUMMER AND WINTER

town by a zigzag course along the almost perpendicular side of a red craggy mountain, which looks
as if it might block out the whole world from
entrance by that route, into the peaceful valley of
Argelez.   Yet along a smooth macadamized road,
excellent as all the public roads in the Pyrenees
are, roll carriages of every description, filled with
the sick, the delicate, the convalescent, and the
gay.   An idea may possibly be formed of the
number of visitors who flock to these mountains,
when I add, that exclusive of diligences, we met
on this day's journey, no less than twelve carriages,
laden with travellers and their luggage, most
probably on their way to distant homes.

Wishing to enjoy what we could of the scenery,
while our horses were resting, we walked up the
old road which ascends directly from the village,
below the new one, and must have presented a
fearful obstacle to the travellers who formerly
passed this way.   From the highest part of this
road we could look into three valleys, with the red
mountain wall to our left, shutting out the sky, and
jutting into the green pastures of Pierrefitte at its
base.   It was a singular, but most lovely scene.
I had beheld nothing like it in the Pyrenees, or
elsewhere.   We stood on a craggy height, with a
torrent far, far beneath us.   Opposite were perpen-

dicular masses of rock, extending to a vast height, sometimes appearing to block in the course of the stream, by meeting those on which we had placed ourselves. And beautiful it was to look down into this stream, and trace out its blue windings at such a depth, yet amongst all this darkness and solitude, to see those green pastures so peculiar to the Pyrenees, sloping down here and there to the edge of the water. Nor was it merely as a picture, that the landscape pleased the eye. It was one to fill the mind with many thoughts; for in the distance was the old chateau, recalling the heroes of Froissart,—then the green valley, with its peaceful herds, and fields of maize,—above it, the red precipice of rock, with that almost miraculous road, constructed by the ingenuity and labour of man,—behind us an inaccessible height,—and beneath, on the banks of the torrent, amongst the green pastures, we caught occasional glimpses of rich groves of walnut trees.

It is in such situations that the mind seems to float, as it were, over the surface of nature, and rather dreams, than thinks. Perhaps we rather feel, than do either; and I confess I was far gone in one of these reveries, when suddenly aroused by my companion, a very charming young lady, exclaiming—"What a delightful place for a pic-nic!"

Now I pretend to no philosophical contempt of

pic-nics, provided they are held in pleasant places; but above all, provided they bring together pleasant people. Yet for a pic-nic in the abstract, considered merely as such, I certainly have no reverence; and yet I suspect there is a large portion of human beings, who think that woods, and streams, and mountains, but especially the Pyrenees, were created for nothing else.

Of this class what troops do we see galloping pell-mell through some of the loveliest of these valleys, and on such horses!—miserable, lean, bony, and mis-shapen, yet so accustomed to the habits of their gay riders, that no sooner do they hear the slash and shout, than off they go, even where the hills are steepest, either up or down, their hoofs clattering over the rocks, with a noise which stuns into insignificance the loudest torrent. Of the exercise of riding I own I am, from long habit, and many early associations, almost foolishly fond; but for what I heard a lady one day describe, as the *absolute sitting on a horse*, I have as little respect as I have for pic-nics in the abstract. I will not describe the costumes of these equestrian parties. All have their tastes; and it is neither amiable nor wise to find fault with the enjoyment of others, because it is not ours; but the hats, of every possible variety of brim, waving in

the wind,—the red sashes worn both by ladies and
gentlemen, I never could tell why,—the white pan-
taloons fastened under the fairy feet of the former,
and the spurs which sometimes adorn their heels,—
with saddles of every shape but what is likely to fit
the back of a horse,—bridles with rusty bits,—and
steeds that would do honour to the knight-errantry
of Don Quixote,—so far as these may be considered to add to the beauty of the landscape, the
scenery of the Pyrenees is rich indeed.

Our road all the way to Cauterets was excellent,
and must have been constructed at no trifling
expense. Towards the conclusion of our journey,
the scene grew wilder and less lovely; and the
afternoon closed with a kind of drizzle, which promised badly for our next day's excursion to the
Pont d'Espagne, and the Lac de Gaube, the two
great wonders that are to be seen by a ramble of
three or four hours from Cauterets.

We found this place much larger than I had
expected. It consists of two or three good streets,
chiefly composed of hotels and lodging-houses, and
was at that time full of people, though the season
was said to be over. This might be one reason
why we were ourselves so much in request as new
comers; for the wheels of our carriage were literally clogged with people recommending themselves

as innkeepers, bakers, and all sorts of things, vying with each other in the excellence and the cheapness of their provisions, all which we knew would be at the utmost rate that could be obtained. Even when we entered our lodging, the crowd pursued us; and not until the evening closed, were we free from those who offered to guide us on the morrow, or to let us horses for the excursion which there was no doubt we had come to make. All this was the more ridiculous, as we had brought our own provisions, meant to stay only one night, and had determined, with the exception of two of our party, to walk to the Lac de Gaube.

Cauterets is in one respect the strangest-looking place in the Pyrenees, being almost filled with Spaniards, to whose exclusive use one set of its many baths is appropriated. We went to see these baths in a drizzling rain; and the heat and steam of the water, with the apparent poverty, and filth of the Spaniards, rendered the place by no means agreeable for a protracted stay. The water which supplies these baths, is conducted from a neighbouring hill in a sort of covered channel; and it is said to be at its source almost boiling, perhaps the hottest of any of these mineral waters; but there is in the town of Bagnères, one almost too warm for the hand to remain in, which makes a favourite resort for the women, who go there to clean their kitchen utensils.

I never saw any people who struck me so much, and yet were so difficult to describe, as these Spaniards. They seem to be all poor, I should suppose all filthy, and yet so dignified, so imposing, and so peculiar in their appearance, that one stands still and gazes at them, as when some distinguished person passes. In detail, few of them are handsome. They have dirty complexions, shrivelled skins, mean features, sharp sunken eyes, and universally brown curling hair, which is evidently guiltless of a comb; yet group them together as a whole, and they make splendid pictures, it is impossible to say how, or why. With their tall gaunt figures, enveloped in the woollen mantle or plaid which they always wear, often concealing one arm, they seem fitted for nothing but mules and mountains. Of their women I cannot say much, having seen so few; but these corresponded well with the men,—tall, meagre, and strange, yet so dignified, that one involuntarily looked again, to see if they were really the wretched, poverty-stricken creatures they appeared, or some fallen remnant of nobility in disguise.

Having allowed ourselves but three days for our journey to Cauterets, we were all extremely anxious about the weather; and when we rose on the morning after our arrival, and saw the clouds upon the mountain sides, down as low as the tops of the houses, we were almost in despair. Soon, however, one pine-covered peak after another appeared, and the day turned out most propitious for our excursion, with a north wind, passing clouds compact and white, and a sky intensely blue.

The whole of the route to the Pont d'Espagne is indescribably fine and beautiful. It differed from all we had seen, in being more wild, and more scattered with pines; while the mountain peaks on each side of the ravine along which we passed, rising through the thin fleecy clouds, which still hung about them, looked of such amazing height and sublimity, that we found it difficult to pursue our route, without stopping too often to wonder and admire. The torrent, too, was diversified by innumerable falls of great beauty and grandeur; one of which, in particular, equals the finest of the waterfalls at Eaux Bonnes, and would far surpass it, but for the sheet of water being broken by a mass of rock, over which it again falls into a deep gulf.

On arriving at the Pont d'Espagne, we found it a simple bridge of pine, over a torrent whose thundering roar seems to shake the foundations of

the surrounding rocks. We stood a long time on
this bridge, watching the foam of the boiling waters
below; and it was here that I saw for the first time
in my life, a rainbow produced by the misty spray.
This bridge is one of the passes into Spain. The
traveller is conducted over it to another point of
view, from whence this world of waters is seen to
still greater advantage. Such is the foam, the
tumult, and the rush of glancing water, that it is
scarcely possible to say how many streams are
meeting in this particular spot. I remember
chiefly the masses of black rock over which the
mighty sheets of water rushed, and the abyss into
which they fell with a bellowing noise like thunder.

After contemplating this scene, we passed again
over the bridge of pines, in order to pursue our
way to the Lac de Gaube. The path now became
more difficult; yet half an hour's steep ascent
brought us out into one of those wide bleak hollows amongst the mountains, which, for want of a
better name, I must call a wilderness plain. As
we entered into this hollow, there rose before our
view the majestic Vignemale, the highest mountain
in France. It is 10,326 feet in height, and its
mighty pinnacles were clothed in glittering snow
which never melts. On either side of the valley
along which we passed, were mountains of no very

Q

interesting character, sloping down to the plain;
and but for the noble Vignemale closing the
valley, the scene would have possessed no particular charm.

The guide had told us it was but an hour's walk
from the Pont d'Espagne to the Lac de Gaube;
yet we continued our walk almost to the end of
the valley, and no lake appeared. At last, on
ascending a ridge of rocks, we beheld this wonder
of the Pyrenees, which, when we had not seen it,
every one told us was more beautiful than anything
else to be found amongst the mountains.   It was a
mere pond—a little green pond, at least so it appeared to me, who had in my recollection the
broad sheet of Derwent water, and more recently
the deep crystal of the Lac Bleu.   For its colour,
however, ample apology was made on the score of
the recent rains; and with regard to its size, I
have no doubt I was greatly deceived by the height
of the surrounding mountains.

It is a solitary spot, without a tree, except the
dark green pines; and without a dwelling, except
the fisherman's lonely hut.   What renders it still
more melancholy, is the circumstance which took
place here about six years ago, and which perhaps
affected us the more, from Mr. Ellis being acquainted with some of the nearest relatives of the

deceased. It is said to have been a bright and beautiful morning, when an English bride and bridegroom, on their wedding tour, went out upon this lake, in the fisherman's rudely-constructed boat, the very same which we saw lying by the shore, than which a more unsafe or unmanageable vessel could scarcely be imagined. Little seems to be known of the awful event which followed, except that those who stood on the shore relate, that when the boat was about the middle of the lake, the figure of the man was seen stooping overboard—that the female, alarmed for his safety, rushed to the same side,—and thus, the vessel being overbalanced, both were plunged into a watery grave.

The bodies were both found, though one of them not until a month after. They were conveyed to England, and buried at Witham, in Essex. There is a rock jutting out a little way into the lake, on which a white marble monument, commemorating this event, has been placed, with an inscription giving a short account of their fate. These words upon the tablet were to me particularly striking,—"*married one month!*" What a conclusion to that portion of life, which mankind have agreed, whether justly or not, to call the happiest in human experience !

I have sometimes heard an expression of wonder, that no attempt was made to save the lives thus awfully brought to their close. This apparent neglect, however, is easily accounted for, by the solitary nature of the place,—by there being but one boat upon the lake,—and by the fisherman to whom the boat and the cottage belong, being on that day absent. There was consequently no one but a guide and one other man on the shore, to witness the calamity. That they could either of them swim, is scarcely probable, from the habits of the people of the Pyrenees; and even if they could, there is an universally prevailing belief, not only that this lake, but that all amongst the mountains, are bottomless; in addition to which, the people always tell you, the water of the lake is so cold, that whoever plunges in must suffer instant death.

After spending an hour by the side of this lake, we set out to return to Cauterets, somewhat refreshed by a dish of excellent peaches, grapes, and plums, brought out to us by the good woman from the fisherman's hut. It was a day on which no one in health could well have been weary. The freshness of the clear cool air,—the sparkling of the torrents,—the deep shadow of the pines, with the sunshine glittering through,—sometimes a little climbing, and occasionally a plain of green turf that sounded hollow under the tread,—now and then the distant tinkling of sheep-bells on the sides of the mountains,—but above all, those lofty and shining peaks that seemed to reach more than half-way to the skies—all contributed to lead us on without counting our steps, through one of the most delightful rambles it has ever been my lot to enjoy.

I had often wished to see pine forests in per-fection, and my wish was this day gratified; for here were pines of every description,—some in their giant structure, apparently unscathed by a single storm, their green fan-like branches tipped with edges of golden yellow,—others stunted, and wrung almost from their hold in the earth, by the violence of the sweeping blast,—others scathed by lightning,—and others crashed, and broken, and swept from their foundation by masses of falling snow, or by the fury of the wintry floods.

In a solitary part of our route we met twelve men, with guns and staves, going out, as I supposed, to hunt the wild goat; but I was a little startled to learn from the guide, that they were going in search of a bear, which had been seen the day before in an adjoining wood.

The route to the Lac de Gaube leads past the principal bathing establishment, about the distance of half an hour's walk from Cauterets. In the morning the path to these baths had been thronged by invalids of every description, most of them carried in little covered chairs, supported on poles. As we returned, the path was deserted, and the baths closed. Had it been otherwise, I believe we were a little too weary to have looked into the bathing-rooms, as unquestionably all strangers ought. We were quite satisfied with admiring their beautiful situation, and the many marble steps which lead up to the entrance of the building. More interesting to me were some other fountains of health, higher up the valley, either too humble or too distant to be visited by any but the poorest class, and those were chiefly Spaniards. At one of these sources, a kind of cave had been cut out of the rock through which the water flows; and in the deep shadow of this cave, a most picturesque group was placed; some of them drinking of the waters, and others resting on the rocks from the fatigues of the ascent.

By way of making the most of our beautiful day, we took a hasty repast at Cauterets, and again crowded into our carriage; our driver, like all French drivers, clattering through the streets, with a cracking of his whip enough to shatter the nerves of all the invalids in the place. We went rapidly

over the excellent road, for it was down-hill all the
way to Pierrefitte; and the man, scorning the
hinderance of a drag, even when descending the
zigzag road along the giant wall which guards the
entrance of the gorge, one of his horses fell, as
might have been expected; and being dragged by
the force of the carriage for some distance on the
ground, was severely bruised, and cut with the
harness.

From Pierrefitte we went again to Luz, to spend
the night at good old Madame Cazeaux', and were
not sorry to find her inn so full, that we were
lodged in a clean new house, looking out upon the
stream and the valley, which extend to Baréges.
I was that night almost too tired to sleep, but I
rose early the next morning, and walked with my
young companions once more on the road to Gavarnie, past St. Sauveur, and then back again by
the hill of the Hermitage, to look most probably
for the last time upon my favourite valley. The
scene was much changed since I had last beheld
it. Hill sides that were green and verdant then,
were now bare and brown; and worse than all,
many of the silvery streams that used to dash and
sparkle along the valley, were totally dried up—
nothing but their grey stony beds remaining to
mark their course. Still there was beauty and

fertility enough, and almost too much, for the eye
and heart to take in at once; and as a scene, the
picture was perhaps mellower and richer than
before.

On descending from the hill of the Hermitage,
we went to see the old church of the Knights
Templars. Here a curious and characteristic little
scene awaited us. A young lady of our party
having chosen to ride that morning, a little boy
had accompanied us to take charge of her horse.
On entering the church, he was sent home with
the horse, looking rather blank without his expected
payment. He soon followed us, however, and
though mass was being said, we saw him hurrying
through the church, in the most irreverent manner, evidently in search of something. He did not
see us at first; but the moment he discovered
we were there, and safe from escape, his whole
appearance changed. He took his place beside
the altar, bowed most profoundly, and even beat
his little breast with folded hands, as if in the
attitude of the most profound devotion; but no
sooner had we turned to go away, than he started
up, hastened round, and meeting us at the door,
demanded his recompense for attentions to the
horse and its rider.

Before leaving Luz, we went to see the curious

manufacture of fine woollen articles, for which this place is so justly celebrated. Nothing can exceed the elegance of some of the dresses exhibited in this establishment, which comprises shawls, scarfs, and almost every article that can be worn, but particularly such as are most light and graceful.

About ten o'clock we set off to return to Bagnères, and passing again through the ravine which leads from Luz to Pierrefitte, we stopped for the last time to look at the little antiquated bridge, the *Pont d'enfer*, which consists of a single arch, spanning a deep chasm, over which was once the only way by Gavarnie into Spain. It must have been thought a work of wonder, when the present road was constructed, and yet modern invention is already busy with another.

On emerging from this gorge once more into the valley of Argelez, I was struck with the conviction, that I had not felt in any part of this little tour the pleasure with which I first visited these scenes. I know not how or why, but I experienced no longer that thrill of joy, that impulse of delight, which had so often animated me before; and I felt convinced, that had we gone, according to our first intention, into Switzerland, much of the beauty and sublimity of that country would have been lost upon us. Was it that the eye was satis-

fied with seeing, or had I lived so long amongst
mountains, rocks, and streams, that they had lost
their poetic character, and settled down into actual
materiality ?

I was not ungrateful for all I had been-permitted
to admire, and to enjoy; yet I was more than ever
impressed with the truth, that in order to enter with
the most intense relish into such scenes as those
around me, one should emerge immediately from
the smoke of crowded cities, after the mind has
been long burdened with social, domestic, or pecu-
niary anxieties.   It is then that the contemplation
of nature in its most sublime and lovely character,
becomes an indescribable refreshment; and in
proportion as the body is invigorated, the mind is
restored to its healthy tone.

Enjoyment, like many other good things,—even
the enjoyment of nature, requires economy to make
it last.   Those who travel for mere pleasure, generally hurry on from one country to another, in
search of that excitement which all have ceased to
afford; and, flying from the Pyrenees to Spain,
or Switzerland, and from thence to Italy or Greece,
they conclude by saying, that "rocks are but
rocks," and that when you have seen one mountain, you have seen another.   No one can feel
more forcibly than myself, that all the beauties

of nature, from the sublimest heights, to the most peaceful and sheltered valleys,—from the foaming cataract, to the rippling stream,—from the loftiest tree, to the simplest flower,—are fit subjects for the poet to invoke, and beyond that, for the Christian to admire; but I feel also that there is more real elevation of mind in the conception of one moral truth which bears upon the temporal and eternal happiness of mankind, than in the highest flights of poetic feeling,—more true satisfaction in the simple act of giving a cup of cold water, in the name of the Redeemer, to one of the least of his disciples, than in spending days, months, or years, in the mere contemplation of what is beautiful or sublime.

CHAPTER XII.

STATE OF AGRICULTURE, AND DIVISION OF PROPERTY
IN THE PYRENEES—EARLY APPROACH OF AUTUMN
—LEAVING ST. PAUL—VIEW OF THE MOUNTAINS
FROM TARBES— REMARKS UPON THE CLIMATE OF
THE SOUTH OF FRANCE—NOTICES OF OLERON, AND
THE VALLEY D'ASPE—CONCLUDING OBSERVATIONS
ON TRAVELLING ABROAD.

WITH all my early prejudices in favour of an agricultural life, I had long been in the habit of thinking, that with a genial climate and a fertile soil to facilitate his labours, where the farmer tilled his own ground, and where that ground was divided into fair allotments, where there were none so powerful as to oppress, and none so poor as to suffer,—man must exist in his most natural and happy state. My favourite system was a plausible one. It never occurred to me, until my residence amongst the Pyrenees, to see how the "thing worked," as the politicians say. Here, however, I beheld it carried out to a degree of perfection, which I had not previously believed to exist in the present state of society.   Here the climate, except for occasional storms, is all that the cultivator of the soil can desire, and the soil itself redundant in vegetation.   Here the peasant almost invariably cultivates his own land, and has all his means of subsistence and comfort within himself. Nor is there that inequality of property to complain of, which is so frequently the cause of unfair assumption on the one side, and of envy on the other.   Here every one has his portion; but that portion is consequently so small, that many of the farms do not exceed three or four acres, and some are only one.   On these little plots of ground, you frequently see all the varieties of maize, grass, wheat, oats, and flax, or the crops by which some of these are immediately succeeded, such as millet and buckwheat; for no such thing as fallow-ground is to be found in the Pyrenees.

Whatever may be the attainments of the French in other respects, they seem never to have learned the true value of time, at least as it is understood in England.   The various little portions of ground appropriated as above described, are seldom separated by a fence; so that when cattle are feeding on the grass, it is necessary they should be tended all the day; and it is no uncommon thing to see

350   SUMMER AND WINTER

an able man employed in this manner. Indeed, wherever either sheep or cattle feed, in the lanes, on the mountains, or amongst the fields, they are invariably watched. The women, however, make this occupation answer two purposes, for they never go out with their cattle, without spinning or knitting all the time. They even knit when they ride; and I have seen them walking home from market on a rainy evening, with heavy baskets on their arms, knitting all the way.

The peasants of the Pyrenees have all which their necessities demand within themselves. They grow their own flax, and one of their most busy occupations is to dress it. They do not steep it in water before beating it, as in England, but spread it on some sloping field or hill side, where it undergoes no other process than what is effected by exposure to the weather. Not only is the flax prepared and woven for their own use, but the wool of the mountain sheep, undyed, is made into jackets, trousers, and petticoats, as well as into various other articles of clothing. Thus supplied with the most common and necessary kinds of dress, their wants are equally simple as regards their furniture and food. A few brass or copper vessels, for their milk, are always used by those who make cheeses, as many of the peasants do, not only of the milk of cows, but of that of sheep and goats. For a churn they have a very simple substitute, being no other than a dried sheep's skin. For keeping wine the skins of kids are frequently used, with the hair inside : and the same article is also converted into a large pocket or knapsack, which the little girls carry at their backs. The skin, when used in this manner, is kept entire, either the head or the tail of the animal being folded over the opening of the knapsack.

All implements of husbandry used amongst the Bearnais, are equally simple in their character. The pole of their little carts is often nothing more than the stem of a tree cut off where it has divided into two branches, so that the ends of the two forks connect with the axletree; and the forks with which their hay is made, are branches or stems of the same description, on a smaller scale. Their ploughing, such as it is, is effected by a sort of double process, requiring four oxen,—two to go before with the coulter, and two others with another implement to turn over the soil. Both these are generally conducted by women. For millet and buckwheat, which succeed immediately to the earliest crops, the soil is merely turned over with a shovel, after which the earth and stubble are burned in heaps, and strewn upon the field. The process of preparing the ground for wheat and oats is simple in the extreme. Both the seed and the manure are strewn upon the land, ploughed in together, then harrowed, and all is finished. The labour of carrying and spreading manure is performed almost exclusively by women, who sometimes carry it on a sort of hurdle into the fields, but more frequently in sacks on their heads. In the valley d'Aspe it is taken to the fields in large woollen sacks placed upon the backs of donkeys.

I find it stated in my journal, that in the beginning of August, the maize in the valley of Campan was waving in all its glory, having attained the height of a man's shoulder, and being still green. At the same time, the reapers had begun to cut the wheat and oats ; and I expected to have seen the yellow corn-fields adorned, as they are in England, with those golden sheaves which have so many pleasant associations. To my disappointment, however, I found that the harvest in the Pyrenees was a very different affair from what it is with us ; for no sooner was the wheat cut down, than it was tied up in bundles, carried away upon the heads of the owners, and stowed into those innumerable little barns which adorn the landscape ; all this despatch being rendered necessary by the dishonesty of the people, which is such, that no one leaves his corn in the field, after it is cut, for a single night. I am sorry to make this confession in relation to the people whose simple lives I had previously thought so enviable; but I am also bound in common justice to state, that even their potatoes, when ready to be taken up, were always watched in the valley of Campan; and that every night, at a certain hour, we saw a lantern placed in the potato-field, and heard the firing of a gun, which announced that the watch had commenced for the night.

The manner of threshing the corn is different in almost all the valleys of the Pyrenees. In that of Ossau it is trampled out by horses. In the neighbourhood of Bagnères, threshing-floors are made for the purpose in the open air, around which eight or ten men thresh out the corn with small light flails; and in some places it is beaten out on trussels. I do not recollect ever to have seen wheat or oats conveyed from the fields in carts, and hay but seldom. Indeed, the use of either carts or waggons is a thing impracticable in many parts of the Pyrenees, owing to the mountainous situation of the farms; while in others, so seldom is there a regular entrance or gateway into the fields, that a cart, when it does pass, must go through a gap in the fence, or through a part of

354   SUMMER AND WINTER

the stone wall, which is often broken down for this purpose. Thus we see the peasants, rather than be at the trouble of making a gateway, lifting the manure over their little fences, and carrying out the produce of their fields in the same manner. Their gates, when they have any, are generally made with a large heavy end, to counterpoise their weight. The stem of a tree, with its thick knotty root, projecting out at twice the length of the gate, generally forms the upper part, and by its weight, makes the gate open on a kind of pivot, or hinge.

Maize and hay appear to be the crops which constitute the wealth of the Bearnais farmer. Of the former, I have already mentioned its various uses, except that, amongst these, I have omitted the excellent beds or mattresses which are made of its leaves when dried. The exact number of successive crops of hay produced on a Pyrenean farm, I am unable to state; because this must always depend upon the situation affording more or less facility for that system of irrigation by which they are so rapidly produced. Every stream of water is here a mine of wealth; and land with facility for being well watered, sells at three times the value of that which is without. The smallest stream from the top of a distant mountain is often conducted with amazing care around the side of a hill,

from whence small lateral, or rather curved lines
are cut, so as to let the water flow at any time,
over the surface of a whole meadow; and nothing
can exceed the vivid colouring of the green terraces thus produced. Tempted by their beauty,
I was only taught by experience to suspect their
real nature; for often when I thought to refresh
my weary feet with the cool soft turf, I found I
was walking in a plashy pool, more deceitful than
a bog. The astonishing rapidity with which these
meadows were again covered with waving grass,
appeared to me like nothing short of enchantment.
I used to amuse myself by watching the haymakers
at work upon these lovely fields; then I saw them
run away barefoot, with the hay upon their heads;
then the little shining streams ran down the slope;
and in a space of time inconceivably short, the
grass was again in a state for the whole process to
be repeated.

Of the uncertain tenure by which the advantages
of one of these mountain streams are held, we had a
good opportunity of judging during our residence in
the valley of Campan. For some weeks, the family
residing at St. Paul being absent, Mr. Ellis and
myself were left with the charge of their domestic
affairs. The gentleman of the house, as is usual with
all gentlemen who possess land in this neighbour-

hood, as well as with the owners of vineyards, allows
to a man who cultivates his land, and who lives on the
farm, one-half of the produce; the hind providing
all the labour, and the landlord supplying all the
seed. Knowing the value of the little stream of
water which supplied the place, the distance of its
highest source, and the many mountain farms it
had to pass in its way from these heights, we were
in constant apprehension lest our water should fail;
and one morning, finding that our fountain in the
garden shade was silent, we set out on a laborious
ascent to the source of the stream, and found at
last that a farmer, living at the extremity of the
highest range of cultivation, and at least three
miles from St. Paul, had taken the liberty of
turning these valuable waters upon his own land.
Such, indeed, is the general want of good faith in
these matters amongst the people of the Pyrenees,
that a man, in the capacity of a guard, is generally
paid by the farmers, to keep watch over the appropriation of the water, and thus protect the rights of
those in whose service he engages. Whether it
was the mere scandal of the place, I am unable to
say, but in our case the guard was reported to be
no more honest than his neighbours; and as an
additional reason why he was unworthy of trust,

we were told, with great emphasis, that he was
" *bien pauvre.* "

It was a source of some anxiety in such a neighbourhood as that of Campan, that our friends had
left under our care an orchard of the most beautiful autumn fruit. I have never seen either apples
or pears so tempting in appearance, as in the south
of France; but though so rich and lovely in their
colouring, those which grow in the immediate vicinity of the mountains, are certainly deficient in
flavour, and keep but a very short time. Great
pains is bestowed upon the pruning and training
of the apple trees, which are seldom allowed to
grow higher than a man can reach; so that their
clustering fruit is by this means more immediately
displayed to view. These apple trees are sometimes trained in the form of a flat screen, sometimes like a cup or vase, and sometimes like a
hollow sphere or globe; but whatever their fanciful form may be, they are closely cut every year, so
that the wood is always short, thick, and vigorous.

Cherry trees are so common amongst the Pyrenees, that in many places they fill the hedge rows;
and it is no unfrequent sight, to see children in the
trees, shaking off the branches, and pigs eating the
cherries as they fall. In our different rambles, we

358   SUMMER AND WINTER

have found both wild raspberries and wild currants, with vast quantities of a kind of bilberry, which, when boiled with sugar, makes a very tolerable sweetmeat. It does not appear consistent with the French taste, however, to eat any thing acid; and this may be one reason why gooseberries are seldom cultivated, because in their green state they would be of no sort of use here. Chestnuts and grapes are the only luxuries the Bearnais people allow themselves, and they appear to like dry bread quite as well as either.

I have said that my prejudices when I first visited the Pyrenees, were all in favour of the kind of pastoral and agricultural life which prevails amongst these mountains. A few months' observation upon the actual state of society, as it exists under these circumstances, was sufficient to convince me, that although natural, and simple, and apparently conducive to human happiness, it is in reality a state but little calculated to promote the moral or intellectual improvement of mankind. That very equality of rank, and comparatively equal distribution of property, for which the theorist in other countries sometimes sighs in vain, is here productive of its necessary result, in the limited sphere of action to which every individual is confined; while that absence of ambition, which we are apt to think contributes to social and domestic peace, renders the peasant of the Pyrenees as poor, as ignorant, and as destitute at the present day, as he was a hundred years ago.

Notwithstanding the genial atmosphere they breathe, the magnificent and lovely scenery by which they are surrounded, and the redundancy of vegetation which characterises the soil they cultivate, the inhabitants of the Pyrenees are for the most part miserably poor, and almost universally destitute of every thing beyond the bare necessaries of life; nor can even these be obtained except at the cost of unremitting labour, pursued upon the same unimproved system which their fathers and forefathers adopted hundreds of years before them. Thus the lives they lead are little calculated to raise them above the animals which share their labour; and the fact of there being no great landed proprietors, or men of wealth or influence amongst them, renders any hope of their condition being ameliorated, too visionary to be indulged. It is indeed pitiable to see the immense labour by which the scanty crops of their short summer are in some situations procured, when a little knowledge of superior methods of cultivation would render the district they inhabit as rich, as it is beautiful. A French writer, in regretting the little advantage

taken of the natural resources of their country, has
spoken of the many streams which "foam with
impatience, and demand to be worked;" and
certainly the whole aspect of nature in these delightful regions, is one of the most inviting that
can be imagined, as a field of operation for the
industry and the art of man.

My remarks upon the state of agriculture are, of
course, confined only to the neighbourhood of the
Pyrenees. I know that there are vast tracts of
land in France presenting a very different aspect,
as to cultivation and produce; although even in
some of these, economy of labour seems to be a
thing but little taken into account; as an instance
of which, it is no uncommon thing to see a plough
drawn by eight large bullocks, two abreast. In
the Pyrenees the owner of one such team would
be a man of wealth indeed. All the animals they
do possess, even their poultry, are extremely small;
and, except in the western Pyrenees, the people
themselves have the appearance of being ill-fed,
and when old, extremely feeble and emaciated. I
could scarcely have believed it, had I not myself
beheld the difference in the aspect and character
of people separated frequently by only a narrow
ridge of mountains. A friend of ours, who made
a short excursion into Spain, told us that such

distinctions were still more observable in passing the frontier. In the course of a ride of two or three hours, he found himself transported into the midst of a totally different race of people, possessing no one point of resemblance, either in person, dress, or habits. On the Spanish side of the frontier, no oxen were to be seen, mules only being used for all the common purposes of labour. Instead of the handsome and becoming dress of the Bearnais peasantry, the whole appearance of the people was wild, forlorn, and filthy; and instead of the thatched cottages and neat barns, which ornament the country on the French side, the Spanish habitations were low and slovenly, and wretched beyond description.

I have already said, that the people in the neighbourhood of Bagnères have not escaped the natural consequences of their country having been for so long a time the resort of idle and curious strangers. They have every appearance of being a people of much lower grade than those of the valley d'Ossau, to whom they are personally as inferior, as their habits and manners are less dignified and independent. Even in the lovely and Arcadian valley of Lesponne, there is scarcely a single woman not frightfully disfigured with the goitre, and there are adjacent villages said to be

R

362   SUMMER AND WINTER

almost peopled by idiots. In my frequent walks I
was perpetually meeting individuals of this description, of all the different grades of mental im-
becility; while in the department of the Lower
Pyrenees, I do not recollect to have seen one.

It is a somewhat melancholy fact, and one which
sufficiently proves the ineffectual method of cultivation pursued in the Pyrenees, that notwithstanding
the salubrious climate, and the indefatigable labour
of the occupants of the soil, the harvest of corn
annually reaped is not more than would suffice for
the maintenance of the people during six months
of the year.

I cannot more appropriately conclude the few
passing remarks I have ventured to make on this
subject, than by some observations of the same
literary friend to whom I have already been indebted, on the general state of France as an agricultural country.

" The French government, three years ago,
published tables of produce from 1815 to 1837.
By these it appears, that only half of the territory
of France is cultivated, so that no advance of
moment has been made, either in her system of
culture, or quantity of produce.

" France is far behind the rest of Europe in the
practical application of the scientific knowledge of

the day. No rail-roads traverse her territory. Merely a short line for pleasurable facility in the vicinity of Paris, at present exists. Her public vehicles are as clumsy as ever. Her great 'water power,' as the Americans call it, is entirely neglected. Her mineral treasures lie untouched. Her fine forests, although wood has risen one-third in value since 1830, only produce four per cent in return, to the proprietors, for want of easy communication. It is estimated that her produce of edible corn is ninety-eight millions of hectolitres, (rather more than two bushels English,) that her people consume only eighty-one millions of hectolitres; and yet such is the difficulty of internal transit, that in the year 1839 the government forbade the export of corn. The harvest that year had been good, yet particular localities were suffering from want, while others were glutted."

The rapid and extreme changes in the weather during the summer we spent amongst the Pyrenees, were such, that though at times astonished and almost oppressed with the brilliance of the sunshine, we were upon the whole as often chilled with the damp and cold. Still we persuaded ourselves that the autumn would be fine and settled, until, while labouring under this delusion, we were surprised about the middle of September, by one

of those storms of snow, which are always regarded
in the Pyrenees as harbingers of winter, and which
consequently drive away the numerous visitors from
the places of public resort.

On the sixteenth of September, after many days
of cold and wet, we looked out in the morning, and
saw the mountains all around us covered with snow.
In our evening walk that day, facing a sharp north
wind, we met with the courier from Baréges, who
told us he had that morning been detained five
hours by the weather, and had found the snow in
crossing the Tourmalet, three feet deep. The season
of his labours in passing from Bagnères to Baréges,
had commenced on the first of June, and would
close on the last day of September, so that the
summer in these regions, may be said to last only
four months.

Baréges is the highest situation in the Pyrenees
to which travellers and invalids resort. In the
winter it is entirely deserted by all its inhabitants,
who go to Luz, and many of the houses, if not all,
are covered with snow. We thought, early in the
month of June, when we spent a night there, that
the place had a strange vault-like feeling; but had
little idea that our lodging had so recently emerged
from its wintry covering. The courier told us this
day, that many of the inhabitants were already

taking their furniture and other property to Luz. It is chiefly in the spring, or when the snows first begin to melt, that those terrible ravages take place in the neighbourhood of Baréges, which every year destroy many of the houses in the town, and considerable portions of the road; and when to these accounts are added the tales the people tell of its being the resort of hungry bears and wolves, an idea may be formed of the savage wildness and dreary desolation of the place. Yet even here, in the summer months, are cafés, and reading-rooms, and I believe ball-rooms too, with many of the accustomed imitations of all that belongs to the gay world elsewhere; and when we recollect that this place was first brought into celebrity by the residence of Madame Maintenon, who brought the young duke of Maine here for the benefit of its healing waters, we may well imagine that Baréges possesses some strong recommendation, to counterbalance so much that is gloomy in its situation, and savage in its scenery.

The first symptom of the approach of autumn, which, however, I was unable to believe in at the time, had been the coming down of the flocks and herds from the mountains. These flocks, which used to fill the roads, had ceased to pass, at least a month before the middle of September. Often

have I looked at the shepherds as I passed them
on the road, and longed in vain to know what were
their feelings on returning again to the abodes of
men, after their companionship with all the sublime
and solitary features of that pathless world which
so long had been their home.   Often have I longed
to ask them where they had found shelter from the
thunder-storms that rolled with such awful grandeur
amongst the hills; where they had slept when the
nights were dark and cheerless; were they had
been when the mountain tops where wrapped in
clouds; and how they had found companionship in
those eagle heights, when days, and weeks, and
months rolled on, and no human voice was ever
near them.   Their answer to these questions would
probably have been a very simple one.   For their
companionship they might have pointed to the
faithful dog; for their shelter, to the mountain
cave, or to the little moveable straw house just
long enough for a man to creep into, with which
they are provided while watching their cattle on
the hills.

The last flock we saw, was one of a hundred
sheep and three goats, which came every night
from the adjoining mountain to lodge in a small
pen, or parc, as it was called, placed for them in
one of the meadows of St. Paul.   This pen was

moved every night, and the shepherd received two francs per day for lodging his sheep there. I had often wondered why there was along with every flock, about the proportion of three goats to a hundred sheep; and we then learned that the mountain dog, so important to the shepherd, was fed while in the mountains, by the milk of these goats. The dog belonging to this flock, used to stay beside the pen all night, while his master went away to sleep. He never attempted to drive the sheep when they went out, but always walked first with his master. I now discovered also, that the sheep which appeared to be led so patriarchally by love for their master, were in reality led by their love of the salt which he carried in his pocket, into which the goats often thrust their noses. I tried the experiment of distributing a little amongst them myself, but it made me quite too popular, and I was obliged to give the matter up; for the sheep and goats of the Pyrenees, notwithstanding the mountain lives they lead for at least four months in the year, have so little idea of fearing any human being, that they scarcely can be made to move out of the way, when you meet them on the road.

The snow which had fallen so early this autumn, never disappeared from the mountains, though summer again smiled in the valleys; and it was a curious sight to see the hills sprinkled with white almost as low down as the chateau of St. Paul, while immediately below its verdant terraces, the people were making hay in the fields.

The cold we experienced at this season, was of very partial extent. Even at Tarbes, the weather was comparatively warm and dry; and the family at St. Paul, on returning from a visit of some weeks to a situation not far distant from Toulouse, told us that they had been all the while in a climate of the most brilliant sunshine, while we had been enveloped in wintry clouds; and that such had been the heat and the glare of the atmosphere with them, that the windows had always been closed in with green blinds, during the middle of the day, while we went shivering from room to room, or looked out upon a landscape half enveloped in snow.

Every one was now hastening from the mountains; and Bagnères, that gay and cheerful little town, which had hitherto presented so lively a scene, was so entirely changed in its character and appearance, as to look as if some great calamity, some plague, or some general desolation, had stripped it of more than half its former occupants. All the principal shops, which during the summer season are supplied by tradespeople from Toulouse, and other towns, were now closed; all its boarding-houses shut up; and the fashionable promenade, a walk of about a mile in extent, which used to be perfectly filled with evening loiterers, was now desolate, silent, and strewn with the dead leaves of the poplars, which came flickering down with every movement of their tall stems.

The general disposition to escape to a warmer and more genial climate, seized us also; but it was not before the 30th of October that we were able to set out on our return to Pau. On that morning we left the old priory of St. Paul—the hospitable home where we had received so much kindness, never, in all human probability, to behold it again, our friends accompanying us at an early hour as far as one of the little bridges, where we had so often sat down to rest in our walks between Bagnères and St. Paul.

The acquaintance which we make with nature is so much like friendship, that when I took my last near view of the majestic Pic du Midi, rising as I had so often seen it, over the dreary forest of burnt pines immediately behind St. Paul, I felt a melancholy satisfaction in thinking I was not leaving it altogether, that I should again see it from a more distant point of view, arrayed in sublimer beauty.

R 3

370 SUMMER AND WINTER

Still there was the limpid Adour with its many tributary streams; the village of Aste, embowered in wood, with its venerable ruins, rich in remembrances of the ancient glory of the family of Grammont; the flowery L'heris, with its noble crest rising above the neighbouring mountains; the shepherd's hut on the far height; the beetling crags that seemed to change their colouring with every variation of the atmosphere; the green terraces; the tall poplars;—these, with the nearer and more familiar objects, down to the cottage gardens by the side of the road, and the idiot boy who used to wheel his barrow with an air of as much importance as if he had ruled a kingdom;—all these, I felt that I should never see again; and such is the intercourse we hold with nature alone, that these had all become as familiar to me as if I had dwelt amongst them from my childhood.

The weather, early on the morning of our journey, had looked doubtful, but as the day advanced it became beautiful in the extreme, and more welcome to my feelings, for the cool freshness which mingled with the brilliant sunshine. Indeed, beautiful as the summer unquestionably is in the Pyrenees, the fine weather of autumn is in my opinion, far more conducive to enjoyment; not the less so, because the aspect of nature then presents that striking effect of colouring, which contrasts the richest tints of foliage with the finest white of mountain snow.

We had often been told that the range of the Pyrenees looked more splendid from Tarbes than from Pau, and we had now an opportunity of judging of this fact for ourselves, the day being most favourable for such a purpose. But whether it is that first impressions are the strongest, or merely that tastes and ideas of beauty differ, we did not think the mountains, when seen from Tarbes, so fine as from the situation in which we had at first beheld them at Pau. They may possibly appear higher, but there are fewer points of distinction. All seem to run into one vast connected line, while from Pau we can see them separate into more distinct ranges, rising from the plains, and running up into the most majestic heights, which maintain a certain degree of individuality, even while blended by the effect of distance into one general line. The Pic du Midi de Bigorre, certainly appears higher from Tarbes, and we have here the advantage of seeing the mountains of Bagnères de Luchon, which are not visible from Pau.

I cannot mention this latter place without a

feeling of regret, that we were never able to
accomplish a journey to it from Campan, from
which place it is reached by a ride of eight or ten
hours across the mountains.   We had ordered
horses for this purpose from Bagnères, more than
once, but were disappointed every time, either by
a change in the weather, or by our horses, as is
frequently the case in this part of France, failing to
come at the appointed time.   Mr. Ellis made part
of the journey, in company with a party of friends,
to the Col d'Aspen, situated on this route, from
whence may be seen at once, three distinct valleys,
and a vast range of snowy and apparently inaccessible mountains.   The carriage road from Bagnères, is said to be scarcely less beautiful and
astonishing, leading into a stupendous defile of
mountains along the course of the river Garonne,
which takes its rise from one of the lakes above
Bagnères de Luchon.

It is no uncommon thing for travellers to speak
in terms of glowing enthusiasm, of the beauty of
the plain of Tarbes.   I can only imagine those
who do so, to have become tired of mountains, and
pleased to get out into a perfect flat, for such it is,
surrounded by richly wooded hills.   Perhaps at
the time we were there, it appeared to the least
advantage; for the Indian corn, which covers

nearly the whole surface, was then stripped of its waving leaves; while nothing remained of it in the fields, but the dry brown stem, with the cob at the top, which the people were then busily gathering; and this state of the Indian corn harvest, sufficiently accounted for the uniformly brown colouring of the country which we had observed from the mountain heights, when looking over this plain, and the extent of country stretching towards Toulouse.

Tarbes appears to be more a place of business, and less of pleasure, than Pau; but like that town, it has its immense barracks, and seems to be half filled with soldiers.   It has its *place* too, or square for public walking; for what could the French do without such a resource?   In vain to them would mountains rise, and valleys slope before their view. Without their public square of bare gravel, and their rows of stunted trees, they would have no spot of ground on which to refresh themselves with a walk.   Even St. Paul, with its cool avenues, and green shades, and verdant turf beneath the feet, was considered a little too *triste* for a lengthened residence; and the lady of the mansion was one day asked by a Frenchwoman, if she did not often drive over to Bagnères to walk on the Coustous.

374   SUMMER AND WINTER

I must not, however, undervalue these most
convenient places of promenade to the stranger,
to whom the general leisure of French travelling
allows, as it did to us at Tarbes, two hours for
breakfast.   Here then I walked, until our vehicle
was ready, with the "snow shining mountains"
stretching in a magnificent range before my view,
alternately looking at them, and turning to objects
less sublime; amongst which I observed that the
whole arrangement of the luggage on the top of
the diligence, was conducted by a woman, who
lifted and stowed all the packages, climbing up and
down with a facility that showed she was well accustomed to the occupation.

I think I never shall forget the balmy atmosphere of that day, rendered perhaps the more
striking to us, from our having lived so long
amongst the sharp air of the mountains, which
differs widely from that of the plains.   I had been
prepared to expect that the climate of the south of
France would be relaxing to the bodily frame, and
consequently depressing to the spirits.   So far
from this, however, I do not recollect once to have
felt during my whole residence in the south, that
causeless and indescribable dejection of mind
which most of the inhabitants of our northern isle
at times experience, and which no one is perhaps

more intimately acquainted with than myself. I
know not whether the malady is mental or physical,
or both; but I believe many of my country people
will bear me out in the assertion, that one of the
greatest drawbacks upon individual happiness, and
one of the greatest hinderances to laudable exertion, which we experience in England, arises from
a want of elasticity of spirit and animal vigour,—
from a sort of sinking of the soul, if I may so
express myself, which often makes the dawn of
each successive morning appear like a renewal of
hopeless conflict; every unexpected event a fresh
hinderance to the course we have to pursue; and
every necessary exertion an insupportable trial. It
requires, I am well aware, a combination of many
causes, before the disease attains this height. It
is not my business now to enter into any farther
remarks upon what these causes are, or may be.
All I wish to state in relation to the subject is,
that in the south of France this peculiar and
apparently causeless depression is seldom known,
except as the result of bodily disease. Nor do I
speak merely from my own experience. I have
the testimony of others to the same fact. The
effect of real affliction is unquestionably the same
in all climates; but in that of the south of France,
supposing the mind to be free from the pressure

376　　　SUMMER AND WINTER

of actual calamity, there is an effect produced by
the clearness of the atmosphere, the brightness of
the sunshine, and the elasticity of the air, which
makes the mere animal sensation of being alive, of
breathing, and moving, a perpetual enjoyment.
All who read these pages, but especially the young,
will be able to realise the kind of sensation experienced, in setting out on a pleasant journey, on a
fine bright morning, in company with the friends
they love best, leaving nothing behind them to
regret, and fancying much before them to invite.
Now something like this sensation seems to return
with every morning, in the delightful climate I
have endeavoured to describe—something which
makes another day be welcomed as another blessing—something which makes the very air we
breathe, at once a refreshment and a balm; which
sends the sunshine like light into the soul, and
which opens all the springs of animal enjoyment,
to flow with fresh vigour through their natural
channels of energy and feeling.

All this, I am aware, may be deemed somewhat
fanciful by those whose feelings are not influenced
like my own, by impressions produced on the outward senses; yet one strong evidence that such is
really the effect of this climate, I have often thought
might be found in the almost uniform cheerfulness

of the native inhabitants of the country. What else, for instance, could enable the poor women to endure fatigue and labour as they do? What else could reconcile them to the life of poverty and privation which so many of them lead? And what else could render them so cheerful and contented, that they have scarcely a wish for higher advantages, or greater facilities than they now enjoy? It may be said that the poor Irish are cheerful under circumstances far more depressing, and with a climate very different from that of Bearn. But the Irish are cheerful in a widely different manner from the Bearnais. Theirs is the cheerfulness of fitful mirth, the lightheartedness of reckless gaiety, more melancholy, more touching in its transient exuberance, than the most uniform and settled gloom. The cheerfulness of the Bearnais is that of regularly animated industry, of the careful husbanding of all the means with which their limited knowledge has brought them acquainted; and thus it never fails them in winter or summer, in storm or sunshine; for each individual having his wealth and his power within himself, and no human influence to conciliate or to fear, he is able to gather in security and peace, the full return of his unremitting activity.

The opinion of Sir James Clarke with regard to

the climate of Pau is, that it is bad for rheumatism, as well as for cases of bronchial disease accompanied with much general relaxation; and that for consumptive patients it is too changeable. He recommends that invalids should arrive in September or October, and leave in May or June. He agrees with all travellers in stating, that the most striking characteristic of this climate is its calmness, high winds being of rare occurrence, and of short duration.

Although more than ever convinced of the many disadvantages belonging to the climate of England, on almost every other ground my prejudices in favour of that country were strengthened by a year's residence in France. With these prejudices it was natural to prefer returning to Pau, to making the experiment of wintering in any place less frequented by the English; for, unlike many travellers, I can truly say that the kindness and social fellowship of the people of my own country, have constituted one of my greatest pleasures while abroad. The town and neighbourhood of Pau are also becoming more Anglicised every year. The addition of many handsome buildings, during the past year, had been made to some of the principal streets; while the increase of many of those comforts of life, to which the English are accustomed to attach at least their full share of value, indicate a disposition on the part of the inhabitants of Pau to render their beautifully situated town still more inviting to strangers than it already is. It is curious, indeed, to see the attempts that are made to meet the wants and the wishes of our country-people, even down to mince-pies on Christmas day!

To invalids, however, there are advantages of far greater importance; for it is in cases of sickness and affliction, that early prepossessions, and home associations, are often awakened in the most lively manner. Here, then, the suffering patient can have the kind attentions of English doctors, there being two regularly residing in the place, with the frequent addition of others visiting it for their own health; and when we consider that many invalids are hastened away from England with very little time for preparation, and often arrive here imperfectly acquainted with the language, the satisfaction of being placed under the care of an English doctor is sometimes one of no trivial importance to the friends of the patients, as well as to the sufferers themselves.

For those English gentlemen who felt the time hang heavily on their hands, there was an English news-room the first winter we spent at Pau. We found on our arrival there the second time, that it had been given up. This loss, however, may be easily supplied, as all newspapers can be sent from England at the trifling expense of one sous. Adjoining what was then the news-room, is an English circulating library and stationer's establishment, where a great variety of English books may be had, including some of the most ornamental works which grace the drawing-rooms of England.

On our return to Pau this time, we were more than ever struck with the loveliness of the surrounding scenery,—the foliage then glowing in the richest tints of autumn, while the mountain heights were clothed in the purest snow. We soon, however, had to experience the general severity of the weather, from which even these sunny regions were not exempt. Cold winds and storms of snow commenced as early as November; and the weather throughout the whole winter was so strikingly contrasted with the first season we had spent at Pau, that we could well believe what the people of the country told us, that the first winter was a specimen of the best—the second, of the worst weather to which their climate is ever subject, nothing like it having been known for the space of at least ten years.

Still there were occasionally those sudden and

astonishing changes which seemed to transport us, in the course of a few hours, to an opposite region of the globe. On no occasion was this more striking to us, than on the day of the funeral of an American gentleman, who had come all the way from Boston, in a state of hopeless consumption. He had been but two months at Pau, and the weather had been most ungenial all the time. On the morning of his death it suddenly changed; and when his mortal remains were committed to the grave, attended by many of the English gentlemen of the place, but by no relative, the balmiest, gentlest air was blowing, that I ever remember to have experienced; while the most brilliant sunshine was rapidly melting the snows, even on the distant mountains.

After one of these pleasant changes, some months later in the spring, Mr. Ellis took the opportunity of making an excursion to a part of the Pyrenees we had not yet visited; and in a short journey of three days, he became convinced, that those who neglect to visit Oleron, and the valley d'Aspe, will leave unexplored some of the most striking beauties of this country.

Leaving the road to Eaux Chaudes, at Gan, he took the route to Oleron, which for five or six miles is extremely hilly, until, on passing Biller, it

382   SUMMER AND WINTER

descends into a broad valley, and becomes level
and good for the remaining distance, about ten
miles.

Oleron was one of the ancient bishoprics of
Bearn.   Its cathedral, though as large as that of
Lescar, is greatly inferior in its style of architecture and ornaments.   Oleron and St. Marie contain a population of ten thousand.   It has several
manufactories, but the traffic it has long carried on
with Spain, is said to be on the decline.   The
numerous and respectable-looking villas in its
suburbs, indicate the prosperity of the place; and
the larger size, and more excellent order of the
fields, afford agreeable evidence of the improved
state of agriculture in this neighbourhood.   A diligence passes daily from Oleron through the valley
d'Aspe, to Jaca, in Spain; and for five francs, the
tourist may thus be conveyed to the farthest town
on the French frontier, the road which runs rather
to the eastward of south winds with the course
of the beautiful river, the Gave d'Aspe, along the
valley of that name, the ascent all the way being
exceedingly gradual, and the road in excellent
order.

On reaching the village of Bidos, which lies to
the left of the road, the traveller is surrounded by
a number of green and beautifully-shaped conical

hills, which lie scattered at the feet of this range of the Pyrenees, and constitute one of the most characteristic features in the scenery. Villages are now seen at intervals on both sides of the valley, which gradually becomes narrower; and at a short distance beyond Escot, the buttresses of lofty sugar-loaf mountains intersect each other, adding greatly to the picturesque effect of the scene, by giving a serpentine form to the course of the Gave, and the road by its side.

Bedous, situated at the distance of three hours' journey from Oleron, is the last post town on this route. It contains about twelve hundred inhabitants, and has one auberge, where, though it cannot boast of greater cleanliness than most French inns in this neighbourhood, excellent refreshments may be had, and saddle-horses procured at a moderate rate. Immediately beyond Bedous, the valley spreads out into a beautiful hollow or plain, around which are seen no less than five respectable-looking villages. In one of these, Osse, there is a Protestant community of thirty families, who in this wild and remote region have retained the faith of the Bible, in opposition to the influence of Rome, to which, others more favoured in many respects, have long since submitted.

A little farther to the right of the circular

384   SUMMER AND WINTER

plain is the village of Accous, the birthplace of
Despourrins, the poet of the Pyrenees, whose songs
in the native language of the people, are not only
held in the highest estimation by the mountaineers
themselves, but are deservedly popular throughout
the whole of the south of France. It is scarcely
possible to imagine a region more fitted to call
into exercise the elements of poetic feeling than
this, or more calculated to give sublimity and
power to the habitual tone of the human mind.
In front of the village is the plain already noticed,
probably about two miles across, highly cultivated,
and adorned with the cottages and villages of the
peasantry. Mountains rise beyond, of varied elevation, some clothed almost to their summits with
grass, or the bright and feathery box waving above
grey jutting rocks of marble,—and others barren,
inaccessible, and apparently covered with eternal
snows; while the secluded valley is intersected only
by the sparkling stream which flows through its
centre, to mingle with the Gave d'Oleron, and
finally to cast itself into the Atlantic at Bayonne.

On the other side of the valley, and behind the
poet's native village, the Christalara and other
mountains of equal elevation and wilder forms,
covered with apparently deeper snows, rear a
lofty and apparently impassable barrier, between

this romantic region and the celebrated valley d'Ossau.   In front of Accous, on the summit of a gracefully-formed hill, partially covered with trees, and traversed by winding paths, a chaste and beautiful obelisk of marble from the quarries in the adjacent mountains, has been erected in honour of the memory of Despourrins, and appropriately associates the recollections of the mountain bard, with the grandeur of the scenery amongst which he, in all probability, found his inspiration and his theme.

The road from Accous to Eggum leads through scenes of grandeur and beauty equal to any in the Pyrenees, especially near the ancient bridge d'Esquelle.   Not far from this place, by a path which leads to Lescun, the traveller may visit a beautiful cascade.   Shortly after leaving the antique village of Estaut, his attention is arrested by a road called *Le Chemin de Manière,* one of the most astonishing designs of a genius to which few things appeared impossible.   It is built up, in some places, from deep parts of the ravine; and in others, actually cut out of the face of a perpendicular rock, at the distance of five hundred feet above the valley, and at an equal distance below the craggy summit of the mountain.   This road was cut by the order of Buonaparte, for the purpose of bringing down timber from the pine forests which crown

s

the mountains beyond. The quality of the timber, it is said, was not found sufficiently good for the use of the navy of France, and the road is now seldom used.

Nearly opposite this road, is the fortified pass called Portalet; and at a quarter of an hour's ride beyond it, thirty miles from Oleron, is Urdos, the last French town; shortly after leaving which, the traveller enters a narrow defile leading into Spain, which can only be passed on mules. From this place, a view is obtained of the craggy summit of the Mont d'Aspe, which gives the name to the valley over which it seems to preside.

The traffic through this valley is great. Not fewer than fifteen thousand mules pass along the road into Spain every year. An equal number pass also through the valley of Ossau, by Eaux Chaudes and Gabas, and probably as many by Cauterets and Gavarnie; and as the French government imposes a tax on each animal imported into Spain, a very considerable revenue must be collected at each of these mountain passes.

Mr. Ellis was much struck with the character of the people in the valley d'Aspe, who appeared clean, active, good-natured, and cheerful, resembling those of Ossau, and far superior to the inhabitants of the department of the Hautes Pyrénées.

This superiority, as well as the general appearance
of order, industry, and prosperity in the neighbourhood of Oleron, may doubtless be accounted for in
some measure, by the facility of communication
between that place and Bayonne. His general
impression was one most favourable to this region
of the Pyrenees, a visit to which will amply repay
the lover of nature in her wildest and most beautiful form.

Having now visited, as far as was practicable to
us, all the situations most admired and most frequented in the Pyrenees, and the time having
arrived for our return to England, we prepared,
with much pleasure, to bid adieu to scenes which,
notwithstanding their many attractions, we still felt
were not our home; and in conclusion, we asked
this serious question, which it ought to be the
business of all travellers to answer to themselves,
on leaving a foreign country—what have we seen
that we desire to imitate? what, that we ought to
study more earnestly than ever to avoid?

I should say without hesitation, that what I have
most admired amongst the French, has been their
obliging good nature, and the simplicity which
characterises many of their habits. Yes, I repeat
it—their simplicity. We are apt to imagine, be-

cause we are more blunt—perhaps because we are
more vulgar in England, that we must be more
simple.   Yet there is certainly a species of vul-
garity—that of *pretension*—from which the French
are comparatively exempt.   In France, a peasant
is a peasant, a shopkeeper a shopkeeper, and
consequently a gentleman a gentleman.   I do not
mean that the last two, or even the first and the last,
are incompatible; but I mean that they are never
farther from being so, than when men are ashamed
to appear what they really are.   In France, too,
there exists a degree of moral courage, which
might put our country to shame, and which consists in daring to be poor—in dressing and living
according to their means, when those means are
extremely limited.   This is what I call simplicity;
and when this is found in connexion with the
influence of Christian principle, how much does
it adorn the character of those whose profession is
one of meekness and lowliness of heart!

The greatest defect I have observed in the
French character, as compared with the English,
is a want of strict regard to the truth; and in this
remark I would be understood to refer merely to
that limited portion of France which has fallen
under my immediate observation.   Even here I

am willing to grant, that half the falsehoods told, are invented for the sake of amusing, or giving pleasure; but if the license to speak what is known to be untrue be once admitted, no human power can stem the tide of evil thus let in, or say for what selfish or mean purpose this license may not be employed. The want of truth is consequently one which neither amiable feeling, nor brilliant intellect, can possibly supply; and if as a nation, the English have more regard for truth in their social and domestic intercourse, than their neighbours on the other side of the channel, long may they cherish a distinction which forms the only true basis of national and individual greatness.

With regard to travelling abroad, an amusement which is generally thought to improve the manners and expand the mind, so far as I have had an opportunity of judging of its effects, I am decidedly of opinion, that except where health requires it, in nine cases out of ten, it is more injurious than beneficial to the English character. I am quite prepared to allow that there are cases, where the religious foundation of the character is well established, and where the mind is already so far enlightened, as to understand and appreciate what is really most worthy of admiration, that great

s 2

390   SUMMER AND WINTER

advantage may result from travelling abroad. Generally speaking, however, such is not the case with those who travel; and to the common order of minds, educated in the popular manner, nothing can be more hazardous to the formation of character, than long-continued travelling abroad. The mere fact of being hurried away from the natural sphere of relative and domestic duties, and kept in a continued state of excitement as to where to go, and what to see next, is of itself, a dangerous experiment for youth to make. But in addition to this, there is the absence of those accustomed barriers of protection, which a religious education places around the family circle when at home. By absolute necessity, some of these are removed when travelling abroad; by carelessness or indifference, others follow; until, in an almost incredibly short space of time, the same individuals have learned to tolerate what they once regarded with horror, and to turn with disgust from what was once esteemed as the highest privilege.

Nor is this change, so often wrought upon the minds of the young, less fatal in its consequences from the gradual and insidious progress which it makes. Perhaps the first encroachment upon religious habits, is necessarily made by the omission of family worship. Next comes the absence of all means of public worship, and so on, until little by little the whole course of life and habit is changed; while on the other hand, the good-natured and amiable affability of foreigners, who are even professedly without religion, combined with that gentleness, kindness, and urbanity of manner, which Christians would do well to imitate, has a startling effect upon the minds of the young, and often leads them to compare the engaging manners of their new acquaintance, who make no pretension to religion, with the bluntness, homeliness, or austerity of some of the religious professors they have left at home.

Superficial as all conclusions drawn from such observations must necessarily be, they are such as the mind of youth is not slow to arrive at; and for this reason, as well as many others, I am convinced there is great danger in bringing young persons of unformed character, abroad. The more we are inured in early life to the performance of practical duty, the stronger will be our moral basis, the more consistent our religious life. Let duty be the goal at which we aim, and pleasure will not fail to be found by the way; but if amusement, even of an apparently wholesome and natural character, be made the business of life, duty will soon be found too irksome to be regarded, and will eventually be either ungraciously performed, or wholly given up.

The business of travelling is to see all that is worth seeing in one place, to lay plans for leaving it, and then to hurry on to another. After years spent in this manner, is it reasonable to expect that a family of daughters will settle down into their relative positions, and remain quietly at home? Will they not rather grow listless when there is no longer any novelty to see? fretful when there is no change to anticipate? and depressed and spiritless when there is no excitement to lead on to exertion?

Far happier in her own feelings, and in her influence upon others, is that unaspiring individual, who having stored her mind with the information of the most intelligent travellers, is satisfied to remain within the home circle formed around the domestic hearth, filling up the measure of daily duty, and willing either to go or to stay, as the good or the happiness of others may require. The mere act of travelling can add nothing to the peace of mind, or the satisfaction with which such a life is accompanied; nor can the absence of what is generally regarded as amusement, take anything from that peace away. If it never happens in the lifetime of such an individual, that duty calls her abroad, she will not be less estimable as a daughter, a wife, or a mother; and if it should occur in her experience, that duty leads her from her native land, she will be one of the first to feel and appreciate all the additional pleasure she is by this means enabled lawfully to enjoy.

THE END.

EDITORIAL NOTES

p. 8, ll. 8–12: *for amongst the writers ... eight or ten years ago*: In the decades previous to Mrs Ellis's travel account, few books on the French Pyrenees had been published in Britain. The most recent ones had been published in the first and second decades of the nineteenth century. After consulting B. Colbert, 'Bibliography of British Travel Writing, 1780–1840: The European Tour, 1814–1818 (excluding Britain and Ireland)', *Cardiff Corvey: Reading the Romantic Text*, 13 (Winter 2004), pp. 5–44, I have found only three travel accounts that include descriptions of the Pyrenees, namely: M. Birkbeck, *Notes on a Journey through France, from Dieppe through Paris and Lyons, to the Pyrenees, and back through Toulouse, in July, August, and September, 1814: Describing the Habits of the People and the Agriculture of the Country* (London: Printed and Sold by William Phillips, 1814); H. Coxe, *The Gentleman's Guide in his Tour through France; Being Particularly Descriptive of the Southern and Western Departments [...]* (London: Sherwood, Neely & Jones, [1817]; and J. Milford, *Observations, Moral, Literary, and Antiquarian: Made during a Tour through the Pyrenees, South of France, Switzerland, the Whole of Italy and the Netherlands in the Years 1814 and 1815*, 2 vols (London: T. Davison, Whitefriars, for Longman, Hurst, Rees, Orme, and Brown and J. Hatchard, 1818). During the European Grand Tour in the eighteenth and nineteenth centuries, visits to the Alps (especially to the main attraction, Mont Blanc) had been the highlight of English travel books regarding the Pyrenees, the mountain range which was seen as the entrance to Spain, a country that was left aside in the interest of the 'Grand Tourists'. Mrs Ellis forgets to mention *Sketches in the Pyrenees, with some Remarks on Languedoc, Provence, and the Cornice*, 2 vols (London: Longman, Rees, Orme, Brown, Greene, and Longman, 1837), by the poet and traveller Mary Boddington (1776–1840), published only a few years before her account on the Pyrenees.

p. 9, ll. 5–13: *narrative of Mr Inglis ... passing notice of Pau*: The general lack of travel accounts on the French Pyrenees is most probably the reason why Mrs Ellis had to rely on a book on Spain – a country in which she was not at all interested – for information on this mountain range: H. D. Inglis (1795–1858), the author of *Spain in 1830*, 2 vols (London: Whittaker, Treacher and Co., 1831), was one of the few who, despite the state of war in the north of Spain, entered the country through the Basque provinces and crossed it from north to south in only eight months. Inglis's account on the French side of the Pyrenees is nevertheless insufficient for Mrs Ellis, as it makes only a few passing remarks about Pau. Nevertheless, Mrs Ellis acknowledges a polite gratitude to this Scotsman's travel account by borrowing from him the motto she uses under the title of her own travel account: 'I know of no pleasure that will compare with going abroad, excepting one – returning home' (Inglis, *Spain in 1830*, p. 307).

p. 11, l. 9: *Pau, April 2ⁿᵈ, 1841*: According to the dates provided by Mrs Ellis in her travel account, she spent approximately eleven months in the area of Pau, spanning from the very last days of December 1839 to 30 October 1840. The preface is, however, signed at Pau in April 1841. Judging by the date of the book's first review, showing that it was published just before June 1841, it seems feasible to suppose that the date and place printed at the end of the preface were added just before the book went to the printing press, and was not an indication that the Ellises were still in Pau at this date.

p. 17, l. 13–p. 18, l. 1: *the routes most frequently pursued by English travellers through France, Switzerland, and Italy*: France, Switzerland and Italy were the fashionable countries to visit during the educational European Grand Tour of the eighteenth and nineteenth centuries. The Iberian Peninsula (and hence, the Pyrenees as its main entrance by land) had remained far from the interest of a large bulk of British travellers until it was deemed more accessible, especially after the publication of R. Ford, *A Handbook of Travellers in Spain, and Readers and Home* (London: John Murray, 1st edn, 1845) and its sequel *Gatherings from Spain* (London: John Murray, 1846). In the late 1830s and early 1840s Spain was mainly visited by the odd health-seeker (Ford himself, who moved to Seville and Granada in search of a benevolent climate for his ailing wife), British and French art-seekers (such as Standish Hall and Baron Taylor, to name but a few), who wished to take advantage of the chaos resulting from the Peninsular War (1809–14), the First Carlist War (1832–9) and the Spanish government's 'desamortizaciones' (the Ecclesiastical Confiscations of Mendizábal from 1835 to 1837 to acquire Spanish works of art for derisory sums) and by other post-Romantic 'odd-men-out' such as George Borrow, who traversed the country trying to sell volumes of the New Testament. Visiting Spain during such turbulent years was almost unthinkable for the majority of women who aspired to travel for pleasure and for an education, and the few that did tread on Spanish soil had preferred a sea voyage to the Peninsula by entering through Gibraltar, Cádiz, Málaga or less frequently Barcelona. This was the case for Maria Witson, the author of *Spain and Barbary. Letters to a Younger Sister during a visit to Gibraltar, Cádiz, Sevilla, Tangier* (London: J. Hatchland, 1837), Elizabeth M. Grosvenor, about whom little is known except for her private cruise in the Mediterranean resulting in *Narrative of a Yacht Voyage in the Mediterranean during the Years 1840 and 1841*, 2 vols (London: John Murray, 1842), visiting only Cádiz, Seville, Tangier, Gibraltar, Málaga and Granada; and Isabella Frances Romer, Marchioness of Westminster, who visited Spain in 1842 as part of a longer journey through France, Egypt and Palestine and wrote *The Rhone, the Darro and the Guadalquivir: A Summer Ramble in 1842*, 2 vols (London: R. Bentley, 1843). Witson's route was a transversal north-to-south journey through France and then from Marseille by boat to Barcelona, Málaga, Cádiz and Gibraltar (followed by a short excursion to Granada). Indeed, in 1840–1 Mrs Ellis did not think it safe enough to cross the Spanish border, no matter how close she was to it several times during her French residence. Coming so close to the French–Spanish frontier was like coming to the very borders of European civilization. After all, with the exception of Lady Elizabeth Holland in the very early years of the nineteenth century, very few British women had dared to do so.

p. 18, l. 5: *Mr Ellis*: Rev. William Ellis (1794–1872), always referred to in Mrs Ellis's travel account as 'Mr Ellis', was her husband. He was an English missionary and a geographical and travel writer on Polynesia, the Hawaiian Islands and Madagascar. He belonged to the London Missionary Society. After his first wife's death, Rev. Ellis married the author of this book, née Sarah Stickney, in 1838. He wrote a biography of his first wife, *Memoir of Mrs Mary Mercy Ellis* (1836).

p. 25, l. 26–p. 26, l. 3: *Notwithstanding the Sabbath ... on other days*: Mr and Mrs Ellis were Congregationalists (a denomination of the Protestant faith) and therefore believed that the Sabbath had to be respected. The French custom of making this day a market day scandalized the author, who seemed to have forgotten that she was in a predominantly Roman Catholic country.

p. 30, ll. 5–7: *I must not ... construction of the language*: Here Mrs Ellis is making a subtle criticism about the teaching of foreign languages in Britain (and indeed, anywhere in the world at the time): no matter how much French literature the educated Britons might have read and learnt, their capacity for oral expression in spoken French in aspects related to daily basic needs for survival (looking for accommodation, for example) were practically non-existent. The teaching of foreign languages during the nineteenth century used to follow the precepts of the so called 'Grammar Translation' methodology, based on an intensive and extensive reading of the French classics and paying little or no attention to the skills of listening and speaking.

p. 36, l. 9: *the nobler sex*: This is the expression Mrs Ellis uses to refer to men. In those days women were on the other hand referred to as 'the fair' or 'the fairer sex', an expression that is still used in current times, although it is now considered offensive by feminists.

p. 40, ll. 13–15: *The peasants of the country ... already wore the look of Spain*: A first sign of Mrs Ellis's prejudices and scant knowledge of Spain and its inhabitants is evident here: Spaniards are, according to her, characterized by their beret-like caps and the cloaks thrown over their shoulders. This description, although more elaborately developed further along in the travel account, remains basically the same throughout the rest of the book.

p. 43, ll. 5–6: *sallow, coarse, and vulgar*: Another of Mrs Ellis's Spanish preconceptions must have been that women in Spain were invariably pretty due to their southern/oriental traits. They had been highly praised by Byron in his *Childe Harold's Pilgrimage* and in his epistolary. Other young Romantics, such as Benjamin Disraeli, author of *Home Letters written by the late Earl of Beaconsfield in 1830 and 1831* (London: John Murray, 1885), contributed to this idea by insisting on the Oriental connection of their beauty.

p. 44, ll. 15–16: *an old college, which appears to be a place of some importance*: The Gothic Cathedral of Aire-sur-l'Adour is dedicated to the worship of Saint Quiteria, who was beheaded in the fifth century. It is a well-known fact that all Catholic cathedrals have seminaries attached to them under the responsibility of a bishop, who is also responsible for the religious services of the cathedral. This unidentified 'old college', which appears to be a place of some importance, could have been a seminary.

p. 44, l. 19: *the battle of Orthez*: In this battle (27 February 1814) the Anglo-Portuguese Army under Field Marshal Arthur Wellesley, Marquess of Wellington, defeated a French army led by Marshal Nicolas Soult in southern France towards the end of the Peninsular War. For more information, see D. Chandler, *Dictionary of the Napoleonic Wars*. (New York: Macmillan, 1979); M. Glover, *The Peninsular War 1807–1814* (London: Penguin, 2001); C. Oman, *Wellington's Army, 1809–1814* (London: Greenhill, 1993) and D. Smith, *The Napoleonic Wars Data Book* (London: Greenhill, 1998).

p. 52, ll. 15–18: *Jurançon ... richness of its wines*: These wines are elaborated from the following grape varieties: Petit Manseng, Gros Manseng, Courbu Blanc, Petit Courbu, Camaralet de Lasseube and Lauzet.

p. 53, l. 18–p. 54, l. 1: *the Pic du Midi de Bigorre ... than it really is*: The 'Pic du Midi de Bigorre' or simply 'Pic du Midi' has an altitude of 2,877 m (9,439 ft).

p. 54, ll. 18–19: *Pic du Midi de Pau*: Here Mrs Ellis is most probably referring to the 'Pic du Midi d'Ossau' (2,884 m, 9,462 ft), towering above the Ossau Valley in the French Pyrenees.

p. 62, l. 10: *Moorish character*: The 'Moorish' appreciation of this Chateau in Pau is gratuitous: the fact that the high black roof of its towers are, according to Mrs Ellis, 'slightly curved inwards', does not confer on them any feature of Moorish art. There are no Arabic elements in the architecture of Pau's Chateau.

p. 63, ll. 5–6: *Jeanne d'Albret*: Jeanne III d'Albret (1528–72) was Queen of Navarre from 1565 to 1572 as Jeanne III. She was the daughter of King Henri II d'Albret of Navarre and Marguerite d'Angoulême and mother of Henri III of Navarre (1553–1610), later crowned King of France as Henri IV.

p. 64, ll. 10–11: *Marguerite of Valois, sister of Francis I*: After converting to Protestantism, Jeanne III introduced the Calvinist Reform in Navarre and Bearne as the state religion of her dominions. Marguerite de Navarre (or Marguerite d'Angoulême or Marguerite d'Orleans), the sister of Francis I and Queen of Navarre, was Jeanne III's mother. Mrs Ellis calls her Marguerite de Valois, a name more widely employed to refer to Queen Margot (1553–1615), a French Catholic princess who married the initially Protestant King of Navarre, who later converted to Catholicism in order to become Henri IV of France after declaring that 'Paris was worth a Mass'. Marguerite de Valois (Queen Margot) was not Francis I's sister but Francis II's sister.

p. 64, ll. 17–18: *her [Marguerite de Valois's] ... high intelectual achievements*: Marguerite d'Angoulême's 'high intellectual achievements' were the writing of two works: *Marguerites de la Marguerite des princesses, tresillustres royne de Navarre* (Lyon: Iean de Tournes, 1527) and, above all, *Heptameron* (1542), inspired by Boccaccio's *Decameron*. She did not finish this last work due to her early death. It contains seventy-two stories told in seven days. Ten travellers are trapped at an abbey due to a storm and are therefore isolated from the outside world. In order to pass the time, each one of them tells a real or an imaginary story, after which the listeners comment in the form of a debate.

p. 64, l. 25: *'Marguerite of Marguerites'*: This idea is evidently taken from one of Marguerite d'Angoulême's best-known works: *Marguerites de la Marguerite des princesses, tresillustres royne de Navarre*. It is also repeated by Mrs Bury Palliser in her *Historic Devices, Badges, and War-Cries* (London: S. Low, Son & Marston, 1870), p. 164. The emblem is reproduced on p. 165 of this book.

p. 64, l. 26–p. 65, l. 10: *And well did she ... a delicate female*: Francis I was captured by accident in the battle of Pavía on 24 February 1525 and subsequently taken to Madrid, where he remained a prisoner until his signing of the Treaty of Madrid in 1526 by imposition of Emperor Charles V. In this treaty France renounced her rights to the Milanesado, Genoa, Naples, Flanders, Artois and Borgogne. As soon as the French king crossed the Pyrenees, he ignored the clauses signed in the treaty. Francis I was nevertheless always well treated in his captivity in Spain. According to Capitán G. Hernández de Oviedo's *Relación de lo sucedido en la prisión del Rey Francisco de Francia* (1535), the royal prisoner was lodged in the Alcázar of Madrid, where the emperor resided. It is there where his conversations with Charles V took place, where he was visited, where he became ill and where he welcomed 'Madama de Alençon' [*sic*], who came to visit and accompany her brother until he was released. Francis I's flight to France accompanied by his sister must have been as fast as possible, but it is doubtful that the latter had to hurry to save her own life. The conditions in which the French king (and presumably his companions, including his sister, 'a delicate female' in Ellis's words) lived while in Madrid do not correspond to the urge to flee to Spain to save their allegedly endangered lives, as implied by Mrs Ellis. In fact, Pero

Megía in *Vida del invictísimo Emperador D. Carlos V* (Lisboa: Marcos Borges, Antón Ribero é Antón Alvarez, 1585) writes that 'Llegado, pues, a Madrid [Francisco I], fué aposentado en el Alcázar y casa Real de ella, teniendo la guardia de su persona el dicho Alarcón con las compañías de España que con él habían venido de Italia; pero la prisión era con toda la soltura y libertad que él quería, y dejábasele salir al campo y a caza cada vez que le placía, y en todo le era hecho el placer y buen tratamiento posible' (Lib, 3, cap. 16).

['Having arrived in Madrid, he [Francis I] was accomodated in the Alcázar and royal quarters there, and was guarded by the aforementioned Alarcón with his companions from Spain who had accompanied him from Italy; but his prison was as free and easy as he wished, and he was allowed to go to the countryside and hunting whenever he desired, and was treated in every aspect according to his pleasure and as well as posible.']

Don Pedro Salazar de Mendoza, who lived in the second half of the sixteenth century wrote in his treaty *Del origen ele las dignidades seglares de Castilla y León* (1618) that 'Fué traído el Rey Francisco I a España ... hasta la villa de Madrid, donde tuvo por prisión el Palacio Real con toda la libertad que él quiso, de caza y pasatiempos hasta que volvió a sus Reinos' (Lib 4, cap. 3). ['King Francis I was brought to Spain ... to the city of Madrid, where his prison was the royal palace and where he was given as much freedom as he desired to hunt and pass the time until he returned to his kingdoms'.]

A Spanish poet of the time, Luis Zapata, wrote in 1566 that

De allí en Madrid el Rey fué aposentado
En el Alcázar Real con su corona
A donde fué servido y fué tratado
Como en París lo fuera él, o en Narbona.
Salióse a pasear acompañado
De Alarcón que guardaba su persona,
Y no tenía de preso otros nublados,
Sino ver par de sí muchos soldados.
(Canto 26, octava 7ª)

The king was lodged there in Madrid
In the Royal Alcázar with his crown
Where he was served and treated
As if he were in Paris or in Narbonne.
He would go for walks accompanied
By Alarcón who was his guard,
And as a prisoner he saw no other clouds,
Than those produced by the sight around
him of many soldiers.
(Canto 26, stanza 7)

Mrs Ellis's accusation that the Catholic emperor had a 'cold-hearted nature' falls flat due to the references made by contemporary witnesses of the royal prisoner's lifestyle while in Madrid. Madama Alençon's 'fearless pleading' for her brother's release, which according to Mrs Ellis nearly provoked her assassination, was opposed by political interests on the part of Spain. Naturally, Francis I would not be released until he signed the so-called Treatry of Madrid. Other historical references, however, explain the king and his sister's return to France as having been made in haste: Queen Marguerite rode on horseback through wintry woods, twelve hours a day for many days, to meet a safe conduct deadline, while writing her diplomatic letters at night. For more information on Marguerite of Navarre, see S. Putnam, *Marguerite of Navarre* (New York: Grosset & Dunlap, 1936);

F. Hackett, *Francis The First* (New York: Doubleday, Doran and Company, Inc., 1937) and P. F. Cholakian and R. C. Cholakian, *Marguerite de Navarre: Mother of the Renaissance* (New York, Columbia University Press, 2006).

p. 65, ll. 15–16: *our unfortunate Anne Boleyn*: Due to Anne Boleyn's key role in the start of the English Reformation, Mrs Ellis uses the possessive as a term of endearment for her. Although most famous for being Henry VIII's second wife and Queen of England from 1533 to 1536, when she was decapitated, as Mrs Ellis states, Anne Boleyn had also been a maid of honour in France in her youth at the court of Claude de France (1499–1524), who was Francis I's first wife and mother to the future Francis II.

p. 65, ll. 23–6: *the most eminent of the early reformers ... Marot, Caroli, Dolet*: A list of influential reformers is added here by Ellis. Apart from John Calvin (Jean Cauvin, 1509–64), she mentions Desiderious Erasmus (of Rotterdam) (*c.* 1466–1536), Gérard Roussel (1500–50, personal preacher of Marguerite of Navarre and Bishop of Oloron), Jacques Lefèvre d'Étaples (or Jacob Faber Stapulensis, *c.* 1455–1536, a Roman Catholic thinker who anticipated the ideas of the Protestant Reformation), Clément Marot (1496–1544, French poet and protégé of Francis I of France), Pierre Caroli (1480–*c.* 1545, a theologian who challenged some of Calvin's ideas) and Étienne Dolet (1509–46), the alleged illegitimate son of Francis I who was accused of atheism.

p. 69, ll. 16–18: *but it is said ... boiling water*: The reference to the employment of servants by the Ellises to prepare their tea whilst residing at Pau is proof of the type of readership that this travel account is addressed to: the upper-middle class or upper class.

p. 71, l. 21–p. 72, l. 6: *hire your own servants ... each article herself*: Mrs Ellis informs the potential upper middle-class or upper-class traveller of the salaries to pay French servants, cooks and *femmes de chambre*. This confirms, once again, the type of reader that the English traveller has in mind: those who can afford to pay a legion of servants abroad. Mrs Ellis is rather critical of these servants, even though she admits that she has not had any bad experiences with them (as she states, she herself found 'a fair average of honesty amongst the French servants'). She is nevertheless being unfair towards a sector of female workers such as cooks by spreading bad rumours about them: she states they 'are all cheats', simply because 'it is said'. She herself insists that it is necessary to watch them at all times, and to keep valuable ingredients such as coffee and sugar out of their reach.

p. 72, l. 27–p. 73, l. 5: *it is related ... Tourné*: The French writer Mrs Ellis is referring to is A. Dugenne, who states 'La ville de Pau n'a produit que deux grands hommes, Henri IV et Tourné!' ['The town of Pau has only produced two great men, Henry IV and Tourné !] (*Panorama historique et descriptif de Pau et de ses environs*, p. 231.) On the previous page, Dugenne had called the latter 'Tourné, restaurateur, le *Véfour* de Pau' ['Tourné, restaurant proprietor, the *Véfour* of Pau']. The anonymous review of Mrs Ellis' book in *Churchman's Monthly Review* states that surely 'Charles John' would be a third. Dugenne is evidently referring to Jean Baptiste Jules Bernadotte, who was born in Pau in 1763 and was later to become King of Sweden in 1818.

p. 80, ll. 12–16: *I have longed to ... days in peace*: The hard lives that female French peasants of the Béarn area lead are depicted as being remarkably similar to the sufferance of the beasts as described by Mrs Ellis (pp. 76–8). By stating that these prematurely aged women should spend their last days 'in a comfortable arm chair by the fire-side of an English cottage ... a neat cap upon her head, and a bible in her hand' (p. 80, ll. 13–16), Mrs Ellis is describing her own version of happiness. She is most surprised that in spite of the hardships that female peasants have to go through in their daily routine, 'still they seem to enjoy life' (p. 80, ll. 6–7).

p. 81, ll. 18–27: *Much of the charm ... native land*: Mrs Ellis criticizes young English girls belonging to the lower classes, who do not dress with the decorum and appropriateness of their French counterparts. This remark is a wink of complicity to the higher social classes in England, her potential readers, who believe in class differentiation and decorum, even in their form of dress.

p. 89, l. 4: *the finest merinos*: The merino sheep is characterized by the high quality and quantity of its wool. This species may have originated in northern Africa and eventually entered the Iberian Peninsula, where it was quickly adopted by the powerful 'Concejo de la Mesta' (an official institution created during the reigns of Ferdinand of Aragon and Isabella of Castile for the protection of cattle, a generous source of income), who monopolized its production for several centuries, subsequently damaging the trade of the omniscient 'manchego' sheep of the centre of Spain. The merino was introduced in France in the eighteenth century and in Britain in the nineteenth century and later exported to her overseas colonies.

p. 90, l. 13: *sous*: The currency in France at the time consisted of francs and sous. A franc had twenty sous. Today the French still use the expression 'être sans sou', 'to be broke'.

p. 91, l. 10: *bargainings*: Mrs Ellis explains the practice of bargaining, which is so characteristic of southern and undeveloped countries. Foreign visitors (mostly English) are overcharged in the belief that they are richer (a statement that implies that she believes that this area of France is indeed economically underdeveloped). Mrs Ellis does not like the idea of having to rely on bargaining and dispute for more reasonable prices. She admits that this is a practice that is mainly characteristic of the French, who are 'so well suited to [this] turn of mind, but for which the English have neither taste nor talent' (ll. 25–6). However, in her acceptance of recommending the use of bargaining she is intending to be consistent with the idea that an English housewife should always see to the economy of the household, even if this means having to resort to bargaining. She then offers a list of prices (provided by an experienced but unidentified English resident in the area) for the use and benefit of the English housewife who is to spend some time in the area.

p. 99, ll. 13–14: *The Reformation in the South-west Provinces of France*: Mrs Ellis is referring to *Notices of the Reformation in the South-West Provinces of France*, by Robert Francis Jameson, published in London by R. B. Seely and W. Burnside in 1839. Jameson, of the Inner Temple, was also the British Commissioner of Arbitration stationed in Cuba between 1819 and 1823. His stay on the Caribbean island inspired him to produce two works: *Letters from the Havana, during the Year 1820* (London: John Miller, 1820) and *Aperçu statistique de l'Île de Cuba; precede de quelques lettres sur la Havan [etc]* (Paris: P. Dufart, 1826). He was also known as a comedy writer, and his works include *A Touch of the Times; a comedy in five acts* (London, 1812), *The Students of Salamanca; a comedy in five acts* (London, 1813) and *Living in London; a comedy in three acts* (London: John Miller, 1815). From Mrs Ellis we learn that he was a judge in several British colonies and that he spent three years in the area of Pau as a resident. For more information on Jameson, see J. Pérez de la Riva and A. Cortés, *La isla de Cuba en el siglo XIX vista por los extranjeros: en 1820* (La Habana: Biblioteca Nacional 'José Martí', 1966).

p. 105, l. 13: *sabbath*: Mrs Ellis's Protestant (Calvinist) sentiment is evident in her disdain of the French people's 'pursuit of pleasure' through dancing (especially on Sundays, the sabbath), and their preference for outdoor amusement, in contrast to English people's inclination for repose at home accompanied by 'many holier associations'. According to her, this French tendency to enjoy their free time outdoors is attributable to the pleasant weather, but also to some 'national or constitutional defect'.

p. 105, l. 26: *sabbath*: The writer insists on the French custom of not respecting the spirit of the Sabbath: apart from going to church, the day is spent by the southern French on too many amusements, which she enumerates: horse racing, horse fairs, plays, dancing and public shows.

p. 106, l. 19: *desecration of the sabbath*: This utterly irreligious attitude of the Béarnais common country and city people (carnivals, religious processions, masques, fêtes, mummeries, and so forth) are described by Mrs Ellis as 'desecration of the Sabbath'. Needless to say, the Ellises not only disapproved of them, but also found them 'devoid of interest', 'conducted without reverence', 'without wit or point', 'childish and grotesque piece[s] of buffoonery', 'entirely without aim', 'aimless stupidity' and not entertaining at all, as they did not inspire a single smile from them. This southern and overt display of entertainment, so devoid of any acute sense of the grotesque or ridiculous contrasts with the Ellises's Protestant seriousness and gravity, which they identify as a typically English national trait: they find the French explosions of speech and gesticulation utterly contrary to the English national demeanour. Passionate (albeit inconsequential) quarrelling is also another of the southern traits of the Béarnais. The Ellises are especially critical of numerous examples of lack of respect towards religious symbols and public displays due to the careless behaviour of the multitude attending the events.

p. 111, l. 24: *Ursuline sisters*: The convent of Sainte Ursule of Pau was founded by Catherine de Sainte Thérèse. The ceremony of the ordination of a group of nuns described in detail by Mrs Ellis takes place in this convent.

p. 116, l. 7: *Duchess of Gordon*: Thanks to the generous donations and purchase of lands during the period spanning 1839–43 by Elizabeth Brodie, Duchess of Gordon (1794–1864), a Protestant temple and colleges – the so-called 'Gordon colleges'– were built in the Pau area. The information provided by Mrs Ellis on this 'amiable lady' and her good deeds for the implantation of Protestantism in the Béarnais area was taken from the *Christian Observer*, 18 (1839), p. 66. The *Christian Observer* was a monthly periodical initiated in January 1802, with Zachary Macaulay as its first editor. From 1875–6 it became the *Christian Observer and Advocate*. For more information on the Duchess of Gordon, see her biography and epistolary *Life and Letters of Elizabeth Last Duchess of Gordon*, ed. S. A. Moody (London: J. Nisbert and Co., 1865).

p. 119, ll. 3–4: *The London Society in the South Seas*: Mr Ellis, the author's husband, was a Protestant pastor and a leading member of the London Society. He had spent many years of evangelization in the South Seas, and would later return to this.

p. 119, l. 27–p. 120, l. 1: *battle between the Duke of Wellington and Marshal Soult*: On 27 February 1814, as part of the Peninsular War (1808–14), Wellington, having succeeded in drawing Soult away from Bayonne, attacked with his Anglo-Portuguese army and defeated this French marshal at Orthez. For more information, see Glover, *The Peninsular War*, pp. 320–2 and Smith, *The Napoleonic Wars Data Book*, p. 500.

p. 122, l. 11: *The Société Evangélique de France*: This society was created in 1833 and was modelled on the Société Biblique (1818) and other British (i.e. The Bible Society), Swiss and Dutch examples. During the 1840s Napoléon Roussel (1805–78) was the main campaigner for the spreading of Protestant ideas in France by founding numerous Protestant schools.

p. 124, ll. 9–14: *cross of the Prince*: Mrs Ellis took this information from Dugenne. She virtually copies the information on the Croix du Prince provided by this French author (*Panorama historique et descriptif de Pau et de ses environs*, p. 346), albeit omitting certain data and facts. The following corresponds to Dugenne's account of the origin of the Croix du Prince in Jurançon: 'Après avoir passé le pont du Gave, on entre immédiatement sur le territoire de la commune de Jurançon. C'est á elle qu'appartienent toute les maisons qui s'étendent, depuis le pont jusqu'à *Croix du Prince*. On donne à la designation de carrefour l'origin que voici: Lorsque Louis XIII vint à Béarn pour y rétablir le Catholicism, il ordenna, ainsi que nous l'avons dit, que toutes les croix que avaient été abattues par les Calvinistes seraient relevées. On se hata donc d'obéir à ses orders et l'on en planta une à cette sortie de la ville. Dès le même jour, le Roi étant allé se promener avec une nombreuse suite de gentils-hommes, et apercevant ce signe révéré de rédemption, mid pied á terre ainsi que tous ceux qui l'accompagnaient et resta quelque temps agenouillé au pied de ce simple monument. Tel fut, dit-on, le souvenir que nos pères voulent perpétuer, en appelant désormais mais ce lieu la *Croix du Prince*.'

['After having crossed the bridge over the river Gave, one immediately enters the territory of the commune of Jurançon. It is to this municipality that the houses which run from the bridge up until the *Croix du Prince* belong. The origin of this cross' name is the following: When Louis XIII came to Bearn to restore Catholicism, he ordered, as already stated, that the crosses which had been knocked down by the Calvinists be re-erected. Subsequently his orders were hurriedly obeyed and one of these was erected at the exit of this town. That same day, the king, who had gone out to ride with his large retinue of noblemen, on seeing this revered symbol of redemption, decided to put his feet on the ground, as did the others who accompanied him, and spent some time kneeling at the foot of this simple monument. It is said that this is the event which our forefathers wished to perpetrate, calling this place from then onwards, the *Croix du Prince*.']

p. 124, l. 22: *Corneille and Racine*: Pierre Corneille (1606–84), most well-known for his work *Le Cid* and Jean Racine (1639–99), author of *Phèdre*, among other plays, were two of the most relevant French playwrights of the seventeenth century and constitute the best representatives of French classical tragedy.

p. 126, l. 9: *The Strid*: The Strid is a treacherous part of the river Wharfe in Yorkshire (England), near Bolton Abby, which has claimed many lives over the years.

p. 127, ll. 21–4: *a noble mansion ... translation of Homer*: Mrs Ellis is referring to the château of Rébénacq, built in the late eighteenth century by the Abbot Paul-Jéréme Bitaubé (1732–1808), a Calvinist pastor who was well known throughout the eighteenth century mainly for his prose translations of Homer's epic poems *The Iliad* (1764, later revised and published in 1785) and *The Odyssey* (1785). For more information on this Franco-Prussian scholar, see P. Hummel, 'Paul-Jérémie Bitaubé, un philologue binational au XVIIIe siècle', *International Journal of Classical Tradition*, 2:4 (Spring 1996), pp. 510–35.

p. 130, l. 26–p. 131, l. 9: *a kind peculiar to the Pyrenees ... terror of the neighbourhood*: Mrs Ellis is describing the Chien de Montagne des Pyrénées or Montagne des Pyrénées (Pyrenean Mountain Dog or Great Pyrenees), a large dog common in the Spanish and French Pyrenees and popularly called 'pastou' in the Béarn area. This breed of dog is ideal for herding livestock and preventing attacks from wolves.

p. 132, l. 25–p. 133, l. 6: *Castel Geloos ... justice in their state*: Mrs Ellis is rather ambiguous in her account of the history of the so-called Castel Geloos [*sic*] or Gelos and its connection with the Viscounts of Ossau. Some other travel accounts in English refer directly or indirectly to the independence of Béarn or Ossau. Louisa Stuart Costello in *Béarn and the Pyrenees. A Legendary Tour to the Country of Henri Quatre* (London: Richard Bentley, 1844), p. 150, approaches the subject thus: 'The most striking object here, is an isolated mount, on the summit of which stand the ruins of a feudal tower, called Castel Jaloux, built by Gaston Phoebus, for the convenience of holding the assemblies of Ossau, there to meet the viscounts who were independent of the kingdom of Bearn. The village of Castets is at the base of the rock, concealed amidst thick foliage: this situation is charming, in the midst of gigantic steeps and rich valleys, with the Gave foaming at its foot.' And in Count Henry Russell's *Pau and the Pyrenees* (London: Longmans, Green and Co., 1871), p. 127, the reader is given the following information: 'Bielle was the ancient capital of Ossau. This valley was a republic under the suzerainty of the viscounts of Bearn. It governed itself, and had its own courts of justice, and absolutely refused to suffer the soldiers of the viscount to enter their little republic. He himself was not recognized till he had sworn to respect its rights and privileges as contained in the ancient *fors.'*

p. 133, ll. 7–17: *an ancient church ... avec lui*: This story seems to be more a legend than a historical fact. The same anecdote is narrated by Louisa Stuart Costello and Sabine Baring-Gould, who both travelled in the area: 'The pillars inside the church [in Bielle] are very celebrated for their extreme beauty; they are of white and blue jasper, found in a quarry near Bielle. A story is told of Henry IV., who greatly admired these pillars, having sent to request the town to make him a present of them, as he found nothing in his capital that could compare with their beauty; he received this answer: "Bous quets meste de noutes coos et de neustes bees; mei per co que es Deus pialars diu temple, aquets que son di Diu, dab eig quep at bejats." ['You may dispose of our hearts and our goods at your will; as for the columns, they belong to God; manage the matter with Him.'] The Ossalais in this showed no little wit; or, if the tradition is not founded on fact, the story exhibits their powers of setting a clue value on their possessions in a striking light.' (Costello, *Béarn and the Pyrenees*, p. 171). 'In one of his bear-hunting expeditions, when a lad, Henry of Navarre had visited the church of Bielle in the Val d'Ossau, and had noticed the columns of Italian marble in the church, the spoils of a Gallo-Roman villa. When he was king he sent to Bielle to have these pillars forwarded to him in Paris. The reply of the villagers was: "Sire, our hearts and our properties are yours, dispose of them as you will; but as to these columns, they belong to God. *Entendez vous-en avec lui.*" (Baring-Gould, *A Book of the Pyrenees*, p. 103.)

p. 133, ll. 16–17: 'Entendez-vous-en avec lui': 'sort the matter out with him' (French).

p. 137, ll. 17–24: *many Spanish families ... their own language*: Spanish refugees. The First Carlist War (1833–40) between the followers of Ferdinand VII's absolutist brother Carlos María Isidoro de Borbón and the followers of Regent Queen María Cristina de Borbón, the surviving wife of king Ferdinand VII and mother of the child Queen Isabella II, more liberal and moderate in her political outlook, must have provoked the exile of many Spaniards from the Basque Country and Navarre, as these Spanish territories bordering the Pyrenees particularly supported Don Carlos's cause. These Spanish exiles moved to France as this country, together with Portugal and Britain, clearly supported Queen María Cristina's cause and therefore sent volunteers to her armies' aid. For more information on the First Carlist War, see J. Coverdale, *The Basque Phase of Spain's First Carlist War* (Princeton, NJ, 1984) and J. Extramiana, *Historia de las guerras carlistas* (San Sebastián, 1978–9).

p. 138, ll. 12–13: *bonnets Grecs ... the orientals*: In Nay the 'Manufacture Royale de Bonnets à la Turque' was created by the Poey d'Oloron brothers around 1740 in order to produce woollen garments for the East and for the Mediterranean markets. However, in the early years of the nineteenth century the traditional clothing industry was on the verge of disappearing, as, being a family business, it could not compete with the appearance of cotton. Bonnets grecs were indeed produced in Nay and exported eastwards. In *Charlotte* Brontë's *Villette*, one of the protagonists, the Frenchman Monsieur Paul, is made to wear 'a defiant and pagan' bonnet grec, usually of red colour (chapter 29). In *Madame Bovary* (1, chapter 6), Gustave Flaubert also mentions the bonnets grecs as part of the garments of the Orientals. For more information on Eastern garments, see *Vers l'Orient européen: Voyages et images Pays roumains, Bulgarie, Grèce, Constantinople*, by L. Cotea (coord.) (Bucureşti: Editura Universităţii din Bucureşti, 2009).

p. 142, ll. 4–14: *When first taken ... affairs of state*: The future Henri IV was sent by his mother, Jeanne d'Albret, to the castle of Coarraze, in the Béarn area, so that he could grow strong and healthy in communion with nature. His guardians were a noble couple of the region, the Baron and Baroness of Miossens, Jean d'Albret and Suzanne de Bourbon-Busset. See V. J. Pitts, *Henri IV of France: His Reign and Age* (Baltimore, MD: The John Hopkins Press, 2009), p. 133.

p. 142, ll. 6–7: *Dis-guished*: Where it says 'dis-guished' it should say 'dis-tinguished'.

p. 143, l. 1: *patois of Béarn*: The popularly called 'patois de Béarn' refers to Gascon, a dialect of the Langue d'Oc or Occitan. It is spoken nowadays in the French regions of Gascony and Béarn and in the Spanish area of the Aran Valley.

p. 143, ll. 16–25: *Gestas ... had to offer*: This same story or anecdote of Henri IV's relationship with the people of Coarraze and the family of the Gestas while living as a young boy in the area is repeated literally by Mrs Ellis in her later work *Fireside Tales for the Young* (London: Peter Jackson, Late Fisher, Son, & Co., 1849), p. 20.

p. 157, ll. 11–15: *one of my companions ... enthusiasm of a poet*: Mrs Ellis is referring to her own husband, Mr William Ellis, in the most laudatory of terms.

p. 161, ll. 5–27: *Gaston Phoebus X*: 'Gaston Phoebus X' as Mrs Ellis calls him, was 'Gaston III of Foix and Gaston X of Béarn' (1331–91), and indeed, he made some major additions to the château of Pau. In his *Livre de Chase* (1387–8) he describes the art of hunting. The historian Jean Froissant (*c.* 1337–*c.* 1410), who visited Gaston Phoebus's court of Orthez in the second half of the fourteenth century, described it as full of splendour in his *Chroniques* (vol. 10, 'Le Cour de Gaston Phoebus (1388–90)' (Paris: Editions Paleo, 2002)). Froissant's *Chroniques* are also relevant to understanding the chivalric revival of the fourteenth century in England and in France, and serve as a major source of information on the first half of the Hundred Years War. For more information on his hunting activities, see C. de Saulnier and A. Strubel, *La poetique de la chasse au Moyen Âge: les livres de chasse du XIVe siècle* (Paris: Presses Universitaires de France, 1994) and J. Cummings, *The Hound and the Hawk: The Art of Medieval Hunting* (London: Weidenfeld & Nicolson, 2001).

p. 162, ll. 2–5: *Gaston XI*: Mrs Ellis makes a mistake here. The real Gaston XI (Gaston II de Foix, 1308–43) did not marry a princess from Navarre, as the English writer states, but Eleonor de Comminges (d. 1365). It was Gaston XI's son, Gaston III de Foix (1331–91) who married Inés d'Evreux, Infanta of Navarre, the daughter of Felipe II of Navarre (known as 'Le Bon') and Juana II of Navarre. Their child was Gaston III de Foix 'Phoebus', XII Count of Foix.

p. 162, l. 19–p. 163, l. 2: *Jean d'Albret II ... the name of Bearn*: There is a great deal of controversy over the papal bulls which were thought to instigate King Fernando of Spain's attack and subsequent conquest of Navarre. See M. I. Ostolaza Elizondo, 'Fernando el Católico y Navarra. Ocupación y administración del reino entre 1512–1515', *Aragón en la Edad Media*, 20 (2008), p. 562.

p. 163, ll. 21–3: *Henry having been ... her brother*: Henry II of Navarre (1503–55) was married to Marguerite d'Angoulême, Francis I's sister. Therefore, King Henry was King Francis's brother-in-law, not his brother as Mrs Ellis states. However, she is correct in her observation that King Henry of Navarre was made prisoner in the battle of Pavia, but that he managed to escape.

p. 165, ll. 5–6: *'Not following lower things'*: The original Latin motto is 'Non inferiora Secutus'. This emblem can be seen in Palliser, *Historic Devices, Badges, and War-Cries*, p. 165. It was also adopted as a motto by Mary Queen of Scots. See M. Swain, *The Needlework of Mary, Queen of Scots* (Carlton, Bedfordshire: Ruth Bean Publishers, 1986).

p. 165, ll. 13–17: *our own Queen Elizabeth ... a Christian soule*: Elizabeth I studied French, and, at the age of eleven, translated from the French of Marguerite of Navarre *A godly medytacyon of the christen sowle, concerninge a loue towardes God and hys Christe, compyled in frenche by lady Margarete quene of Nauerre, and aptly translated into Englysh by the ryght vertuouse lady Elyzabeth doughter to our late souerayne Kynge Henri the. viij*. Wesel, April 1548. See J. Mueller and J. Scodel's edition of *Elizabeth I: Translations, 1544–1589* (Chicago, IL: University of Chicago Press, 2009).

p. 166, l. 20–p. 167, l. 2: *Jeanne d'Albert ... to the church*: In 1541 Jeanne d'Albert was forced by her uncle King Francis I of France to marry Guillaume, duc de Clèves (duc de Jülich-Berb-Ravensberg-Kleve-Mark) (1516–92). Jeanne was twelve and was whipped and dragged to the altar as she stubbornly refused to be married. The marriage was annulled four years later. See Mrs J. Robinson (née Freer, Martha Walker), *Jeanne d'Albret, Queen of Navarre, 1528–1572* (London: Hurst and Blackett, *c.* 1861), pp. 15–32, N. L. Roelker, *Queen of Navarre: Jeanne d'Albret, 1528–1572* (Cambridge, MA: Belknap Press of Harvard University Press, 1968) and B. Berdou d'Aas, *Jeanne III d'Albret. Chronique (1528–1572)* (Biarritz: Atlantica 2002).

p. 170, ll. 16–17: *This has already been done by abler hands than mine*: Mrs Ellis could be referring to Rev. S. A. Laval's *A compendious history of the Reformation in France and of the Reformed churches in that kingdom from the first beginnings of the Reformation to the repealing of the Edict of Nantz, with an account of the late persecution of the French Protestants under Lewis XIV; extracted out of the best authorities*. London: H. Woodfall for the Author, 1738, 2 vols.

p. 172, l. 23: *Beza*: Théodore de Béze (1519–1605) was a French poet and Calvinist humanist and theologian. His best-known work is *Histoire ecclésiastique des Églises Réformées au royaume de France* (1580). It was re-edited in 1841 in Lille: Imprimerie de Leleux. He also wrote a biography of Calvin. For more information on Béze, see A. Defour, *Théodore de Béze, poète et théologien* (Genève: Droz, 2006).

p. 172, l. 27: *Cardinal Ferrara*: Cardinal Ferrara (Ippolito d'Este) and the Jesuit Father Diego Laynéz were the Pope's legates sent to confront Théodore Béze and Peter Martyr Vermigli at the Colloquy at Poissy, September 1561, with the mission of effecting a reconciliation between the Catholics and the Protestants (Huguenots) in France. It was a failure, as they did not agree on the issue of the Holy Communion. The Protestants did not believe in the concept of transubstantiation as the Catholics did (Laval, *A Compendious History*, p. 515). Catherine de' Medici (the queen mother and regent) and her young son King Charles IX of France were present during the debates. For a more detailed account on the conversations held at Poissy, see Laval.

p. 173, ll. 10–12: *Jeanne d'Albret ... rites of the reformed church*: Jeanne III d'Albret Queen of Navarre, converted to Protestantism in 1560 after Béze's stay at her court in Nérac. However, if she converted in 1560, this was not after her husband Antoine de Bourbon's death, as Mrs Ellis states, as he died in 1562 (Berdou, *Jeanne III d'Albret*, p. 522). During Antoine de Bourbon's last two years of life the married couple had overtly shown their religious leanings. Whereas Jeanne d'Albret had converted to Protestantism, her husband still remained a Catholic. For more information on this event, see Lyman, who states that her conversion took place in 1561 (*Queen of Navarre*, p. 125) and Berdou, who affirms the date as 25 December 1560 (*Jeanne III d'Albret*, p. 522).

p. 174, l. 26. *Gaillart*: Mrs Ellis is referring to Charles Gaillard, Bishop of Chartres.

p. 175, ll. 14–19: *Marguerite of Valois ... one of the victims*: Marguerite de Valois, also known as Marguerite de France and Queen Margot, was King Charles IX's sister and the daughter of Henri II of France and Catherine de' Medici. She married Henri II of Navarre, a Protestant king who converted to Catholicism to avoid death on 18 August 1572. He later became King Henri IV of France. Marguerite de Valois was therefore queen twice. The massacre of St Bartholomew took place only a few days after Marguerite de Valois's marriage to the King of Navarre. This mass murder began on 23 August in Paris and went on for several weeks in the provinces. The Catholics killed thousands of Huguenots, including relevant leaders, who were still in Paris after having attended the wedding ceremony of the Protestant king. For more detailed information on this historical event see M. P. Holt, *The French Wars of Religion 1562–1626* (Cambridge: Cambridge University Press, 2005).

p. 177, ll. 5–12: *Catherine, Soissons and Lorraine*: Catherine de Bourbon (1559–1604) was the only daughter of Queen Joanne III and King Antoine de Navarre. She was a stout Calvinist. She was forced to marry a Catholic aristocrat, Henry Duc de Lorraine, but she died childless. She had not been allowed by royal order to marry her lover, her cousin Charles de Bourbon, Comte de Soissons (1566–1612). For more details on her love affair with Soissons and its political implications, see *Lettres inédites de Catherine de Bourbon, princesse de Navarre*, recuillies par Ernest Fréville et Sainte-Marie Mévil, 1857.

p. 179, ll. 18–23: *Charles Jean Bernadotte ... 1763*: Charles Jean Bernadotte was born in Pau in 1763. After becoming a marshal in Napoleon's Army, he was made King of Sweden and Norway in 1818 as Karl XIV Johan, after resigning his French nationality and his Catholicism. He died in 1844. See F. Favier's *Bernadotte. Un maréchal d'Empire sur le trône de Suède* (Paris: Ellipses 2010).

p. 182, l. 22–p. 183, l. 11: *Madame Caudan*: The spelling of this aristocrat's name does not match that given by Dugenne as 'Madame la vicomtesse de Candau'. Dugenne reproduces this same story (*Panorama historique et descriptif de Pau et de ses environs*, pp. 222–3) quoting from the memoires of Madame de Genlis, Stéphanie Félicité Ducrest de St-Aubin, comtesse de Genlis, or Madame Brûlart, (b. 25 January 1746, d. 31 December 1830). This sad story is proof of Mrs Ellis's scant sympathy for the instigators of the revolution, who attacked the social classes to whom she addresses her books.

p. 187, l. 20: *John Haydock*: The entrepreneur Haydock was evidently one of the thousands of Britons that crossed the English Channel to visit France when the Treaty of Amiens was signed in 1802, by which all hostilities between France and Britain during the French Revolutionary Years were ceased. Soon after, in 1803, Napoleon broke the peace terms and imprisoned thousands of Britons trapped in Paris, who would only be released when he was finally deposed in 1815. Haydock, probably due to the fact that he resided in Pau, sufficiently far from Paris, must have gone unnoticed and therefore was not disturbed and was able to keep his profession of mechanic, hence his numerous inventions, as Mrs Ellis informs us.

p. 189, l. 18: *Ivanhoe*: Ivanhoe was a novel written by Walter Scott in 1819. Mrs Ellis compares the rural landscape of the area of Pau to the one described in chapter 1 of Scott's novel. Scott describes the landscape where Gurth takes his herd of swines, in the following terms: 'The sun was setting upon one of the rich grassy glades of that forest, which we have mentioned in the beginning of the chapter. Hundreds of broad-headed, short-stemmed, wide-branched oaks, which had witnessed perhaps the stately march of the

Roman soldiery, flung their gnarled arms over a thick carpet of the most delicious green sward; in some places they were intermingled with beeches, hollies, and copse wood of various descriptions, so closely as totally to intercept the level beams of the sinking sun; in others they receded from each other, forming those long sweeping vistas, in the intricacy of which the eye delights to lose itself, while imagination considers them as the paths to yet wilder scenes of silvan solitude.'

p. 191, ll. 9–10: *the Emperor, Napoleon and Josephine*: According to the official website of the town of Gelos (http://www.gelos.fr/Histoire-et-presentation/Histoire-et-presentation [accessed on 10 March 2012]), on 22 July 1808, Napoleon and Josephine stayed at the castle of Gelos long enough (approximately 17 hours) to sign a series of decrees concerning Pau, which it lists.

p. 200, ll. 1–2: *of Roman origin*: The Roman name was 'Benebarnum' according to R. Vernier's *Lord of the Pyrenees: Gaston Febus, Count of Foix (1331–1391)* (Suffolk: Boydell and Brewer, 2008), p. 15.

p. 200, ll. 9–14: *The church of Lescar*: This distinguished nobleman who built the church of Lescar in the year 980 to expiate his guilt over a murder seems to be Bishop Arsias Raca, Bishop of Acqus in 982 (according to M. Faget de Baure in his *Essais historiques sur le Béarn*, published in Paris, Imprimerie Denugon, 1818, p. 49), or Arsius/Arsivus/Arsinus, according to the Abbot Hugues du Tems, who authored *Le Clergé de France ou Tableau historique et chronologique des Archevêques, Evêques, Abbés, Abbesses & Chefs des Chapitres principaux du Royaume, depuis la fondation des Eglises jusqu'à nos jours* (Paris: Delalain, 1774), p. 441. However, nothing is mentioned in these sources about his guilt for some grave sin or murder.

p. 200, ll. 21–3: *a very extensive traffic … the Saracens*: The first cathedral built in Lescar in 1062 was an obligatory stop on the St Jacques's Pilgrimage to Santiago de Compostela (Spain). For this reason, I very much doubt that 'the extensive traffic' in the area near Oleron and Jaca in Aragón (Spain) was 'entirely monopolized by the Saracens.' Indeed, King Sancho Ramírez, known as Sancho I of Aragon and V of Pamplona (*c*. 1043–94), had made Jaca the court of Aragon in 1077, encouraging French artisans to settle in the area and fostering the St Jacques pilgrimage through Jaca and Pamplona. For more information about Sancho I, see E. Sarasa Sánchez (ed.), *Sancho Ramírez, rey de Aragón, y su tiempo (1064–1094)* (Huesca: Instituto de Estudios Altoaragonenses, 1994).

p. 202, ll. 4–11: *a celebrated musician … through all eternity*. Dugenne mentions that this 'celebrated musician' was Pierre de Lancelot (*Panorama historique et descriptif de Pau et de ses environs*, p. 453).

p. 204, ll. 2–3. *Barnabite college*: The Barnabites, or Clerics Regular of Saint Paul (*Clerici Regulares Sancti Pauli*) is a Roman Catholic order founded in 1530 by three Italian aristocrats, St Anton Maria Zaccaria, Barthélemy Ferrari and Jacopo Morigia, and was approved by Pope Clement VII in 1533. The popular name 'Barnabites' came from its association with the church of St Barnabas in Milan, acquired by the institute in its early years of foundation. See C. Tondini di Quarenghi, 'Barnabites.' *The Catholic Encyclopedia*.vol. 2. (New York: Robert Appleton Company, 1907) at http://www.newadvent.org/cathen/02302a. htm [accessed 24 April 2012]. This former Barnabite college in Lescar described by Mrs Ellis was created by Bishop Jean de Salettes in 1622 and promoted by Henri IV in 1624 by sending a few Barnabite priests to inhabit it with the mission of preaching and teaching the local youth. It became highly prestigious in terms of the education provided, thanks to Father Fortuné de Colom, and was especially relevant as its religious and educational mission was carried out while Protestantism was at its height in the area of Béarn. The

French Revolution and the anti-secularization of its laws set a deadly blow to the college and in 1793 it was closed down and converted first into a prison, then a military hospital and then a cotton factory. In 1845, after persistent claims of the town of Lescar, it was again converted into an educational establishment, l'Ecole Normale d'Instituteurs des Basses-Pyrénées. See http://www.lescaramisvieillespierres.asso.fr/pages/lescar_cite_historique.html#ANCHOR_Txt20 [accessed 2 May 2012].

p. 204, l. 22: Sauvegarde du roi: 'the refuge of the king' (French).

p. 214, l. 15: Jardin Anglais: 'English Garden' (French).

p. 220, ll. 11–15: *Since this time ... neighbouring valley*: Not even when on holiday does the couple cease in their missionary zeal.

p. 221, ll. 15–26: *Women's sketches*. Mrs Ellis's educational interest leads her to criticize how English women are educated: their only achievements seem to be in looking for 'picturable' scenes abroad to copy and then to collect the resulting sketches for their albums, which, however, they hardly ever manage to draw.

p. 224, l. 23: *those frightful goitres*: A goitre is a swelling of the thyroid gland which can lead to a swelling of the neck or larynx, usually caused by iodine deficiency. It has nothing to do with bathing in or drinking water coming from the melted snow as Mrs Ellis believes.

p. 227, l. 14: *izard, a kind of wild goat or chamois*: Mrs Ellis is referring to the Pyrenean chamois (*Rupicapra pyrenaica*), a type of goat antelope.

p. 230, l. 2–p. 233, l. 14: *Pierrine Gaston*: Mrs Ellis makes a physical and psychological description of this French peasant who she has befriended which would make any husband jealous.

p. 237, l. 5. *Parisian*: Mrs Ellis uses the term in the sense of 'fashionable', in contrast to anything that is not Parisian, that is, rural, country-like, and therefore unfashionable.

p. 244, l. 15: *Byron*: A quote from Lord Byron's closet tragedy *Manfred* (act 1, scene 2). Manfred is preparing to throw himself from the Jungfrau Mountain but he will be saved at the last minute by a chamois hunter who pulls him back to the edge:

> And you, ye crags upon whose extreme edge
> I stand, and on the torrent's brink beneath
> Behold the tall pines dwindled as to shrubs
> In dizziness of distance, when a leap
> A stir, a motion, even a breath, would bring
> My breast upon its rocky bosom's bed
> To rest for ever – wherefore do I pause?
> ... Thou winged and cloud-cleaving minister,
> Whose happy flight is highest into heaven,
> Well may'st thou swoop so near me ...
> ... How beautiful is all this visible world!
> How glorious in its action and itself!

p. 254, l. 10: *The sanctuary of Notre Dame, at Betharam*: The Sanctuary of Notre-Dame de Bétharram (not Betharam as Mrs Ellis writes) is a Roman Catholic chapel built in commemoration of miracles carried out there by the Virgin Mary in the fifteenth century. Mrs Ellis takes advantage of her visit to the sanctuary to criticize the overtly commercial interest of the Catholic Church, which allows the selling of souvenirs and other 'amulets' in the place.

p. 255, l. 20–p. 256, l. 6: *I was suffering great anxiety ... attended with danger*: Here Mrs Ellis implies the reason behind why she spent a few months in the south of France. It was not for any special interest in sightseeing but for her husband's (presumably, mental) health. He was in a 'precarious state of health' (p. 255), unable to expose himself to the intense rays of the sun (shocking in someone who had worked for years on end as a missionary in tropical climates). Mrs Ellis's comment that only those of 'robust health' or those 'unaccustomed to painful affections of the head' could enjoy what she calls a 'hurried tour through the Pyrenees' (p. 256) indirectly reveals that her husband was neither of these two. It is my opinion that Mr Ellis was suffering from a depression.

p. 257, ll. 19–21: *How much would one ... a cup of tea!*: Mrs Ellis, reluctant traveller to the south of France, is overtly showing her wish to go back to England, her nostalgia symbolized by 'a refreshing wholesome cup of tea' that she is literally craving. Her early descriptions of the Arcadian Pyrenean landscapes and picturesque clean and orderly villages have turned to complaints about rural life: lack of cleanliness or comfort, filthiness, ugliness and the shapelessness of the people, their unhappy conditions, their unappetizing meals, etc. She complains there is no soap in many places and she is tired of the repetitive menu of stewed meat covered in a thick sauce and vegetables fried in lard.

p. 263, l. 19–p. 264, l. 4: *good old Madame Cazaux*: The only food and drink Mrs Ellis now enjoys is 'good wholesome English dinners' that Madame Cazaux's hotel provided and 'something like respectable tea' made in a 'veritable kettle' there.

p. 265, l. 20–p. 267, l. 21: *in order to calm ... tumultuous passions*: Mrs Ellis is trying to explain that the 'stirrings of anxiety and apprehension, which the accustomed habits of the world have rendered second nature' can be treated or calmed by a residence in the countryside. She is perhaps referring to her own husband's 'stirrings'.

p. 268, l. 6: *the Fort of St. Marie ... subject to his sway*: Mrs Ellis is alluding to the pillaging and razzias that the Black Prince (Edward of Woodstock, Prince of Wales, Duke of Cornwall, Prince of Aquitaine, son of King Edward III of England and father of King Richard II of England) and his English troops carried out in the south of France in August–September 1356.

p. 269, l. 9: *Cagot*: Dugenne speaks explicity about the Cagot people (*Panorama historique et descriptif de Pau et de ses environs*, p. 311–14), quoting M. Faget de Baure's *Essais historiques sur le Béarn*. Mrs Ellis summarizes most of what Dugenne says from p. 270, l. 5: 'It is impossible ' to p. 271, l. 2. 'amongst the country people'. However, unlike the author of *Panorama historique et descriptif de Pau et de ses environs*, she does not quote her source, which is no doubt Dugenne once again.

p. 270, ll. 11–15: *their name may have come ... rest of the people*: Mrs Ellis does not mention the other theory that Dugenne quotes from Faget de Baure, who stated that their name could also have originated from two words 'caa goth', meaning gothic dogs, (*Panorama historique et descriptif de Pau et de ses environs*, p. 337). The Cagots constitute a dark chapter of French history which they understandably seem eager to forget. Cagots were considered to be inferior and made to suffer constant discrimination by their fellow villagers: they were made to live apart from the rest of the population, use a door in the church which was only for them, they were not allowed to go barefoot for fear of spreading disease, they would have to use a rattle to announce their presence, they were not allowed to eat with non-Cagots and were buried separately in their own cemeteries. The list of their prohibitions is enormous and worse still, these prohibitions were backed by laws. During the French Revolution, these laws against Cagots were abolished and from 1789 this downtrodden group of society became slowly incorporated into the rest of the French population of the area or emigrated. For a vision of the Cagots from the nineteenth century see H. D. Inglis, *Switzerland, the South of France and the Pyrenees in 1830* (Edinburgh: Constable and Co., 1931), pp. 97, 128–34, F. Michel, *Histoire des races maudites: de la France et de l'Espagne.* (Paris: A. Franck, 1847) as well as Baure, *Essais historiques sur le Béarn*, pp. 121–3 and, more recently, B. Cursente, 'La question des "cagots" du Béarn. Proposition d'une nouvelle piste de recherche', and E. Porqueres I Gene, 'La chaleur des cagots. Lèpre et inscription généalogique de la marginalité', both in *Les Cahiers du Centre de Recherches*, 21 (October 1998) and G. Robb, *The Discovery of France: A Historical Geography from the Revolution to the First World War* (New York: W. W. Norton, 2007).

p. 270, l. 12: *gafo*: In Spanish this word refers to a curving of the fingers and the toes (*Diccionario de la Real Academia de la Lengua*) and from the same origin, 'gafedad' refers to a symptom of leprosy whereby fingers and sometimes toes became excessively curved.

p. 277, ll. 18–25: *Lady Clara ... Todie Toslip*: Baring-Gould (*A Book of the Pyrenees*, p. 169) recorded this very same anecdote, but stated it was not true. However, she is also equally as vague about which book she is quoting from when she states: 'A French guide-book asserts that at the spot an English lady, the Lady Clara, standing on the bridge, recited the celebrated soliloquy of Hamlet, in this fashion: "To die, to slip!" and then flung herself into the abyss. No such an incident ever occurred there'.

p. 280, l. 5: *Milton's ... angels*: Mrs Ellis is making an allusion to John Milton's *Paradise Lost*, book 6 (1667).

p. 280, ll. 16–17: *the rose of Switzerland*: Baring-Gould (*A Book of the Pyrenees*, p. 9) mentions 'the Alpen rose, Rhododendron ferrugineum' as growing in the Pyrenees.

p. 283, ll. 22–3: *the highest waterfall in Europe*: The Gavarnie Falls (422 m) is not the highest waterfall in Europe, as Mrs Ellis says – it is the Mongefossen (655 m) in Norway. The Gavarnie Falls is, however, the highest waterfall in France.

p. 285, l. 10: *Breche de Rolande*: La Brèche de Roland is a natural gap which forms part of the border between France and Spain. It measures 40 m across and 100 m high, and lies at an altitude of 2,804 m among the cliffs of the Cirque de Garvanie. The 'warrior from whom it derives its name' was Count Roland (Charlemagne's nephew). In the famous medieval poem, *La Chanson de Roland*, Durendal, the name of the sword which had been bestowed on Count Roland's uncle by angels, was used by Count Roland to fight off thousands of Moors, allowing Charlemagne's armies to retreat into France. In order to avoid the sword being appropriated by the Moors, Roland tried to destroy it by creating the Brèche de Roland. However, it was indestructible, so he had to hide it under his body.

p. 286, ll. 21–2: *twelve skulls of the Knights Templars*: The village of Gavarnie used to belong to the Knights Templars. Legend has it that these twelve skulls, which can be seen in this church, correspond to the twelve Knights Templar, who legend states, were decapitated there when the order was dissolved in 1312. The historian Thomas Keightley, in his *Secret Societies of the Middle Ages* (London: William Clowes and Sons, 1837), p. 296, states that this story is probably incorrect but does not give any reasons for this supposition.

p. 288, l. 4: *Meg Merrilies*: This is the name of a witch-like gypsy character in Sir Walter Scott's *Guy Mannering or The Astrologer* (Edinburgh: James Ballantyne and Co., 1815, 2nd edn), where she is described as having 'dark eyes' (p. 128) and 'supernatural strength' (p. 129), addressed as '*malefica* – that is to say Mrs Merrilies' (p. 131) and indeed considered to be 'a most mysterious and unaccountable personage' (p. 271). Scott's contemporary, the poet John Keats (1795–1821), wrote a poem based on Scott's fictional character titled 'Meg Merrilies'.

p. 291, l. 16: *The waters of Baréges*: In R. Hooper's *A New Medical Dictionary* [etc.] (Philadelphia, PA: M. Carey & Son, Benjamin Warner, and Edward Parker, 1817), p. 124, we find that these sulphureous and alkaline waters (reaching a temperature of 131° F) are employed in the Baréges baths as thermal waters, that is, for external use. *The Cyclopaedia of Practical Medicine* [etc], edited by J. Forbes, A. Tweedie and J. Conolly, vol. 4 (London: Sherwood, Gilbert, and Piper, and Balwin and Cradock, 1835), p. 485, mentions the building of a military hospital at Baréges and the characteristic sulphuretted hydrogen smell of its waters. *Green's Encyclopedia of Medicine and Surgery*, vol. 1, by J. W. Ballantyne (W. Green, 1906) p. 102, mentions the highly stimulant thermal baths and douches of the area and its healing properties thanks to the 'baregine' or organic matter consisting of an alga (*leptomitus sulphurariua*).

p. 293, l. 17: *kraals of the Africans*: 'Kraal' is an Afrikaans and Dutch word for a roughly circular pen for cattle or other livestock, surrounded by a palisade or mud wall. Mrs Ellis seems to be using this term as a synonym for hut, cottage or any other primitive type of lodging.

p. 299, l. 11: *Frascati*: This term is used by Mrs Ellis as a synonym for a gambling house. Her use of this term (which is also the name of an Italian city), is no doubt inspired by a successful novel, *Frascati's; or Scenes in Paris*, 3 vols (London: Henry Colburn and Richard Bentley, 1830) by Major John Richardson (1796–1852), a Canadian army officer, prolific novelist and journalist. Here, the word 'Frascati' referred to a famous Parisian café, restaurant and gambling house.

p. 303, l. 8: 'Pour passer le temps': 'To kill time' (French).

p. 303, l. 20: *Abbé Torné*: Pierre Anastase Torné (1727–97) was a French bishop, revolutionary politician and philosopher. He preached at Versailles and even pronounced the funerary oration at Louis XV's funeral in 1774. However, in 1793 he resigned as an abbot and married. He joined the Revolutionary cause during the French Revolution. He retired to Bourges and later to Tarbes, where he held a post as a librarian with the mission of saving numerous manuscripts connected to the Revolution. He was rejected by his family and died forgotten by everyone in 1797. See 'Pierre Anastase Torné', in A. Robert, E. Bourloton and G. Cougny, *Dictionnaire des parlementaires français, de 1789–1889* (Paris: Bourloton, 1891) vol. 5, p. 430.

p. 306, l. 16: *monastery of Medous*: In his second edition of *Travels through Spain, in the Years 1775 and 1776* (London: J. Davis, 1787), vol. 2, p. 311, Henry Swinburne adds the account of a journey from Bayonne to Marseilles and also mentions the 'convent of capuchins at Medous'. He does not refer to it as 'old and ruinous' as Mrs Ellis does, although perhaps by the time of the latter's visit it had become that way.

p. 321, ll. 12–13: *Lamartine*: Alphonse Lamartine (1790–1869) was a French writer, poet and also a politician. He was a member of the Académie française and Minister of Foreign Affairs. He declared the II Republic from the main balcony of the town hall of Paris. By the time he visited St Paul, Lamartine had published *Impressions, souvenirs, pensées et paysages pendant un voyage en Orient, 1832–1833, ou Notes d'un voyageur*, better known as *Voyage en Orient* (1835), hence Mrs Ellis's allusion to him as an 'eastern traveller'. *Jocelyn* (1836), *La chute d'un ange* (1838) and *Recueillements poétiques* (1839) are just a few of his famous poetic works. Lamartine was at the peak of his poetic career when Mrs Ellis was in France, hence his multitudinous welcome at St Paul. His most famous poem is the semi-autobiographical 'Le Lac', which was published in his *Méditations poétiques* (1820).

p. 322, ll. 1–2: *Lady Hester Stanhope*: Lady Hester Stanhope (1776–1839) was a British traveller, adventurer and archaeologist. She began as a private secretary to her uncle William Pitt the Younger. She travelled extensively in the Orient (Athens, Constantinople, Rhodes, Egypt, Palestine and Lebanon). Dr Meryon, her private physician, published *Memoirs of the Lady Hester Stanhope as Related by Herself in Conversations with her Phy-*

sician, 3 vols (London: H. Colburn, 1845). As Mrs Ellis rightly indicates, Lamartine did visit Lady Stanhope in her own house in Sion (Lebanon), the result of which was a chapter titled 'Visite à Lady Esther Stanhope' in his *Impressions, souvenirs, pensées et paysages pendant un voyage en Orient* (1835).

p. 322, ll. 19–20: 'brave montagnard': 'brave highlander' (French).

p. 335, l. 11–p. 336, l. 1: *We have been told ... wine which speaks to the throat*: This very passage (between pp. 335 and 336) is repeated literally in the *Literary Gazette and Journal of the Belles Lettres, Arts, Sciences, for the Year 1841* (London: Robson, Levey, and Franklin, 1841) p. 388, by an anonymous reviewer/advertiser of Mrs Ellis's book, which he/she writes in combination with two other travel accounts: *The Manners and Customs of Society in India, &c.*, by Mrs Clemons (London: Smith, Elder and Co., 1841) and the anonymous *Sketches in Erris and Tyrawly* (Dublin: Curry; London: Longman & Co., 1841). Some passages are merely copied from each book and the readers left to decide whether they wish to read them or not. Curiously enough, the section of the literal copy of the aforementioned excerpt from Mrs Ellis's book is titled 'The Pyrenees. English in France: French Beggars, &c.'

p. 338, ll. 23–4: *This language, which is properly that of Bearn, is a mixture of French and Spanish*: Gascon is one of the six dialects of the romance language Occitan together with Provençal, Languedoc, Limousin, Alpine and Auvergne. Gascon is spoken mainly in Gascony and Béarn and in the Aran Valley in Spain. See P. Courteault, *Histoire de Gascogne et de Béarn* (Paris, 1939); A. Puech, *Histoire de Gascogne* (Auch, 1914) and C. Dartigue, *Histoire de la Gascogne* (Paris, 1951).

p. 338, l. 27: *Despourrins*: Cyprien Despourrins (1698–1759), as Mrs Ellis states, was a poet from Béarn who wrote in the Béarnese form of Gascon. His poems, or 'cansous' were published in *Poésies Béarnaises* (Pau: Vignancourt, 1827), pp. 4–66.

p. 339, ll. 9–15: *the Basque ... Spain in the year 1492*: There is no connection between Basque and Arabic whatsoever. Besides, the Arabs who left the Peninsula in 1492, after the conquest of Granada (in the south of Spain) by King Ferdinand V of Aragon and Isabella I of Castile, did so by crossing the channel towards North Africa. Those who remained in Spain after the Christian Reconquest were exiled to the mountain area of the Alpujarra in the province of Granada.

p. 339, l. 21: montre: 'wristwatch' (French).

p. 341, l. 10: *Indian corn*: this was the original term for maize or corn which was then shortened simply to 'corn'. Nowadays, 'Indian corn' refers to a variety which is also known as 'flint corn'.

p. 340, l. 25: *Marshal Soult*: Marshal Soult, Jean-de-Dieu Soult (1769–1851) was a French general and statesman, three times prime minister of France, and honoured with the distinction of Marshal General of France. See F. Hulot, *Le maréchal Soult* (Paris: Pygmalion. 2003).

p. 342, l. 18: *Lord Elgin*: Thomas Bruce (1766–1841), seventh Earl of Elgin, most famous for taking the marble sculptures of the Parthenon, Greece, to England. These are now commonly known as 'the Elgin Marbles'. The information that Mrs Ellis provides on Lord Elgin's imprisonment in the Béarn area could have been taken from Walter Scott's 3 volumes of *The Life of Napoleon Buonaparte, Emperor of the French. With a Preliminary View of the French Revolution* (Philadelphia, PA: Carey, Lea & Carey, 1827), vol. 2, pp. 54–6.

p. 349, l. 8: *Don Quixote*: A literary character created by the Spanish novelist Miguel de Cervantes Saavedra (1547–1616), the protagonist of *Don Quijote de la Mancha*, published in two parts in 1605 and 1615. It has become the symbol of idealistic and old-fashioned knight-errantry.

p. 353, l. 23: *Vignemale*: Mrs Ellis affirms that this is the highest mountain in France. This is incorrect: the highest one is Mont Blanc, in the French Alps. The Vignemale (10,820 ft; 3,298 m) is the highest in the French Pyrenees.

p. 354, l. 15: *Derwent water*: Derwent Water is one of the most beautiful lakes in the Lake District of Cumbria as well as being the widest in England, hence Mrs Ellis's mention of its 'broad sheet'.

p. 376, l. 26–p. 377, l. 15: *A friend of ours ... wretched beyond description*: Mrs Ellis is being utterly unfair by using the references that a friend of hers has given of the country consisting of a four-hour ride on the other side of the French frontier. By doing so she is spreading unfair prejudices about a whole country.

p. 378, ll. 16–19: *the same literary friend ... an agricultural country*: Mrs Ellis has taken this information from exactly the same source that was used in E. Arnolt, *L'Institut Journal des academies et societes et travaux scientifiques de la France et de l'étranger* (August 1841), p.126.

p. 381, ll. 16–17: *Madame Maintenon ... young duke of Maine*. Madame de Maintenon (Françoise d'Aubigné, 1635–1719) was the governess of Louis XIV's two illegitimate children when she became his mistress (and later his second wife). Louis XIV's oldest illegitimate child was Louis Auguste de Bourbon (1670–1736), Duke of Maine. Madame de Maintenon and the Duke of Maine visited Baréges in 1675, when the duke was only a child of five. From then on, Barége became a fashionable resort. See also H. D. Inglis [Derwent Conway], *Switzerland, the South of France and the Pyrenees*.

p. 390, l. 24–p. 391, l. 1: *that causeless and indescribable dejection of mind ... than myself*. This is a clear allusion to what I presume to be her husband's depression. The symptoms, as described by her, are 'sinking of the soul', 'hopeless conflict', 'causeless depression' (p. 391), which, according to her, is so frequent in England and so scarce among the people of the south of France.

p. 393, l. 27: *Sir James Clarke*: Sir James Clark (1788–1870), of Scottish origin, was a renowned physician in his day. He travelled to the south of France, Switzerland and Rome and researched the effect of climate changes on disease. He was appointed physician to the Duchess of Kent and to her daughter, Princess Victoria, who later, as the Queen of England, appointed him as her Physician-in-Ordinary and granted him a baronetcy. Among his works are *The Influence of Climate in the Prevention and Cure of Chronic Diseases, more particularly of the Chest and Digestive Organs: Comprising an Account of the Principal Places Resorted to by Invalids in England and the South of Europe; a Comparative Climate of their Respective Merits in Particular Diseases and General Directions for Invalids while Travelling and Residing Abroad* (London: Thomas and George Underwood, 1829), and a *Treatise on Pulmonary Consumption, Comprehending an Inquiry into the Causes, Nature, Prevention and Treatment of Tuberculous and Scrofulous Diseases in General* (Philadelphia, PA: Carey, Lea, and Blanchard, 1835).

INDEX

For Product Safety Concerns and Information please contact our EU
representative GPSR@taylorandfrancis.com Taylor & Francis Verlag GmbH,
Kaufingerstraße 24, 80331 München, Germany

Batch number: 08158359

Printed by Printforce, the Netherlands